Social Synthesis

How is it possible to understand society and the problems it faces? What sense can be made of the behaviour of markets and government interventions? How can citizens understand the course that their lives take and the opportunities available to them?

There has been much debate surrounding what methodology and methods are appropriate for social science research. In a larger sense, there have been differences in quantitative and qualitative approaches and some attempts to combine them. In addition, there have also been questions of the influence of competing values on all social activities versus the need to find an objective understanding. Thus, this aptly named volume strives to develop new methods through the practice of 'social synthesis', describing a methodology that perceives societies and economies as manifestations of highly dynamic, interactive and emergent complex systems. Furthermore, helping us to understand that an analysis of parts alone does not always lead to an informed understanding, Haynes presents to the contemporary researcher an original tool called Dynamic Pattern Synthesis (DPS) – a rigorous method that informs us about how specific complex social and economic systems adapt over time.

A timely and significant monograph, *Social Synthesis* will appeal to advanced undergraduate and postgraduate students, research professionals and academic researchers informed by sociology, economics, politics, public policy, social policy and social psychology.

Philip Haynes is Professor of Public Policy in the School of Applied Social Science at the University of Brighton, UK.

Complexity in Social Science

This interdisciplinary series encourages social scientists to embrace a complex systems approach to studying the social world. A complexity approach to the social world has expanded across the disciplines since its emergence in the mid-to-late 1990s, and this can only continue as disciplines continue to change, data continue to diversify, and governance and responses to global social issues continue to challenge all involved. Covering a broad range of topics from big data and time, globalization and health, cities and inequality, and methodological applications, to more theoretical or philosophical approaches, this series responds to these challenges of complexity in the social sciences – with an emphasis on critical dialogue around, and application of these ideas in, a variety of social arenas as well as social policy.

The series will publish research monographs and edited collections between 60,000–90,000 words that include a range of philosophical, methodological and disciplinary approaches, which enrich and develop the field of social complexity and push it forward in new directions.

David Byrne is Emeritus Professor at the School of Applied Social Sciences, Durham University, UK.

Brian Castellani is Professor in Sociology and Head of the Complexity in Health and Infrastructure Group, Kent State University, USA. He is also Adjunct Professor of Psychiatry, Northeastern Ohio Medical University.

Emma Uprichard is Associate Professor and Deputy Director at the Centre for Interdisciplinary Methodologies, University of Warwick, UK. She is also co-director of the Nuffield, ESRC, HEFCE funded Warwick Q-Step Centre.

For a full list of titles in this series, please visit www.routledge.com/Complexity-in-Social-Science/book-series/CISS

Agile Actors on Complex Terrains
Transformative realism and public policy
Graham Room

Social Synthesis
Finding Dynamic Patterns in Complex Social Systems
Philip Haynes

Social Synthesis

Finding Dynamic Patterns in Complex Social Systems

Philip Haynes

Routledge
Taylor & Francis Group
LONDON AND NEW YORK

First published 2018
by Routledge

2 Park Square, Milton Park, Abingdon, Oxfordshire OX14 4RN
52 Vanderbilt Avenue, New York, NY 10017

Routledge is an imprint of the Taylor & Francis Group, an informa business

First issued in paperback 2019

British Library Cataloguing-in-Publication Data
A catalogue record for this book is available from the British Library

Library of Congress Cataloging-in-Publication Data
A catalog record for this book has been requested

ISBN: 978-1-138-20872-8 (hbk)
ISBN: 978-0-367-37124-1 (pbk)

Typeset in Times New Roman
by Apex CoVantage, LLC

Contents

Illustrations

Figures

Tables

Boxes

Acknowledgements

Routledge has been a major supporter of the dissemination of research and scholarship about complexity theory and it's relevance to the social sciences, including the promotion of this series. My thanks to the editorial staff Emily Briggs and Elena Chiu for their support in developing this monograph.

My thanks to the *ESRC Complex methods network* and its leaders: Professors David Byrne, Brian Castellani and Emma Uprichard. The new method presented in this book, Dynamic Pattern Synthesis (DPS) was first presented at the *ESRC Complex methods network* in February 2015 at the University of Warwick, and the feedback and encouragement from the network members was pivotal in providing the inspiration and motivation to write this monograph.

During the last year I have collaborated with the ESRC Centre for the Evaluation of Complexity across the Nexus (CECAN) and have become an Associate of this innovative research programme. I am grateful to the CECAN team for their support.

Chapter 3 contains two macro case studies with data previously collected at the country level, or summarised and calculated as country aggregates, this for the purposes of the DPS applied in the chapter.

Macro case study 1 about health and social care in Europe is compiled from the Survey of Health, Ageing and Retirement in Europe (SHARE) data.

This monograph uses data from the generated easySHARE data set (DOI: 10.6103/SHARE.easy.500), see Gruber et al. (2016) for methodological details. The easySHARE release 5.0.0 is based on SHARE Waves 1, 2, 3 (SHARELIFE), 4 and 5 (DOIs: 10.6103/SHARE.w1.500, 10.6103/SHARE.w2.500, 10.6103/SHARE.w3.500, 10.6103/SHARE.w4.500, 10.6103/SHARE.w5.500) (see also Börsch-Supan, et al., 2016). The SHARE data collection has been primarily funded by the European Commission through the FP5 (QLK6-CT-2001–00360), FP6 (SHARE-I3: RII-CT-2006–062193, COMPARE: CIT5-CT-2005–028857, SHARELIFE: CIT4-CT-2006–028812) and FP7 (SHARE-PREP: N°211909, SHARELEAP: N°227822, SHARE M4: N°261982). Additional funding from the German Ministry of Education and Research, the U.S. National Institute on Aging (U01_AG09740–13S2, P01_AG005842, P01_AG08291, P30_AG12815, R21_AG025169, Y1-AG-4553–01, IAG_BSR06–11, OGHA_04–064) and from various national funding sources is gratefully acknowledged (see www.share-project.org).

Macro case study 2 is about the implementation of the euro currency and its impact on member countries. This study of macroeconomic dynamics is adapted and extended from a previous Cluster Analysis published by the author and Haynes, J., as 'Convergence and Heterogeneity in Euro Based Economies: Stability and Dynamics', in *Economies* 2016, *4*(3), 16; doi:10.3390/economies4030016 (www.mdpi.com/2227-7099/4/3/16). My thanks to Jonathan Haynes for his advice and contribution with the preliminary research study. The new research analysis of this dataset published in Chapter 3 uses only the 12 euro member countries joining in 2002 and does not attempt to include new members joining the currency between 2005 and 2016. The previous modelling also included later euro members. The version of the research published in this book makes much more extensive use of Qualitative Comparative Analysis (QCA) than the earlier version and therefore offers an innovative and original DPS approach (the earlier version of the data analysis used a more conventional historical statistical comparisons). Data for Macro case study 2 is provided by Eurostat, the European Central Bank (ECB) and Organisation for Economic Cooperation and Development (OECD). Eurostat data is publicly available at: http://ec.europa.eu/eurostat. European Central Bank statistics are publicly available at: www.ecb.europa.eu/stats/ OECD statistics are publicly available at: http://stats.oecd.org/

In Chapter 4, the meso case study is compiled from a variety of UK data sources. London population projections are provided as public information via The London Datastore at https://data.london.gov.uk/. The London Datastore is a free and open data-sharing portal and was winner of the 2015 ODI Open Data Publisher award. The data is copyright of The London Datastore, which is part of the office of the Mayor of London and the London Assembly. London health outcomes are provided by Public Health England and are available as public data via https://data.london.gov.uk/. Additional London health and social care data are made available via The Health and Social Care Information Centre, and at the time of editing was available to the public via www.hscic.gov.uk/.

In Chapter 5, the micro case study is compiled using the same easySHARE data used in Chapter 3 (for full details about this data, and acknowledgements. please see information above about the dataset and its sources and funding).

My thanks to Jane Haynes for her advice and support with the preparation of the final manuscript.

Abbreviations

CA	Cluster Analysis
CS	Crisp Set
DPS	Dynamic Patten Synthesis
ECB	European Central Bank
EU	European Union
GDP	Gross Domestic Product
GDPPPSI	GDP purchasing power standard per inhabitant
HICP	Harmonised Indices of Consumer Prices
LTIR	Long Term Interest Rate
OECD	Organisation for Economic Cooperation and Development
QCA	Qualitative Comparative Analysis
SHARE	Survey of Health, Ageing and Retirement in Europe

Introduction

How is it possible to understand society and the social problems it faces? What sense can be made of the financial markets, government interventions and ability of the economy to be integrated with the needs of society? How can citizens best understand the course that their own lives take and the relationships they have with others and the opportunities available to them? These issues are at the core of social science and especially the application of empirical research to the social sciences. What research tools and methods are available to answer such questions?

Although statistical generalisations are argued about in the social sciences and some become accepted and highly influential on governments, each person has their own individual and unique experience. This is a deeply personal experience and each makes their own conclusions about the reasons for their own life course. But our own subjective experience invokes rapid and strong feelings and emotions. When each individual scrutinises these with the insights of social science, including better self-understanding our own cognitive psychology, it is immediately apparent that a range of cognitive biases distorts our subjective and singular perceptions (Kahneman, 2012). Cognitive 'system two', characterised by slow and reflective thinking, tries to overrule system one with its fast and instinctive reactions, but it is far from always successful.

When starting to reflect on social science and how it is best researched, scholars are calling on the rationalistic part of their brain, where slower and reflective thoughts can restrain their more conditioned, preprogrammed immediate urges and responses. Similar, but older than the influence of psychology, is the influence of the academic discipline of history, where collective and recorded accounts of the past seek to inform us about what might happen in the future and perhaps offer some means for forecasting the future to plan accordingly. But looking in the rear-view mirror is not the best method to drive forward.

The more formal way that social scientists discipline their approaches to get the benefits of a more reflective and rational approach is via their aim to be more objective through research and research design with its structures and focus on specific research aims and questions. Such methods of social research also require a review of past knowledge, a constant comparison with the context of previous relevant research and literature.

Social Science gives us two fundamental research approaches to draw upon: the quantitative and qualitative. These have evolved over the decades in the minds of scholars to be characterised by having different strengths and weakness in their application and therefore their ability to answer certain types of questions. Quantitative approaches are better when issues of scale are important and where there is a good chance of sharing scale definitions of the concepts that are being problematised. If the starting research questions are less clear, and the definition of questions and problems of interest disputed and contested, the underlying concepts are abstract and probably in need of further debate and definition. In such circumstances, qualitative research methods are more appropriate to use. But a quantitative versus qualitative dualism is false. The differences are paradoxical. A completely satisfactory prior consensus never defines quantitative research concepts and measures; all concepts and how they are measured evolve and are disputed. Qualitative research is never completely inductive and exploratory; it too will be influenced by prior subjective experiences and disciplinary-based conceptual constructions. Qualitative research will share some interest in the scaling of quantification and relative comparison. As (Bryman, 2008, p. 4) notes in his seminal discussion of the 'paradigm wars':

> [T]he often stark contrasts that are sometimes drawn up in accounts of the differences between quantitative and qualitative research possibly exaggerate the differences between them.

The approach of the research proposed in this monograph is at the interface of the quantitative and qualitative approach. The methods product of this book is called Dynamic Pattern Synthesis (DPS). It uses quantitative data to help make qualitative decisions about the evolving of social patterns, but it also searches for these patterns by applying a method of synthesis rather than analysis.

Synthesis is the combining of elements to form something new. Or in the words of Major and Savin-Baden (2010, p. 63): 'Synthesis by definition means taking parts and developing them into something whole.' It is the antithesis of analysis. Analysis is where something is deconstructed into its constituent parts. The construction of the universe is an extraordinary history of synthesis, of the ever-increasing emergence of new things from basic matter. Others refer to this as the evolution of complexity. It is both emergence and innovation.

> Emergence refers to the way in which particular combinations of things, processes and practices in social life frequently give rise to new emergent properties. The defining characteristic of emergent properties is their irreducibility. They are more than the sum of their constituents, since they are a product of their combination, and as such are able to modify these constituents.
>
> (Carter & New, 2004, p. 7)

Much science and social science has historically been concerned with analysis, with reducing things to components, as if by deconstructing something and seeing the parts one will understand how they came to fit together. Analysis can work well in some circumstances. Much operational maintenance of mechanical systems works through analysis. A problem is diagnosed using a trial and error approach to examine the reducible parts of the system, until a problem is identified in a specific part of its operation. Car mechanics and domestic water system plumbing are two such pragmatic applied scientific examples.

In contrast synthesis argues for a good understanding of the whole, to be sure about how the mechanical details work. Synthesis has a juxtaposition with systems and systems thinking. As Burns (2007, p. 21), notes: 'Systemic thinking means "taking into account the whole", and seeking meaning in the complex patterning of interrelationships between people and groups of people.'

The argument of this book is that social scientists need to discover new ways of researching and understanding social synthesis. The focus of this monograph is to propose and demonstrate a mixed method that begins to deliver on this challenging task. This new method is DPS.

The structure that follows in the book is explained below.

Chapter 1 explains the underpinning methodology arguing that the combination of complex systems theory and critical realism as applied to the social sciences provide an authoritative grand narrative of social systems and that the behaviour and values and beliefs which evolve within these systems helps to define their key characteristics. It is argued that this reality requires a further adjustment of the methods that social science researchers use, especially in the disciplines of economics, sociology and sub disciplines of policy studies.

Chapter 2 proposes the new method to be called Dynamic Pattern Synthesis (DPS) that is fit for the critical realism challenge that complex systems demand. There then follow a series of case study chapters that demonstrate use of the method and its ability to add understanding to different aspects of complex social systems.

The third chapter presents two macro examples. The first is the synthesis over time of the aggregate family and health circumstances of older people in European nations through the financial crisis of 2007–08. The second example examines the countries that share the euro currency after 2002, as they evolve together on new economic path, interlocked by new economic interactions that were apparently designed to make them converge towards shared economic objectives. This chapter explores how countries evolve in comparative relation to each other, bearing in mind that they also coexist increasingly in a relatively open global market place where both capital investment and labour move across national borders and create new economic patterns.

Chapter 4 moves to present a meso, organisational level case study. This examines a set of large local government organisations in the London area. These are administrative London boroughs that assess and provide social care services to older people. These organisations, while separate legal entities and discrete public services, also coexist and cooperate and compete in an area of public policy and managed a health care economy that is regulated by national government. Therefore, the paradoxical separation and interdependence of these organisations, alongside their existence within a national health and wider social environment, means they are very much emergent and partially codependent sub systems, making a typical example of a large complex social system. The case study charts their similarities and differences, identifying similar types of boroughs and outliers, and it charts their progress and evolution over time. This case study follows a focused three year period from 2010 to 2012.

The final case study in Chapter 5 explores social dynamics at the individual, micro level. It does this by examining the journey of a group of older people born in the same year in Sweden. Again, these are cases that have a unique journey, but also people who interrelate with their society, its changing attitudes and provision of services and social codependencies. These social factors therefore influence each person's outcome.

Chapter 6 assimilates the conclusions from the case studies and the learning from the trialling and testing of this new method of Dynamic Pattern Analysis. It reflects on what has been achieved and the scholarly tasks ahead.

1 Methodology

Towards a representation of complex system dynamics

Introduction

This chapter considers the use of complexity theory in the social science in the last 25 years. The growing application of complexity theory in the social sciences followed the adaption of ideas from complexity science into the natural sciences. The method of Dynamic Pattern Synthesis (DPS) as proposed, developed and demonstrated in this book has its roots in two theoretical and methodological approaches to social science: complexity theory and critical realism. The growing recognition that complexity theory has implications for social science is changing the approach to the research methods used by social scientists (Byrne & Callaghan, 2014; Castellani & Hafferty, 2009). Social researchers informed by complexity theory see the need for methods that can take account of the strong interactions between people in social systems and that the way these interactions occur leads to indeterminate and difficult to forecast outcomes. Rather than looking for fixed causal laws, researchers turn their attention to less stable patterns of association that might suggest temporal causal patterns, these being patterns that change over time and can even reverse in their interactive effect in future relationships. Kauffman (1995, p. 15), a seminal figure in complexity science, notes that all of life 'unrolls in an unending procession of change'. It is this constant change that feeds the need for research to understand dynamics. This chapter will explore the theory of complexity theory and consider how it is influencing social science methodology and its connections with the domain of critical realism and the mixed methods that result. As Byrne and Callaghan (2014, p. 8) remarked in their seminal review of the influence of complexity science on the social sciences

> When we say complexity theory we mean by theory a framework for understanding which asserts the ontological position that much of the world and most of the social world consists of complex systems and if we want to understand it we have to understand those terms.

Complexity science

The classical reductionist method

Complexity Theory has its origins in contemporary scientific methodology and it questions the universality of the assumptions of Newtonian reductionist methods. Sir Isaac Newton, argued to be one of the greatest scientists of all time, and Lucasian Professor of Mathematics at Cambridge University from 1669–1701, was much involved in the discovery of some of the most important predictable laws of science, for example, gravitation force and its effect on objects on the earth, including the motion of tides, but also its effect on planets in the solar system.

Similar to Newtonian laws, reductionist methods premise that if research analyses the micro detail of physical matter it will be possible to deduce how higher order entities and their forms function. For example, the discovery of microbiology in medicine explained the causes of bacterial related diseases and therefore if drugs could be discovered to kill the destructive microbes, a cure was guaranteed. This classical scientific approach has certainly had historical influence on the development of the social sciences. As Byrne (2002, p. 6) writes:

> Traditionally, quantitative social scientists have tried to construct a social mechanics that can generate predictions of future states on the basis of the measurement of variables in the same way in which Newtonian mechanics predicts through the measurement of forces.

Some early social scientists questioned such a mechanistic view. For example, Durkheim, himself, questioned the Newtonian principles of science, even though he is often regarded as a social scientist with much investment in a classical scientific method.

> It is in the very nature of the positive sciences that they are never complete. The realities with which they deal are far too complex ever to be exhausted. If sociology is a positive science, we can be assured that it does not consist in a single problem but includes, on the contrary, different parts, many distinct sciences which correspond to the various aspects of social life.
>
> (Durkheim, in Thompson, 2004, pp. 13–14)

But it is not only social science that has challenged the classical and mechanistic view of science. Much of the new science of complexity has emerged from within the physical sciences also.

Beyond reductionist science

Twentieth century postreductionist scientific theories like thermodynamics, quantum mechanics and complexity theory supplemented the Newtonian explanation by exploring how dynamic and creative change can occur through the emergence of order at the micro level. One such example is the law of thermodynamics.

> In classical mechanics, time was reversible, and therefore not part of the equation. In thermodynamics time plays a vital role. This is perhaps best expressed in the second law of thermodynamics, which states that the entropy of a system can only increase. Entropy can be seen as a measure of disorder in a system.
>
> (Cilliers, 1998, p. 8)

In addition, quantum theory or quantum mechanics is the science of the smallest building blocks of physical materials, atomic and sub atomic particles. Instead of reducing the particles to predictable laws, quantum mechanics demonstrates that such particles behave probabilistically rather than deterministically. In 'Quantum leaps', particles will pass through barriers and boundaries, or behave differently in sub atomic structures, in unpredictable probabilistic ways, rather than always responding to precise deterministic rules (Frisch, 2014). Sub atomic matter may behave simultaneously as a particle and a wave and may demonstrate surprising future behaviours in terms of their movement, location and consequences. Quantum physics and the study of sub atomic particles resulted in a science of wave motions and probability events, rather than a fixed and highly predictable movement of its component parts.

Such phenomenon challenge single dimensional and highly predictable versions of science. Quantum theory implies that increased analysis of scientific detail will not solve all understanding, but instead micro detail may have dynamic, random and chaotic characteristics that are not easy to predict. This has similarities with complexity theory, where the interaction of physical materials can be dynamic and unstable, resulting in analogous historical patterns of interaction, but never a completely identical outcome. For example, different outcomes might result when the same apparent processes are observed at differing levels and scale. Weather systems are the most obvious physical examples, but neurological and cognitive systems can also be understood by applying complex theoretical and methodological frameworks.

One of the earliest technical acknowledgements of scientific complexity that could not be easily explained by fixed rules of motion was Poincare's three body problem. This demonstrated that the movement of three celestial bodies subject to gravitational forces was theoretically unstable and chaotic and not easy to determine by the laws of motion. In general, the movement of three celestial bodies was found to be nonrepeating and thus not reducible to an outcome based on the known laws and rule of gravitational forces. Subsequent reflections on Poincare's problem suggest that the patterns of stability usually observed in the relationship of three celestial bodies are created by a combination of resonance and gravitation. The influence of complexity science has therefore resulted in a different view of the universe. It is no longer seen as governed by entirely mechanistic laws, but rather viewed as an evolving complex system. It is dynamic not static. This book will argue that this complex reality means that social and economic researchers need to be careful about the methods they use and should consider selecting methods which can see the changing dynamics of complex systems and are not blind to the likelihood of unstable change. The relationship of time with social interactions and change is episodic and not stable or linear in its combined impact. An example of this is 'sensitivity to initial conditions'.

Sensitivity to initial conditions

In the 1960s, an American meteorologist, Lorenz, was programming a mainframe computer to model the weather when he noticed that a small mistake in an input led to very large results in the model output. This was heralded as the discovery that small changes in initial conditions could have exponential results. It has since been referred to as the 'butterfly effect', given the conclusion that a butterfly flapping its wings in Brazil might cause a hurricane in Texas. More fundamentally it raised significant challenges for Lorenz in terms of the theoretical possibility of building a computer program that could really model a large-scale weather system based on local data inputs. Many scientists came to know this phenomenon as 'chaos' (Gelick, 1988).

Such sensitivity to initial conditions has been argued to apply to the historical evolution of economies in the study of social systems. Getting products to market first, and marketing them first, may make exponential success much more likely. Once that a given number of consumers have made the purchase and others begin to copy their behaviour (because they also want the product), a rapid positive feedback loop develops. It is much harder for later producers of the same invention to be as successful. But within this change may be a random effect. For example, if two companies get similar inventions to the market at the same time, it may be luck, or randomness, as much as their advertising strategy that makes one more successful than the other. Examples of this might be the PC and Apple computer, the Betamax and VHS video tape. While companies claim their success is down to marketing and product quality, we cannot always be sure that this was the reason and cannot rule out an element of randomness in rapidly generating consumer patterns of feedback.

If one of two similar products get market supremacy early on in a product life cycle, due to customer behaviour and feedback, this can also be linked with the concept known as 'path dependence' (Room, 2011, pp. 16–18). In other words, if the historical path of events is tracked, the observer finds critical points of time and transforming events that explain the longer-term trajectory and a resulting period of stability and dominance which follows the initial conditions (Boulton, et al., 2015).

These early theoretical observations about the importance of initial conditions and subsequent different random paths were later replaced by an appreciation that disorder and instability is often mixed in with periods of order and stability over time. As the late Paul Cilliers said:

> Complex systems are neither homogeneous nor chaotic. They have structure, embodied in the patterns of interactions between components.
>
> (2001, p. 140)

Change becomes episodic (Boulton, et al., 2015) rather than chaotic. Systems might periodically get into situations that put them on the 'edge of chaos' and more likely to experience substantial change, but such a system state is not permanent. This mix of order and disorder is what we have come to know as complexity, rather than chaos.

The dynamism of micro order in complex systems and the ability of 'small things' to create novel outcomes can also be considered with regard to the emergence of new forms of order.

Emergence

Perhaps the most important scientific finding with respect to the understanding of complexity science rather than chaos was the discovery of emergent order in biochemistry by the Nobel Prize winner Ilya Prigogine. He demonstrated that open physical systems could result in dissipative structures that were dynamic and far from equilibrium. Given that simple scientific rules at a micro and local level could result in innovative and creative structures led Prigogine and others to conclude that a given state of order is not deterministic over time. Knowing things by reducing them to detail and examining their past cannot necessarily guarantee a predictable outcome. The chemical reactions studied by Prigogine and his research team showed that simple rules and behaviours led to the emergence of complex patterns rather than simple predictable outcomes.

Smith and Jenks (2006) summarise the importance of Prigogine's work. Systems reorganise and change far from equilibrium when driven by entropy. This is not a mechanical or deterministic process. Such change is irreversible and unlikely to return to an exact previous system state. The nature of such change is, in part, statistical and random, following patterns of probability. At the micro level, Smith and Jenks (2006, p. 95) conclude:

> Prigogine's studies lead us to a new conception of material probablity. The microspcopic properties of matter, such as substance, particles, molecules, largely independent of each other at equilibrium levels, begin to act together at macroscopic levels at far-from-equilibrium conditions, charged by thermo-dynamics.

This dynamic change also takes place at a relatively high level in the system, rather than in just micro parts, so that a large number of elements and their interactions are involved. This is the discovery of a creative and dynamic world that is best understood by searching for similar patterns rather than singular causes. At the macro level, Pawson and Tilley (1997, p. 72) state: 'The balance of mechanisms, contexts and regularities which sustains social order is prone to a perpetual and self-generating reshaping'.

Relatively new research methods, like Agent Based Modelling (ABM), put more emphasis on the bottom up emergence of actor behaviour to create novel social behaviour and seek to demonstrate the collective results of models of agent behaviour (Gilbert, 2008). Perhaps the best-known example is Schelling's (1971) model of ethnic segregation in urban populations, where it was demonstrated that, even if agents were tolerant of ethnic difference, if they nevertheless mildly preferred ethnic similarity in their choice of neighbourhood, over time ethnic segregation would follow. In more recent times, Bar-Yam (2005) has presented a similar type of argument about the causes of ethnic violence in civil stress such as was experienced in former Yugoslavia in the 1990s. In sum, relatively small scale incidents and decisions can quickly get scaled up to represent a social phenomenon with devastating larger scale effects in the macro system.

Byrne (2004, p. 55) neatly summarises the importance of emergence for the social sciences.

> The important thing about complex systems is that they have emergent properties. They are inherently non-analysable because their properties, potentials and trajectories cannot be explained in terms of the properties of their components.

If complexity theory demonstrates the importance of system dynamics and reveals the ever-important emergence of change and innovation, it is also important to rethink the notion of the relationship between the individual and society and how separate and joined social sub systems and systems interact in an unstable world. The scientific concept of 'autopoiesis' has been used to explore these challenges in the social sciences.

Autopoiesis

Another seminal moment in the development of complex systems theory was Maturana and Varela's (1992) proposal of the concept of 'autopoiesis'. This is a cell or system that can maintain or reproduce itself. It can refer to itself in a social process, it is 'self-referential'. Luhmann (1995) expanded these concepts in sociology and applied the principles of autopoiesis to social systems. Here was a branch of systems theory that turned its attention to the unity of a case within a system, or a part of a system (or sub system) and its ability to keep itself discrete from external systems and the environment. This allowed onc component to be identified as 'different' while still operating as part of something else. This leads to an important area of research and scholarship that debates the relative openness or closure of complex systems.

Autopoiesis is something of a paradox for social systems in terms of social differences to physical systems. Cilliers (2001, p. 141) expresses the following concern.

> An overemphasis on closure will also lead to an understanding of the system that may underplay the role of environment. . .if the boundary is seen as an interface participating in constituting the system, we will be more concerned with the margins of the system, and perhaps less with what appears to be central.

While autopoiesis emphasizes the autonomy of living systems, Maturana and Varela (1992) also proposed how autonomous systems interact with other systems and their external environment, via ontogeny and structural coupling. Ontogeny is the situation of a living organism and how it relates to its external environment. The mix of internal and external influences and the dynamic of internal coherence is further reflected on in the seminal work defined by Maturana and Varela that defines ontogeny (1992, p. 74).

> Ontogeny is the history of structural change in a unity without loss of organisation in that unity. This ongoing structural change occurs in the unity from moment to moment, either as a change triggered by interactions coming from the environment in which it exists or as a result of its internal dynamics. As regards its continuous interactions with the environment, the cell unity classifies them and sees them in accordance with its structure at every instant. That structure, in turn, continuously changes because of its internal dynamics. The overall result is that the ontogenic transformation of a unity ceases only with its disintegration.

Luhmann (1995) also attempted to address such linkages regarding social systems and proposed examples of 'structural coupling' in social systems. Structural coupling is the recurrent interactions between two systems that results in a formal linking of communication or similar between them. Maturana and Varela (1992, p. 74) explain structural coupling as:

> Two (or more) autopoietic unities can undergo coupled ontogenies when their interactions take on a recurrent or more stable nature. . .in these interactions, the structure of the environment only triggers structural changes in the autopoietic unities. . .The result will be a history of mutual congruent structural changes as long as the autopoietic unity and its containing environment do not disintegrate: there will be structural coupling.

Luhmann sought to apply such an understanding to much larger scale social systems, for example, the operation of two different sub systems in society like the rule of law and the functioning of the economy. He hypothesized that while these were fundamentally different in form, concepts and language, they could be structurally coupled in specific ways, to allow them to share certain forms of communication. This enabled them to coexist in the wider social environment. Whereas much sociology has focused on deterministic structures, for example that separated peoples into rich and poor, the elite and those with no power, Luhmann – like other complex systems theorists – saw the routes of this real separation as being in the accepted forms of communication and that these forms could restrict and shut down movement in social systems. This leaves many areas of society appearing formally closed and restricted while paradoxically open to the uninformed gaze of others.

Autopoiesis shows that it is quite possible for social and economic systems to be unstable, dynamic and changing whilst at the same time also relatively closed and restrictive to the experience of individual people. Cilliers' (2001) implies we may have to think about boundaries differently, as social codes and 'filters' that are permeable in certain situations, rather than as fixed structures with different sized 'real' gateways.

Indeed, Cilliers (2001, p. 140) suggests that boundaries in social systems are more about 'forms' of closure in open systems rather than defined by rigid and impermeable structures of closure.

> Complex systems are open systems where the relationships amongst the components of the system are usually more important than the components themselves. . . . One way of dealing with the problem of boundaries is to introduce the notion of 'operational closure'.

Operational closure has some similarities to Luhmann's (1995) idea of 'structural coupling' and how movement between systems is restricted by communication rather than physical barriers. This challenges a structural approach to understanding systems that puts too much emphasis on features like hierarchy. Cilliers (2001, p. 143) therefore adds the comment:

> Hierarchies are not that well-structured. They interpenetrate each other, i.e. there are relationships which cut across different hierarchies.

At the level of social systems, sociologists like Archer (1982) have argued that the process of interactions between people, organisations and institutions, from the past to the present, is best theorised as 'morphogenesis', as these interactions lead to future change within the systems themselves. This type of theorising about system structures puts the emphasis for understanding structures and boundaries on analysing the interactions and communications across these boundaries. Whilst these interactions could be used to maintain a stability of the existence of parts, it also recognises that over time single parts may not survive and may ultimately disintegrate back into the larger environment. Again, we see the mix of stability and instability, order and disorder, over time. Archer (1982, p. 458) argues that the sequential nature of morphogenesis and its emphasis on 'system endings' is one key reason for its realism over other social theories.

Having considered the core complexity theory concepts of initial conditions, path dependency, emergence and autopoiesis, the importance of energy, interaction and communication to determining the construction of order and organisation is evident. Feedback processes within these processes of system interaction are a further important concept to consider.

Feedback

Change that occurs because of interaction can also be identified as related to the concept of feedback. Events and interventions invoke responses. Responses to social and economic events take the form of social interactions. These interactions can reinforce more change as people copy behaviour traits. Alternatively, interactions can check, modify and perhaps limit change. They do this by diminishing copying and stopping the scale of behavioural reinforcement. There are many examples of such behaviour change and checking in social systems. Consumer trends often follow periods of intensive reinforcement and positive feedback, as increasingly more people desire to own a specific product. Advertising is used to continue to drive such a process of reinforcement. Conversely, if a government or similar public authority sees such a social behaviour pattern change as having unethical social consequence, it will act to dampen or even stop the feedback process. Government interventions like regulation, taxation, imposing custom duties and licensing can all be used to check behavioural feedbacks. If behaviour is made more financially expensive, people might be less motivated to copy it. Government policy and practices therefore need an understanding of the interactive processes of feedback in social systems and sub systems if they are to change behaviour to achieve good social outcomes.

If the concept of feedback assists an understanding of the typology of interactions and their implications in complex systems, the patterns that interactions form can be thought of as networks.

Networks

Paul Ormerod (2012) has described how the scaling up of feedback patterns in a market or wider society produces networks. If an initial idea or product does get copied, this copying can rise exponentially, quickly resulting in a network of communications that is dominated by some people and cases over others. Once an idea is established as successful for a reasonable period, it then becomes easier to scale it up. It is easier for a millionaire to become a billionaire than for any one individual to become a billionaire. Someone with a thousand social media followers is likely to move much quicker in securing their next thousand than someone registering for the first time. While such exponential scaling up of behaviour and trends in networks helps to explain the stubborn features of poverty and inequality in society and why government intervention is needed to address them, another feature of networks is that they often inhibit a nearest neighbour and geographical bias also.

Many networks are characterised by local branches and locally located connectors. Despite the arrival of the internet and the sharing of social media messages worldwide, much human contact is still with people who are geographically close. One key determinant of network construction and communication remains locality. It is argued that many internet communications are with people in close proximity, for example in larger offices or in the towns and cities that people inhabit. Geographical social patterns overlap with social media patterns and they are not mutually exclusive in their forms. So called, ‘small world’ networks are primarily constructed around geographically close or historically close relationships. The occasional links out from these small and intense clusters are through people (connectors) who move or travel in certain roles, but remain in close psychological contact with the other locally based members.

Social network analysis can quantitatively count and plot the patterns of interaction that take place between a given number of people. It can identify the 'connectors', people who often hold greater power in social communications because patterns of communication movements become established through them more than others. For example, in larger organisations, the connectors can be middle operational managers who manage local teams but also have communication across regional divisions and up to senior managers (Haynes, 2015). Their key role in organisational communications becomes essential to the future success and survival of the organisation. The study of patterns of communication through social network analysis and theorising about resulting types of network patterns is a key element of research to better understand complex social systems.

Summarising the influences of complexity theory

Complexity theory challenges the way in which social research engages with the social world. Society is dynamic and not static. Change both occurs at the micro and macro level and in inconsistent ways. The central characteristic of this dynamism is the interactions between people and collective groups of people and the communications that they share or fail to share. This dynamic of interactions is not in a perpetual state of randomness, disorder and chaos. Societies seek order. Patterns of order result. Social research seeks to identify these patterns, but with a humility that accepts such patterns may change their configurations, subject to time and space.

Many scholars and writers have tried to summarise the contribution of complexity theory and its understanding of complex systems to the social sciences. One of the best resulting and seminal definitions was contributed by the late Paul Cilliers (1998, pp. 3–4) and his useful summary is paraphrased below.

1 Complex systems consist of many different cases and elements and the system is defined by the interaction of these cases and elements over time.
2 While it is necessary to have many elements for a system to be complex this is not sufficient to define the characteristics of a complex system. What really characterises a complex system is the interaction between the elements. This interaction is dynamic, not static. The forms of interaction and communication between the elements change over time.
3 The forms of interaction and communication in a complex system are rich in form and detail. Cases and elements are influenced by numerous others.
4 Most interactions within a complex system are short range. That is, they involve communications with cases and elements that are nearby and are neighbours. Therefore, there are limits to the complexity of interactions in complex systems. Every case and element does not communicate directly with all others in a synchronous fashion. The interactions follow network patterns and these patterns have similarities.
5 Given the above, individual elements in the system are often ignorant of the behaviour of the system as a whole, so an element responds to information

that is available to it locally or that has come from specific places or routes in the system.

6 Nevertheless, some interactions are longer range and with far away elements. But even in these cases, the number of modifications and linkage points is relatively small for any one communication. As a result, system interactions follow a relatively small number of steps when contrasted with the complexity of the system.

7 Given the predominance of short range and small steps in complex interactions the communication is subject to feedback loops where communications and the behaviours associated with them get repeated or challenged. Repetition or reinforcement is often described as positive feedback. Challenging the basis of a communication, or attempts to change feedback, is often described as negative feedback. These two characteristics of interactions underpin the structure of complex system interactions and communications and the resulting patterns of similarity and difference across the system.

8 In the main complex systems are relatively open. They interact with an external environment and other systems. There are however, some limits and restrictions to their openness which gives them partial boundaries and characteristics of definition and distinctiveness.

9 Complex systems are far from an equilibrium 'balanced' state. Dynamic flows of energy maintain and change the way the system is organised, and this is necessary for its survival in the environment.

10 History is important evidence for understanding complex systems. As systems evolve over time, their present is always in part influenced by their past. This is in addition to the influence of their current internal dynamics and external influences.

Understanding system change as patterns

The central argument of this book is that if social and economic research methodology accepts the complex nature of the social systems, research needs to move towards a better understanding and measurement of the complex process through which dynamic patterns result and evolve.

Researchers seek to identify patterns in complex systems that converge over time to similarity. A starting state of relationships doesn't necessarily give one much idea about the future course of direction or what kind of future pattern formation a current state will later result in. It is observing the process of the emergence of order over time that permits macro patterns to be monitored and understood. Macro similarity can then be identified. Order and continuities may become evidence, but these are not predictable on the basis of a first, single time point and cross sectional study. It is repeated observation of phenomena and how it behaves over time that brings insight and meaning to the scientist who observes dynamic systems.

Meteorology is typical of such a complex physical system. Weather is inherently dynamic and unstable. Forecasting is only possible for a given locality and in the short term. Medium term forecasting is error bound. As the Realist philosopher Bhaskar (1978, p. 119) notes:

> Theory is never disconfirmed by the contrary behaviour of the uncontrolled world, where all our predictions may be defeated. Meteorology provides an instructive example here. We can have very little confidence in the ex-ante predictions of weather forecasters, because of the instability of the phenomena with which they have to deal.

Meteorologists try to improve their forecasting by studying historical patterns of what has evolved from similar previous conditions and path dependencies. Different historical scenarios are observed. This is not improved prediction based on increased intensity of analysis of physical micro details, like barometric pressure and wind speed. The synthesis comes from macro observation of historical patterns.

As Cohen and Stewart (1994, p. 442) note:

> Reductionism is great for quantitative aspects of internal details. In contrast, our current understanding of external large-scale effects is mostly descriptive and qualitative, geometric rather than numerical. We can recognise a hurricane from a satellite photo, but we can't tell what it is going to do.

These kinds of dynamic and emergent systems are not just physical. Such descriptions are of great relevance to the social, political and economic systems that interest social scientists.

Patterns are not necessarily hierarchically defined, where structure imposes on individuals and determines predictable outcomes. Kontopoulos (1993, p. 226) has argued that complex social systems need to be stood as 'heterarchical' and not hierarchical.

> Any theory that speaks of levels of phenomena that are semi-independent from each other and entangled with each other in other than totally ordered, asymmetrical ways, that is levels that are partially ordered or nonlinearly ordered, is a heterarchical theory.

Therefore, rather than the whole being a sum of its individual parts, or there being a strong top down structural determinism of the behaviour of the parts, heterarchy describes the complex relationship between macro and micro system levels given the emergent properties and behaviours defining the system. There is consequently an under determination of structures and boundaries (Cilliers, 2001; Haynes, 1999, p. 23). But research needs to search for patterns in this emergent world.

The emergence of similar macro patterns over time, sometimes from different starting points, events and contributing factors results also in the conclusion that 'the same outcome can follow from different combinations of conditions' (Ragin, 1999, p. 1225). Social scientists have had to rethink their approach to causality. Olsen (2014) describes the existence of multiple paths to the same outcome as 'equifinality'. Identifying variable patterns and how they change the experience of cases is a different task to arguing and demonstrating that 'X causes Y'. As Collier (1994, p. 34) observes in his discussion of Roy Bhaskar's realist philosophy: 'The events that we can ordinarily observe are not invariably preceded or followed by any other constantly conjoined event'.

Similarly, Cilliers (1998, p. 107) applies this to our understanding of complex systems:

> In our analysis of complex systems . . . we must avoid the trap of trying to find master keys. Because of the mechanisms by which complex systems structure themselves, single principles provide inadequate descriptions. We should rather be sensitive to complex and self-organising interactions and appreciate the play of patterns that perpetually transforms the system itself as well as the environment in which it operates.

The high degree of interactions within complex systems creates these uncertainties and diversity with the causality of outcomes. As Byrne (2011, p. 23) remarks: 'Complex systems are characterised above all else by emergence, by the possession of properties which are not amendable to description in terms of the elements which describe the system.' Cases and elements may not change, but there can be a different configuration of their relationships. Cilliers (1998, p. 90) discusses this as a form of self-organisation within the system:

> The capacity for self-organisation is a property of complex systems which enables them to develop or change internal structure spontaneously and adaptively in order to cope with, or manipulate, their environment.

Interventions into social systems, therefore, contribute to the myriad of interactions and are likely to change the emergent patterns of relationships and behaviour. For example, interventions may invoke defensive reactions from those in the system. These might be referred to as conservative self-organisation, because some are trying to preserve the state of the system and prevent change. As Pawson (2006, p. 33) says about public policy interventions: 'Interventions are open systems and change the conditions that make them work in the first place'. Performance management regimes set up by social organisations to measure outputs and outcomes are notorious for having unintended effects on behaviour of people working in the system and therefore often changing the nature of any cause and effect patterns that do exist (Haynes, 2015). Similarly, setting up a research process may itself influence the results that are found. Social interactions and their possible effects are widespread. Social research needs to examine the emergence of patterns over time and the degree to which cases become similar or different because of these changing patterns of interaction. This is rather different to classical approaches to cause and effect, where there is a cross sectional prediction of a dependent variable from its independent determinates. Such models give the results for a 'typical' case, rather than patterning the movement of real cases.

Arguably the social science discipline that has seen itself more as a classical reductionist and predictable science in recent decades is economics. The subject has been accused of 'physics envy' because of its turn to complex mathematics to theorise on the relationship between businesses and consumers operating in the market place. Economics has been argued to fail because it has attempted to form hierarchical mathematical models that are based on numerous underlying assumptions about how people behave. It has been unable to embrace the emergence of new interactions.

Complexity in economic systems

Paul Ormerod, in his critical deconstruction of economics published in 1994, found fault with several of the scientific assumptions of economics and argued for an explanation based on a complex systems perspective. At the core of his critique was the failure of the rational economic consumer to behave in a singularly rational manner and with a one-dimensional sense of 'value'. Instead, Ormerod noted, different values and different beliefs could motivate consumers, thus allowing them to be motivated by cooperation and altruism as well as personal survival and financial gain. Likewise, given the complexity of such values and motivations, Ormerod (1998) challenged the economic concept of market equilibrium where the sum of a single rationality would always balance supply and demand and allow the price mechanism to operate as a singular and ultimate rational operation and mechanism of perfect allocation. Complexity undermines such a balanced mechanistic view of the economy. He noted that classical economics could not give an adequate account of hidden economies and illegal/criminal economies and their importance to many people's existence. Alongside his work, behavioural economics was emerging as a sophisticated challenge to the neoclassical idea of the rational economic consumer, suggesting that consumers could be far from rational, or subject to different rationalities and perspectives (Kahneman, 2012). Such critical approaches to economics question the domination of market values in contemporary social life, given that a critique of liberal market economics undermines the belief that the price mechanism always represents a true comparative measurement of relative value (Sandel, 2012). By implication, these new economic writers have demonstrated that a price can be 'wrong': either too cheap or too expensive, because the consumer never has perfect information and knowledge (Ormerod, 1994). Other writers, including the Director of the London School of Economics at the time of the financial crash, added to this critique of neoclassical economics after the great economic upheaval of 2008 (Davies, 2010). After the fall of neoclassical economics, it is necessary to approach economic systems as dynamic and often emerging into new forms of existence. They are fundamentally about human behaviour. As behaviour and communication feedback between suppliers and customers changes, new market behaviour results. Economic policy and interventions must adapt rapidly because of diverse and changing behaviour, and they cannot remain static. Consumer behaviour changes and evolves by processes of feedback and emergence.

In 1996, the economist Roger Bottle wrote a seminal text entitled the *Death of Inflation*, where he argued, based on events in Japan, that the world was about to enter an economic era where the key political economic concerns of national economies and their policy makers would have to adapt from controlling inflation to managing debt (Bottle, 1996). Twenty years later, so called 'advanced economies ' like the US, UK, Eurozone and Japan are indeed struggling to manage debt in a zero inflation and ultra-low interest rate economic environment. This illustrates a dynamic and changing interaction between price inflation and interest rates. It illustrates how fundamental dynamic change in social systems can be, in terms of it destabilising traditional relationships, data patterns and understandings.

Ormerod, Rosewell, and Phelps (2009) similarly made a rebuke of the idea that the relationship between inflation and unemployment (as previously expressed by the theory of the Phillips Curve) was deterministic, or fixed within boundaries of concurrent movement. Historically, the Phillips Curve relationship had led to a policy interpretation that reducing unemployment would lead to a trade-off with rising inflation. While it may be that in some social and economic circumstances reductions in unemployment result in price inflation and that this is linked to wage inflation, this is not necessarily always the cause. In fact, since the new millennia many national economies have experienced a rather different pattern of relationships: an expanding labour force, but in the context of increases in part time and low paid employment, increasing women in the labour market, rising work poverty and rising inequality. This has occurred alongside the opening of national borders to capital flows that encourage production to move to countries with lower labour costs. The 'supply side' became ever more competitive, undermining the power of organised labour (Turner, 2008). The end result, in the developed West, was an overall price environment that was not inflationary and prices did not inflate to meet conservative central bank inflation targets.

The great financial recession of 2008 was diagnosed as a crisis of unstainable credit growth, not just money liquidity, but many economic and policy observers still feared price inflation above all other economic woes. Some predicted the new and unconventional central bank policy of quantitative easing (creating liquidity by purchasing financial assets like government treasury bonds) would cause rapid rises in inflation. It did not happen. Indeed, Japan had by then struggled for 20 years with deflation and high levels of debt that it had been unable to reduce in value through reinflation over time. During 2015, the Federal Reserve Bank of the US continually speculated about when it would eventually raise base interest rates, but the Chief Economist of the Bank of England (Haladane, 2015) questioned in September, 2015 if interest rates and inflation in advanced economies would ever return to normal positive levels or whether a new era of money and monetary policy had begun. All this illustrates how in complex economic systems interactions can fundamentally change known key variable patterns. Past trends and key relationships cannot be assumed to remain forever as rigid economic laws to predict the future.

These sea changes in the interaction of microeconomic variables and their eventual combined outcomes illustrate well the dynamic interaction of human action and changing behaviours of governments, firms and consumers in the economy and how the combined macro outcome of interactions and dynamics shifts its social patterns over time. Precise prediction of detail is very difficult, but the overall changes in the form of social and economic patterns that result can be observed over time. Some historical patterns may repeat themselves. The great depression of the 1930s caused by excessive credit expansion and debt deflation had some parallels with the recession of 2008, but also some differences. In many social and economic circumstances, the best that social research can offer is to identify the nature of changing patterns, this as a guide to decisions and intervention rather than seeking to provide precise estimates of exactly what will happen. The main dimensions that can assist social researchers in seeing these patterns is to build their measurement models on the relatively solid foundations of time and space.

Time and space

A social world of dynamic change, where cases like people, organisations and nations constantly interact and evolve creates considerable challenges to the researcher who seeks understanding of such systems. Understanding social systems and their evolution is formidable. Nevertheless, two aspects of the system environment can assist the research process. The first is the deterministic nature of time, or the temporal dimension, and the second is the slow evolution of physical space, the geographical features on which any social system operates. As Byrne (1998, p. 67), remarks: 'The issue of time and changes in time is of course central to any consideration of the dynamics of complex social systems.' Likewise, Cilliers (1998, p. 4) comments: 'Any analysis of a complex system that ignores the dimension of time is incomplete, or at most a synchronic snapshot of a diachronic process.' Andrew Sayer has made a substantial argument about the vital contribution of space to social science research. For example, he says:

> The spatial form is not a constraint upon pre-existing non-spatial social processes but is constitutive of those processes: there is no such thing as non-spatial processes.
>
> (2000, p. 121)

And,

> Space is a necessary dimension of all material phenomena, social ones included, in that they have spatial extension and spatial exclusivity and sometimes a limited range of shapes.
>
> (2000, p. 129).

Of course, even the space dimension – physical geography – has dynamic aspects. The physical environment is always changing, but its relationship with time – when compared with human time over the life course – is relatively stable and predictable. In our lifetime, the physical movement of tectonic plates is relatively small. Permanent change in physical geography is seldom rapid at the macro level, even following the dynamic instability of volcanic eruptions, earthquakes and storms. There may be considerable micro local disruption, but for the majority in global society, there is little immediate effect on the human experience. These deterministic elements of time and space in the social environment give the researcher two dimensions on which to build substantive understanding of complex social systems. Sayer (2000, p. 111) makes the argument below:

> There are well known contrasts between space and time: time has only a single dimension, while space has three; movements are reversible in space, but time is irreversible; but while many things can exist at the same time, two things cannot exist in the same place at the same time (the property of physical exclusivity). Any social science which conceptualizes its objects in ways which contradict these properties – like neoclassical economics, for example – is taking serious risks.

But, conversely, Sayer also argues that the monetarisation and marketisation of social life weaken the deterministic presence of time and space, as, for example, people who hoard money in investments and use it later and in a different place. 'Money allows us to choose with whom we exchange and provides a store of value across space and time' (Sayer, 2000, p. 117). Such transfers of money as a form of power have been a macro lever for economic and social change encouraged by the rise of globalisation.

Cilliers (2001, p. 142) cautions on the multidimensional nature of boundaries in complex organisational systems and that space does not necessarily define them.

> Parts of system may exist in totally different spatial locations. . . . If the components of the system are richly interconnected, there will always be a short route from any component to the 'outside' of the system.

Also, given that social systems are largely constructed and determined by the nature of their communication flows, aspects of communication such as the media and internet further complicate any understanding of social system boundaries and the emergence patterns and their relationship with physical space. While modern social features like electronic money and internet traffic do to some extent change and undermine the defining features of time and space on social life, the argument in this book is still that time and space offer firm foundations on which to build understandings of social change. As Sayer concludes, many of the great challenges that face social science 'concern the way in which things are juxtaposed in space-time' (2000, p. 154).

In summary of the argument of this chapter so far, complexity theory provides a fundamental critique of deterministic and rigid, hierarchical and structuralist approaches to science and social science. It provides a powerful argument for a methodological approach that can deal with an evolving and unstable world. This is a social world where entities and cases (that are as individually complex as human beings and their organisations) coexist together in a constant tension of stability and instability, navigating through periods of order and disorder. In this world, the task of social researchers who seek to understand the social and economic world is more about identifying patterns that are contingent on time and space than it is about proving permanent rules of causation. One methodological approach has already established such a method for understanding the social world and has already evolved to influence working research methods, especially in public policy and service evaluation. This approach is 'critical realism'.

Critical realism

Critical realism is a philosophy of social science that attempts to combine the approach of science to physical materials with the interpretations of social culture and behaviour offered by social science. Critical realism acknowledges the associated progress in understanding and predicting the behaviour of the physical world and combines this progress with the ontology of social constructionism in the social world, where beliefs, values and perceptions determine much of how people behave and interact with each other. Critical realism has many of its roots in the philosophy of Roy Bhaskar (1978), who distinguished between Transcendental Realism (when people apply a scientific method and interpret scientific results) and Critical Naturalism (the dynamic framework of values and beliefs that people use to construct their understanding of both the physical and social world). Pawson (2006, p. 18) says that realist methodology 'steers a path between empiricist and constructivist accounts of scientific explanation'.

The evolution of the philosophy of realism into a research method can best be summarised as the conclusion that different methods need to be applied to different questions.

> To understand the differentiated character of the relation between subject and object we must therefore abandon the usual methodologists quest for the holy grail of a single model for all purposes.
>
> (Sayer, 1992, p. 152)

Byrne (2002, p. 27) has presented a juxtapostion of complexity theory with critical realism, saying that 'we can understand such systems in a realist frame of reference'. The result, he argues, is that we need models that allow us to understand the essential processes of the systems we observe without oversimplifying them in mechanical and static ways. Boulton et al. (2015) caution that we need models, but also need to accept that they will never succeed in capturing reality. The measurement of variables continues in social science quantitative work, but these measurements have to be understood as 'variable traces' that only partially represent real cases. In other words, a mean average score allows us to begin to locate many cases in their relation to this aggregate score, but we derive more information and better understanding from also seeing the full distribution of such scores (and the probabilities of such variation). The latter detail enables the research to relate to the real experience of each individual case. Variable traces are also merely points in time, indicators of where a case was, but never end points. Cases continue to evolve and change in their relationships with each other and this is defined by many variables and their interactions, not just one. Byrne (2011, p. 32) summarises this as:

> A complex realist take regards measurements as generally being not accounts of things in themselves which can be abstracted from the complex systems they describe, the cases – the traditional understanding of variables – but rather as variate traces of the trajectory of those cases.

If the starting point of social research is about people in their social settings, persons as individual cases in social science are unique and never identical. Even identical twins have some differences. Cases are soft entities that do not have hard and permanent physical identities. Science can link people to unique physical traces such as fingerprints and DNA, but this does not tell us everything about them. People change over time. They grow old and take on different physical features and conditions. Their psychological condition constantly changes and adapts, moulded by their past, but always interacting in creative ways with others and their environment. As a result, cases can have inconsistencies. A psychological test score taken by a person at the beginning of the week is repeated and gives a different score at the end of the week. Once people form into social collective cases, such as families, neighbourhoods and organisations, these inconsistencies and unpredictability multiply. It becomes especially difficult to summarise the behaviour and culture of a collective entity like a social organisation or institution. When studying cases in social science, it is often important to focus on similarities and differences, in the context of space and time, rather than to search for fixed entities and permanent causal rules. Critical realism acknowledges the formidable problems that social science faces understanding the complexity and indeterminacy of social life. It suggests that different research methods are likely to be needed to answer different types of questions and challenges, and this depends on the phenomenon being studied.

One division in realist approaches is the degree to which researchers still see the tools of traditional methods, whether they are qualitative or quantitative, as the driving force in applied research. Pawson (2006, pp. 18–19) explains this division as a reaction to the dilemma of how to respond to open and indeterminate social systems (which are explained in this book as complex systems). On the one side of the realist debate, Pawson argues, is a philosophical approach with the dominance of applied philosophy like that of Bhaskar (1978). This is likely to lead to research led by a normative turn although still seeking to justify values by demonstrating traditional research evidence. This approach is criticised for being potentially elitist and idealistic. On the other side of the debate are those who have started their approach more with the pragmatics of method and they therefore seek a 'new empiricism'. Pawson places himself and his work in this latter camp. The method of DPS proposed in this book also falls into this empiricist tradition.

This leads to important issues about order within the research design of social science research (Harrits, 2011). One argument is that a more traditionally scientific approach comes first (via deduction and formal measurement) and then is followed by an inductive and exploratory approach towards ontology and meaning. In effect, a scientific proposition and measurement is then placed in the context of values, beliefs and ethics. Some realists argue the opposite – that research should start from an inductive sense of ontology – being clear on the place of values and beliefs, and the moral and subjective intervention of the research. Formal measurement follows this. Indeed, the relationship between the methodological phases here can be more concurrent (Johnson & Onwuegbuzie, 2004) while acknowledging an awareness of human subjectivity. Likewise, Morgan (2007, p. 73) argues for a pragmatic approach to combining methods that is both realistic and ethical rather than founded on a single philosophical basis:

> The great strength of this pragmatic approach to social science research methodology is its emphasis on the connection between epistemological concerns about the nature of knowledge that we produce and technical concerns about the methods that we use to generate that knowledge.

In a later article, he argues that pragmatism can be based on values from political philosophy rather than necessarily driven by a practical need to do research that works in a specific setting (Morgan, 2014).

Critical realism seeks to clarify the subjective and ethical duty of social research, because researchers, through their humanity, are always in some way part of the phenomena that they research. They are always linked to the research respondent and their environment and because of the existence of this link, a shared humanity is the essence of the researcher's ontological being. Research cannot easily isolate human subject matter into controlled experimental conditions, but should understand the dynamic and changing properties of the social context (Hawe, et al., 2009). The approaches to critical realism already documented and tested in the previous social research literature are therefore an important progress in the application of methods that can deal with the challenge of social and economic complexity. Dynamic Pattern Synthesis evolves from these traditions.

Case similarity and difference

At the core of developing a social research method to understand social complexity is the issue of case definition (Ragin & Becker, 1992). Social order in a large part depends on the integrity of the case. This integrity relates to the previous discussion in this chapter about ontogeny. Individual human beings are recognisable as discrete living systems. They have a beginning and an ending and change through the life course, but are nevertheless identifiable and recognisable as human actors. There remains the paradox of case closure and how cases hold a discrete identity that is juxtaposed with their openness to other systems. The same is true of higher order human cases, like institutions and organisations. They are recognisable for their closed separation that makes them identifiable from other entities, but they are also highly dependent on other systems. The integrity of the case is therefore fundamental to social research. The task is to understand the journey that these cases take over time (given that they all have beginnings and ends) and how similar and dissimilar they are to others, in relation to that journey. A difficult balance must be struck between research, on the one hand, that overly summarises the experience of cases by being overly dependent on models that seek an aggregate or average representation and which, on the other hand, over-emphasises the unique differences of all cases and cannot find any useful patterns of similarity. The experimental method starts out by isolating a limited number of independent effects and then checking differences that result from applying one effect. In social research, the results of these experiences are rarely conclusive in their effect size. Small differences demonstrated by the effect that is applied are subject to tests of inference. Is any difference discovered beyond the possibility of just being a chance occurrence of difference, and is it larger enough to be generalised to a larger population? These probability tests, sometimes applied to quite unsubstantial differences in quantitative effect, have come to have a huge footprint on the practice of social research. The historical practice is that these kinds of experimental approaches need to be replicated and repeated using incremental adjustments over time in order to add areas of knowledge and theory. This is an important part of such research practice. It is all too easy for any one experimental finding to lose its humility about the reality that it just has one piece of the historical jigsaw in its possession. The worst outcome of the experimental approach is when researchers start to confuse statistics of inference with those about real effect size. The underlying 'elephant in the experimental room' is that some diversity is remaining in the experience of individual cases, regardless of small aggregate differences in effect that are found to be statistically significant.

An important and welcome development in economics has been the tendency to present trend research models as a probabilistic fan, where the outer boundaries of likely futures and the degree of uncertain movements of key variables between maximum and minimum futures is evidenced. An example is some of the UK Office for Budget Responsibility (OBR) consideration of a range of possible impacts on the UK growth and public finances in November, 2015 (http://budgetresponsibility.org.uk/). This type of practice is a move towards a more honest portrayal of uncertainty in social research. The politics of UK Brexit demonstrated a huge frustration with economic modelling and presented a challenge to the social research arena in terms of how to model uncertainty and an unprecedented new political and policy situation.

Central to these concerns about the practice of the study of cases is ignoring that uncertainty in future replication of variable based models. This uncertainty is created because cases interact and feed back to each other. Cases are changing and constantly adjusting to the variable information that they receive. Part of the answer to this instability is to measure and examine how cases move and change over time in relation to each other and to see what patterns remain.

Convergence and divergence

When considering case similarity and difference over time, previous methodological research has focused on the issue of convergence and divergence. That is the extent to which cases become more similar, or less like each other. Convergence as a concept is well documented in both macroeconomics and public policy research. Several different definitions and measurements of the concept have resulted. Classical quantitative approaches to convergence identify a key variable of social or economic performance and look at the extent to which cases become more similar in their performance for this variable (Buti & Turrini, 2015).

Whether a group of cases converge over time as indicated by a single variable can be measured by the coefficient of variance. This divides the standard deviation by the mean. A reducing coefficient over time indicates convergence. The coefficient of variance is prone to being skewed by outliers. An alternative single variable measure of convergence is the Gini coefficient. This has the advantage of considering the proportionate contribution of each case score to the changing distribution, where a score of 0 is perfect convergence towards equal distribution. Nevertheless, the Gini coefficient has been criticised for overrepresenting the central area of a distribution and under-representing changes in the tails of distributions. Therefore, in a distribution of incomes, extreme changes in poverty and wealth may not be reflected in the Gini coefficient, if most cases score in the middle percentiles and these cases do not change very much.

Single measures of convergence put emphasis on the social and economic relevance of the chosen indicator. Popular examples are measures over time of changes in income per capita and average income.

More recent developments in measuring convergence have attempted to use multivariate approaches. Beta regression convergence uses a combination of an independent variable (or variables) to regress the average change over time of a key dependent variable. A negative beta regression slope demonstrates convergence. There are several likely problems with the validity of such an approach. The inputting of different independent variables will give different results (Benedek, et al., 2015).

More recent attempts at measuring convergence that seek to increase the validity of what is being measured have included Cluster Analysis. With such multidimensional approaches, convergence is a final qualitative judgement dependent upon how similar or different cases are after they have been subject to a range of indicator measures over time (Irac & Lopez, 2015; Haynes & Haynes, 2016). The development of the method of DPS in this book, using repeats of Cluster Analysis over time, with further consideration of variable effects through the application of Qualitative Comparative Analysis (QCA) to the same datasets, is intended to be a better and more complex assessment of whether cases converge or diverge over time. This reflects a complex social reality, that while cases may change to be more like each other in some respects, they may simultaneously become less similar regarding other characteristics.

Complex causation

One of the most important ontological repercussions of complexity approaches is that different patterns of phenomena, behaviour and events might lead to the same outcome. While for some academics this raises general and fundamental issues about whether complexity can be applied to speculative causal modelling, most still agree that modelling is of value if done with humility and with an acceptance of the severe limitations which can result for the use of modelling based applications and forecasts (Boulton, et al., 2015). Models have practical uses, but will always fail in some circumstances.

Cilliers (2001, p. 138) notes that dynamic interactive feedbacks within complex social systems, such as organisations, raise formidable challenges to understanding what is happening and who is responsible for it.

> When there are lots of simultaneous, nonlinear interactions, it soon becomes impossible to keep track of causal relationships between components.

The social scientist Charles Ragin (Ragin, 1987) has led important theoretical work in the last 30 years to operationalise understandings of multiple causes of the same outcome in logical explanations, primarily through the method of QCA. Qualitative Comparative Analysis compares the extent to which cases share variable characteristics and then looks for multivariate patterns amongst the cases studied.

Different variable patterns may lead to some cases experiencing the same outcome (Cartwright, 2007, p. 35). So, the use of case based methods often leads to a rejection of a singular model of variable causality. While some variables may be found that are a necessary part of the explanation of a specific outcome for a group of cases, these variables may not be sufficient on their own to provide a complete explanation of causality. The following quotation about the cause of disease illustrates this.

> Genes may be necessary causes of disease and disease outcomes but other than for some conditions with very well established mendelian inheritance patterns they are not sufficient causes.
>
> (Byrne & Callaghan, 2014, p. 254)

An example of 'necessary but not sufficient' causality is indicated in Table 1.1.

Table 1.1 Causality: necessary, but not sufficient

Genetic profile AND x = disease
Genetic profile AND poor diet OR low exercise OR high stress = disease
Genetic profile is necessary and the prime implicant, but not a sufficient causal factor in isolation from other factors

Bhaskar wrote about these difficulties when understanding causation in his seminal account of realism.

> Now it is a characteristic of open systems that two or more mechanisms, perhaps of radically different kinds, combine to produce effects; so that because we do not know ex ante which mechanisms will actually be at work (and perhaps have no knowledge of their mode of articulation) events are not deductively predictable. Most events in open system must thus be regarded as 'conjectures'.
> (1978, p. 119)

Bhaskar (1978, p. 125) called the imperfect process of human reflection that proposes what causal and associated powers might be induced from the observation of events and data, 'retroduction'. This, he pointed out, was not 'prediction'.

Zachariadis et al. (2013) provide us with a more recent interpretation of retroduction:

> Retroduction allows researchers to move between the knowledge of empirical phenomena as expressed through events to the creation of explanations (or hypothesising) in ways that hold "ontological depth" and can potentially give some indications on the existence of the unobservable entities.

In other words, retroduction attempts to take some evidence found at one level of reality and then to reflect on its meaning at some deeper level. This gives further explanation and meaning to what has been already been evidenced. (Carter & New, 2004).

Bhaskar (1978, pp. 48–50) defines the resulting modification of causality as 'generative mechanisms'. This concept takes account of the central concerns of realism, namely the limitations of human perception and understanding, and the environmental discontinuties imposed by time and space. Applied social science research has to accept some limitations in its ability to generalise from one situation to another (Sanderson, 2000).

While there has been a tendency in the history of social research to see quantitative and qualitative research as a dualism, with very different strengths and weaknesses, many of those influenced by critical realism now caution against that. No longer is quantitative research seen as having the superior contribution to explaining causation. For example, Bryman (2004, p. 170) has argued that quantitative and qualitative research may have as many similarities as differences, for example, in their application to test and modify theories and concepts and speculate about causation. Sayer modifies the language of causality to the consideration of 'connections' and reminds us that realism always places causality into an environmental context that includes its space-time location.

> Realists seek substantial connections among phenomena rather than formal associations or regularities. In explaining associations, they seek to distinguish what must be the case from what merely can be the case. Explanation

> of the social world also requires an attentiveness to its stratification, to emergent powers arising from certain relationships, and to the ways in which the operation of causal mechanisms depends on the constraining and enabling effects of contexts. Realists also recognise the concept-dependence of social phenomena and the need to interpret meaningful actions, though since reasons can be causes, this is not something separate from or alternative to causal explanation.
>
> (2000, p. 27)

The historical path that a relationship between cases and variables has taken can be one key route by which the researcher discerns patterns, but this is not necessarily path causality. Again, contextual circumstances may be highly significant in their influence.

> When social science tries to focus on what seems a uniform pattern of behaviour it soon discovers that it is shaped by historical forces, with the result that it may occur in one culture and not the next.
>
> (Pawson, 2006, p. 18)

The concept of path dependency, considered earlier in the chapter, confirms that while the system's starting point is not deterministic, it can have a major influence on its future possibilities. As Kiel and Elliot (1997) argues, the initial starting point of a social system has influence on its later behaviour. Historical study can help with seeing the shape of what might emerge, but it struggles with the reality that the re-emergence of political and economic events will never be identical but only keeping certain characteristics in the future. This is very much a qualitative judgement about how patterns evolve. As Kauffman (1995, p. 300) says, historians are: 'looking for the web of influences that kaleidoscopically interact with one another to create the patterns that unfold'.

Empirical realists like Pawson (2006, p. 21) still seek generative models of causation. They seek 'outcome patterns' rather than 'outcome regularities'. The fact that there are some consistencies over time in pattern repetition provides a causal basis. This provides evidence of a generative mechanism, as long as it is accepted that these mechanisms may not be consistent over time and space and there are always some missing elements of the causal models that have not been fully appreciated and understood. This is because of the nature of complexity. The concept of causality remains, but its permanency has been modified.

Another key aspect of generative mechanisms in social science research with human subjects is the subject's perception and understanding of their involvement in the process being researched. For example, one key reason a generative mechanism might apply in one situation and not another, is because the culture and belief systems of those in the second situation are completely different. This is an often-cited reason for the 'failure' of developed world overseas aid projects in countries that are less wealthy and industrialised, or why an organisational change project applied successfully in one company does not work in another. The context and mechanism need to be considered concurrently. Part of the context is the subjective basis of human observation and experience. This is the 'relative autonomy of consciousness. . .the fact that people can interpret the same situation differently' (Sayer, 2000, p. 134).

In their seminal definition of realist explanation Pawson and Tilley (1997, p. 71) state:

> The basic task of social inquiry is to explain interesting, puzzling, socially significant regularities (R). Explanation takes the form of positing some underlying mechanism (M) which generates the regularity and thus consists of propositions about how the interplay between structure and agency has constituted the regularity. Within realist investigation there is also investigation of how the workings of such mechanisms are contingent and conditional, and thus only fired in particular local, historical or institutional contexts (C).

It is also important to consider that causality may have a random or probabilistic element (Frisch, 2014). This might also be described as 'luck'. For example, research may demonstrate that successful entrepreneurship is largely dependent on a mix of getting the right finance, training and creativity, but that it also depends on some chance interactions with other entrepreneurs. While an entrepreneur can seek out and act to put themselves into the right social networks and meeting places to achieve this, there will be an element of probabilistic chance about whether they meet certain individuals who can add maximum value to their own inventions. Getting into the right networks and meeting places to achieve this is sometimes described as 'making your own luck', but it is also problematic in that one can invest large amounts of time in social and internet based network communications without the certainty of knowing one will encounter the right kinds of people. Randomness can have some influence on social outcomes.

Methodological conclusions

A methodology that accepts great complexity of its subject matter will have relevance in both science and the social sciences. The core principles of this methodology in the social sciences are now summarised at the end of this first chapter.

Simplicity evolves towards complexity, both in the physical realm and the behaviour that results. Examples are the evolution towards complexity and diversity in institutions and markets, types of families and types of community.

This evolution towards complexity is characterised by the diversity of interactions and communication between elements, and so systems are highly relational and interconnected and how a social system evolves very much depends on how the people within it are connecting and communicating, and what feedback is reinforced and what feedback is checked and balanced. Examples are negotiations in roles and relationships, changes and movement in the labour market, buying and selling and stockholding in market places.

In addition, complexity is characterised by both time periods and places that are a mix of instability and stability and stability. This mix of order and disorder can be understood as stable and identifiable patterns and the subsequent breakdown or evolving of these patterns and their re-emergence in similar or different shapes. Over history, some strong underlying patterns may be observed, some are unstable and short term, others are persistent and long term, and others break down in the short term, but still re-emerge again over the longer term. To better understand complex systems is to search for these patterns.

Reductionist methods cannot understand complexity alone. Observing the detail does not always explain higher order phenomena. As the late John Urry remarks:

> Complexity argues against reductionism, against reducing the whole to the parts. . . . It emphasizes how positive feedback loops can exacerbate initial stresses in the system and render it unable to absorb shocks to re-establish the original equilibrium.
>
> (2003, p. 13)

Complexity does include some manifestations of hierarchy. Systems are comprised of levels and scales of organisation and behaviour that are both separate from each other and connected to each other. The interaction of these levels and scales is dynamic and not constant, so that at some points in time the interaction is exponential and at other points in time it is negligible and constrained by other factors. It is also argued by complexity theorists that the structure of scales is recursive, that is, there are aspects of similarity and pattern running right through it from the macro to micro.

> A large system of linear elements can usually be collapsed into an equivalent system that is very much smaller. Non-linearity also guarantees that small causes have large results and vice versa. It is a precondition for complexity.
>
> (Cilliers, 1998, p. 4)

The structure of systems is also understandable by observing its heterarchy – that is the structures that exist horizontally across the system – as well as vertically from top to bottom.

But complexity theory and critical realism caution against a preoccupation with social structures. In complex systems interactions, the forms of communications the interaction takes and the feedbacks it communicates are all important to the journey of evolution the system is taking.

The trend of interactions within levels and scales, and across levels and scales, is both far from equilibrium and has the characteristic of long distributional tails, where outliers have a more substantive effect than would be predicted by a normal distribution. For example, income distribution tends to have positive distribution with a long tail of high scores. This has also been described as it is easier to become a billionaire once you are a millionaire, than it is to become a millionaire in the first place.

Mixed methods

As previously stated, this book is concerned with mixed methods, with seeking the best skills and access to evidence offered by quantitative and qualitative methods.

> When dealing with complex phenomena, no single method will yield the whole truth. Approaching a complex system playfully allows for different avenues of advance, different viewpoints, and, perhaps, a better understanding of its characteristics.
>
> (Cilliers, 1998, p. 23)

Decisions must be made about which methods are appropriate for the system ontology being explored.

> Predictive, statistical and iconological models . . . should be restricted to those ontological levels in which collective social phenomena can be legitimately treated as a statistical aggregated phenomenon, that is, as being composed of additive, numerable, and interchangeable individual units. . . . Structural, ideal typical, or narrative history models of . . . processes can be deployed with maximum effectiveness in those very areas where predictive, statistical, and iconological patterns are least suited to those upper ontological levels in which cultural products, historically specific events, and collective symbolic processes are the rule.
>
> (Harvey & Reed, 1997, p. 314)

The development of a new combined method to be called Dynamic Pattern Synthesis in this monograph seeks to take a pragmatic view towards applying a new research method to the task of unmasking social and economic complexity.

Conclusions

The exploration of methodology in this chapter has argued that complex social systems are evolving in emergent and dynamic ways and are often not reducible to mechanistic causal explanations that hold for long periods of time. These methodological arguments are not new and have been offered for several decades by leading scholars like David Byrne and Roy Bhaskar.

> This is a new kind of 'social engineering science', a rational programme not of assertion based on absolute prediction, but of social action based on specification of the multiple but not limitless range of urban options.
>
> (Byrne, 1998, p. 166)

> If science is to be possible the world must be open; it is men that experimentally close it. And they do so to find out about structures, not to record patterns of events.
>
> (Bhaskar, 1978, p. 126)

What is needed is a diversity of methods, and reflexivity when methods are not working so they can be adjusted and combined with pragmatism. Qualitative judgements and observations are as important as mechanical quantitative measurements and solutions.

Social science has to seek to explain this dynanmic change. It operates its research and scholarship methods in a highly dynamic environment. Elliott and Kiel (1997, p. 74) say that new methods are needed that: 'attempt to capture the multiple interactions extant in complex systems while also incorporating the multiple outcomes and behaviors that result from complex system behavior'.

Since the 1990s, progress has been made in assessing and using existing quantitative and qualitative methods that are best able to cope with the dynamic characteristics of the social world (Byrne & Callaghan, 2014). Cluster Analysis and QCA are two such examples of methods applied to understand complexity and change. This is an approach that has learnt from the pragmatism of critical realism as advocated by Byrne (2002).

> The principles . . . we have to deal with are complex systems – non-linear, far from equilibric and evolutionary complex systems – and that we can understand such systems in a realist frame of reference.
>
> (Byrne, 2002, p. 27)

In the next chapter, it is argued that the strengths of Cluster Analysis and QCA as methods can be combined and repeated over time to give a new and more robust approach to gaining insights into complex social systems and their dynamic properties and changing patterns.

The purpose of the newly proposed mixed method, that has characteristics of both quantitative and qualitative research methods, is to search for patterns and pattern stability over time. It is an approach that seeks to be case based, but using variables to indicate the changing characteristics of these cases, the similarities and differences.

In a world of such dynamic change the combined method presented in the subsequent chapters of this book is used to develop models of case based patterns. These are partial models that can never be complete, given the impossibility of knowing and including all the likely interactions and parameters of influence created by dynamic change. But these emerging partial models give some idea of the places of stability and instability that exist in our social and economic world and how the cases studied are navigating them.

As Cilliers (2001, p. 138) has advised:

> It is impossible to have a perfect model of a complex system. This is not because of some inadequacy in our modelling techniques, but a result of the meaning of the notions "model" and "complex". There will always be a gap between the two. This gap should serve as a creative impulse that continually challenges us to transform our models, not as a reason to give up.

2 The method

Introducing Dynamic Pattern Synthesis

Introduction

In this chapter the aim is to consider the use of methods that can deliver the complex methodological requirements of the previous chapter.

The concept of synthesis was defined in the introduction to this book as the making of a whole from constituent parts. But it is more than a 'reverse reductionism'. In social science, synthesis refers to the social phenomenon that occurs when people act together. The results are greater than the sum of parts. Many social developments are only possible when people act together in communicated and coordinated ways. Social institutions like families, religious organisations and economic organisations are such examples. They are a complex synthesis of human behaviour and they are dynamic and always changing to some extent. In the real world of social synthesis there are no permanent physical boundaries, the people define any boundaries themselves and the rules and codes of interaction.

> It is often difficult to define the border of a complex system. Instead of being a characteristic of the system itself, the scope of the system is usually determined by the purpose of the description of the system, and is thus often influenced by the position of the observer.
>
> (Cilliers, 1998, p. 4)

> Even syntheses have to be selective.
>
> (Sayer, 2000, p. 151)

The approach of meta-analysis has often been associated with synthesis in that it attempts to draw together the conclusions of several studies and then concludes on the overall findings. Nevertheless, if it does this in a mechanistic process it may reproduce validity problems inherent in reductionist designs, rather than leading to a dynamic synthesis (Borenstein, et al., 2009). For example, a quantitative and statistical approach to meta-analysis may do little more than combine the sample size of numerous small studies so that rather small differences in effect can be generalised to a larger population. Meta-analysis, if built around a synthesis of similar studies with positivist methods and statistical analytical techniques, may ironically ignore the addition of much contextual evidence (Pawson, 2006, p. ch 3)

Byrne (2004, pp. 54–55) has considered the role of the multilevel modelling as a statistical attempt to deal with complex social systems. While he acknowledges the progress made in isolating different levels of explanation like the structural (ie: hospital or school) from individual measures, he is concerned that it is still fundamentally a variable centred model that seeks variable aggregates as explanations that are independent of cases. Therefore, multilevel modelling does not fully engage with the complexity of open systems and the unpredictable paths that cases can take, these trajectories being generated by shared emergent properties.

Using the qualitative paradigm, some scholars have also examined synthesis as a method for combining previous studies and deriving a combined benefit from them (Major & Savin-Baden, 2010). The more open and inductive approach of qualitative methods makes the researcher less likely to fall foul of the problem of reproducing the limitations of a given statistical method many times over, but replicating errors of measurement and judgement that invalidate theoretial patterns can still be an issue to be aware of in more qualitative approaches. It is argued that when quantatative approches are used, it is more straightforward for those scrutinising systematically the work of others to identify the likely measurement and calculation problems.

Other researchers have previously attempted to find a dynamic method for dealing with the complex evolution of social and economic change over time. For example, Ferragina et al. (2013) proposed the use of Multiple Correspondence Analysis (MCA) to examine the dynamics of developed countries' welfare state sub systems changing in relation to each other in the international economic system.

Some previous attempts have been made at Dynamic Pattern Analysis (DPA), in particular using spatial, visual and mathematical methods in geographical applications. Aleskerov et al. (2014) developed a mathematical model for evaluating the evolution of Russian regions and classified them based on their strategies and operations over time. Identifying patterns was at the core of their project.

> The term 'pattern' refers to a combination of values of some features such that objects with these feature values significantly differ from other objects.
>
> (Aleskerov, et al., 2014 p. 1)

Leong et al. (2009) carried out a form of DPA to analyse spatial-temporal crime relationships. Here dynamic pattern analysis aimed to identify changing spatial patterns at different times of the year. It did this by combining event data with the clustering of spatial data and the mapping of temporal data. The resulting patterns identified were: similar spatial patterns but occuring at different points of time, an interactive connection between two geographical places that could be linked to a social phenonema, and other forms of associations linked to events, places and times.

Cilliers (1998, p. 24) has argued that there are two different methodologies for modelling complex systems: 'logical rules versus connectionist'. He makes a powerful argument for the use of a connectionist approach. The Dynamic Pattern Synthesis (DPS) model developed in this book starts from an essentially logical rules basis, in its application of Cluster Analysis to explore similarities and differences between cases. By repeating this mathematical method over time and observing the movement of cases, the method of DPS also applies a qualitative element of interpreting the macro movement of connections. In this sense theoretical statements are concluded on the basis of observations of what happens to the connections between cases. One problem is that case connections are nevertheless synthesised into a macro expression of variable scores and, therefore, limited in how real they are to the reliability of the variables inputted into the method. Nevertheless, all modelling is a partial representation of what is happening in a complex system and the qualitative interpretation over time is the critical element that gives the model its dynamic and 'added value' element.

It is considered in this book that it is reasonable to try and model complexity, but that it must be done with a humility given that a model will never be complete and always subject to errors. As Cilliers (2001, p. 137) says:

> We cannot deal with reality in all its complexity. Our models have to reduce this complexity in order to generate some understanding. In the process, something is obviously lost. If we have a good model, we would hope that that which is left out is unimportant. . .The underlying problem with models of complexity is, however, even more serious. No matter how we construct the model, it will be flawed, and what is more, we do not know in which way it is flawed.

With these sobering words in mind, the chapter now progresses to explain the first element of DPS; that is the application of Cluster Analysis.

Cluster Analysis

Cluster Analysis (CA) is a quantitative case based method that uses variable scores to measure how similar or different cases are to each other. Aldenderfer and Blashfield (1984, p. 9) remarks that CA is a method for both 'developing a typology or classification' and 'investigating useful conceptual schemes for grouping entities'. CA creates a mathematical argument for reasons as to why cases can be colocated in sets. CA is not the only method that attempts to categorise cases in this way. Everitt (1993) illustrated with examples that some basic descriptive statistical techniques can be used to begin to explore the similarity and differences between cases. For example, three dimensional scatter plots allow cases to be respresented visually in accordance with their scores for three scale variables.

Byrne (2002, p. 127) gives a helpful definition of the essential characteristics of CA as a method.

> Clusters. . .can be understood as something like prototypical classifications systems. There is no requirement that all members of a cluster should be alike on all the variate traces which have been used to construct the clusters. In contrast, a cell in a multidimensional contingency table is a polythetic class because all cases in that cell are identical in terms of all the measured variate

> traces which have been used in constructing that cell. If we think of cells as classes, even if somewhat inflexible polythetic classes, then we can handle our interpretation of them in a different way.

There are many different sub types of CA. These are different according to the mathematical method used and how this is applied to calculations with the available data. Differences may occur in how formulae are used to assess if the cases are similar or not (for example, either prioritising measuring their similarity or their difference), or by starting a mathematical process based on reducing clusters to the minimum number of possible groupings first, or – alternatively – considering the maximum number of groupings first.

In the main, because CA involves running many calculations to examine permutations of possible relationships between cases, the method tends to be used with a relatively small numbers of cases (relative in terms of what is now normal experience with quantitative methods), although two step Cluster Analysis is an exploratory form of CA that is now offered by computer programs like SPSS which allows for an exploration of larger datasets for possible groupings, also using both categorical and scale data.

Cluster Analysis can be used as an exploratory method, to see how many clusters computer modelling identifies and the characteristics of these clusters, but it can also be used to confirm a specific hypothesis about the number of clusters present in a dataset.

As with many types of mathematical and statistical modelling, researchers need to be aware that CA will generate different results when running the different optional algorithms and calculation methods that it offers (Everitt, 1993). When using CA as an exploratory tool, the researcher needs to guard against 'statistical artefacts', that is, patterns that are purely mathematical and have no useful interpretation in real life. The qualitative interpretation of the social science researcher about 'what' any clusters identified really are in the context of a theoretical literature and language is an extremely important task. Like all quantitative methods, therefore, the researcher needs to theorise the design and resulting choice of clusters. The decision about how to conceptualise resulting clusters and validate them alongside previous research and literature and available qualitative contextual research is as important as the data analysis itself. Cluster Analysis cannot be used to find a single perfect classification of clusters. As with other types of statistical and mathematical modelling in the social sciences, the aim of the method is to use the approach to make the best possible argument about the existence of clusters. When combining CA with a complex systems approach to theory and methodology, CA is particularly useful for examining the changing cluster patterns in a dataset over time, as it then becomes a useful tool for examining dynamic social patterns and seeing how interactions and relationships between cases are changing the very identify of those cases as individual identities.

Cluster Analysis is primarily used as a case based method. It holds cases constant while comparing them (Uprichard, 2009). It does not isolate cases on the basis of individual variable characteristics and then look for a sum of variable characteristics that gives an average or aggregate score for all cases. As Williams and Dyer (2004, p. 78) note:

> Unlike variable analysis one begins from the case and seeks characteristics held in common, rather than beginning with the characteristics and seeking their association with cases.

Cluster Analysis: specific approaches

The first distinction in CA methods is between monothetic and polythetic approaches.

Monothetic cluster definitions depend entirely on one variable. For example, countries are allocated to GDP clusters according to their relative score and proximity to each other when comparing those scores. An example of an economic variable that could be used for such a monothetic definition is GDP per capita in US dollars.

Polythetic cluster definitions depend on more than one variable. This is the approach offered by modern statistical programs. In bivariate and multivariate CA the difference between cases can no longer be calculated by a single subtraction of difference in scores. Instead, it is common to use an equation based on Pythagoras's Theorem and calculated from the hypotenuse of a triangle formed by the available data points. When three or more variables are added to the CA the same approach is extended and applied. Given the further dimensions, the approach to the calculation is known as an *n*-dimensional space and algorithms like Euclidean distances are used to calculate measures of dissimilarity between the cases. The Euclidean distance can be squared to give greater weight to objects that are farther apart and, therefore, it is also possible to use the square root of this calculation.

Distance measures

Several different measures of distance are available in contemporary multivariate CA. They have different consequences in terms of their effect on the final model. This is because when calculating the distance between cases with multiple variables and *n*-dimensional spaces, different methods will result in different measurements for this spatial distance, according to the mechanics of the differing algorithms.

Euclidean distances based on multiple variables can be disproportionately influenced by variables with larger values. This is also true for other distance measures. For this reason, data transformation to create standardised variables is often applied before data is entered into a CA. One common approach is to calculate z scores for all variables (where z equals the data observation minus the sample mean average then divided by the sample standard deviation). Nevertheless, there will be some research situations where, for example, due to issues of social realism and modelling this realism, the researcher wants to permit differences in variable scales and scores to be able to affect cluster definitions and groupings.

There are several other distance measures offered when working with interval or scale variables by contemporary statistical programs. The city block

'Manhattan' calculation is the average distance between two cases as calculated from the available variable dimensions. The Chebychev distance algorithm finds the maximum difference between two cases based on the available variable differences. Distance measures can also be partially use defined. For example, SPSS offers a Customised Power measure where the user defines the power and root. Power is the weight that the user wants to apply to individual dimensions of difference and the root is used to mitigate the weight that is placed on larger differences between cases.

If working with a set of categorical variables, computer programs like SPSS also offer distance measures based on chi square and the phi coefficient.

Hierarchical and nonhierarchical CA

The second distinction when considering possible approaches to CA is between hierarchical and nonhierarchical methods.

When hierarchical methods are used, no prior assumption or specification of the number of clusters to be identified has to be used. Although in practice, such a request can be used in a computer based hierarchical cluster methods procedure, and it is an option in many modern statistical software products that offer hierarchical CA. Nonhierarchical methods usually require a prior specification of the number of clusters to be computed.

The most common method with nonhierarchical CA is k-means. Here only interval and scale variables are used and the computer undertakes many repeated calculations to determine the most efficient allocation of cases to a given number of clusters. These calculations are based on maximising significant differences between the averages scores for cases in each cluster and have some similarities to the methods used in traditional Analysis of Variance (ANOVA).

Hierarchical cluster methods algorithms either start with all cases as separate and individual entities that need to be joined, or with all cases in one single cluster that require disaggregation. Starting the method with all cases as separate is referred to as an 'agglomerative' approach. Beginning the hierarchical procedure with all cases together in the same set is frequently called a 'divisive' approach (Aldenderfer and Blashfield, 1984; Pastor, 2010).

Hierarchical clustering methods have the problem of a tendency to produce clustering artefacts in the latter stages of their calculations. For example, when using agglomerative approaches, the later stages will merge most cases into two final clusters that have little theoretical basis for social categorisation. Likewise, once a hierarchical process has linked or separated cases at an early stage in its mathematical calculations, it cannot later reverse that judgement, as it continues to make additional links or separations with other cases. There is therefore a limit to the number of dimensions of similarity and difference that it can consider in any one series of calculations (Everitt, 1993). The researcher can to some extent counteract this limitation by running numerous different models for consideration before making a final qualitative judgement about the most meaningful patterns discovered.

Clustering algorithms

Cluster Analysis can use a range of mathematical algorithms to calculate the order of agglomeration or division. An important matter with the choice of algorithm is to know that the method chosen will impact the resulting cluster definition and patterns. For this reason, some researchers prefer to run several models trying different clustering algorithms before deciding on the most valid and reliable result to report. The ideal methodological approach is to make a judgement that is both informed by knowledge of the method and likely consequences of the algorithm, and to juxtapose this with research realism about the nature of resulting clusters. This second aspect is an important qualitative judgement of the research that is informed by previous knowledge and theory, not least the results of any similar historical studies.

One approach to clustering algorithms is to use the average values for cases to form first clusters and then the resulting averages for clusters to decide any further modifications. Unweighted pair-groups, also often called centroid Average Linking, calculates the central tendency of the inputted data points and positions cases according to these scores. When applied during a hierarchical process, cases may move quite noticeably into other clusters as the central position is recalculated, but this is mitigated to some extent by the hierarchical order already initiated. Therefore, a secondary effect maybe a disproportionate impact for one case that exaggerates its subsequent similarity to an extension (or reduction) in clusters.

The furthest neighbour method uses the greatest dissimilarity score between a case in different clusters. It is argued that applying this method tends to result in constricted clusters of similar cases and less outliers.

In contrast to the furthest neighbour calculation, the nearest neighbour method finds the least dissimilarity between the cases in different clusters. As a result, it is reasoned that it tends to find the opposite general pattern to furthest neighbour calculations, which is more dispersed and separated clusters. This has applications when researchers wish to maximise the differences in their classifications and avoid overgeneralising cases.

Clustering 'within groups' calculates cluster membership using the cluster central tendency while minimising variance within a cluster. This again increases the likelihood of constricted clusters with smaller memberships and can be useful when seeking to create homogeneous groups.

Dendrogram charts

The most popular way to visualise how cluster methods are working and the structure of resulting cluster patterns, and the differences between applying different methods to the same data, is by using a computer software sub menu that allows the printing of CA dendrogram graphics. This is possible in SPSS, but dendrograms are not produced by default in this software and have to be selected in a sub menu (an SPSS example is given below, later in this chapter).

When using agglomerative hierarchical clustering the dendrogram is a tree like structure with branches, where the analysis starts with the top of the tree or smaller branches, as all cases are treated separately at the beginning of the analysis. In Figure 2.1, as the dendrogram is horizontal the imagery of the tree has fallen from its base on the right-hand side, so that the small branches are to the left. In the first stage of analysis, look at the detailed branches on the left. Small clusters, often just pairings with some remaining outliers, are created. Next, moving across the diagram towards the right side of the page, the analysis proceeds to find further linking branches to agglomerate the small clusters. In the hierarchical analysis, the first cluster formation is measured against all other cases and once cases have been joined in a branch they cannot be later separated. Finally, the computer analysis joins all the branches in a single trunk. In Figure 2.1 below, the dendrogram joins Ayesha and Jayne first, as being most similar, then adds Mark and finally Li Wei.

The interpretation here is that Mark and Li Wei are not similar, because they are not joined together early in the analysis (the analysis proceeds from the left side of the dendrogram to its end point on the right-hand side). The dendrogram 'rescaled distance cluster combine' is a measure of similarity, where Jayne and Ayesha are joined at point 1 on the scale and Li Wei is not joined with any other cases until the final point 25. The remaining decision for the data analyst is whether Mark, who joins Jayne and Ayesha at point 7, is judged to be in the cluster or not. This

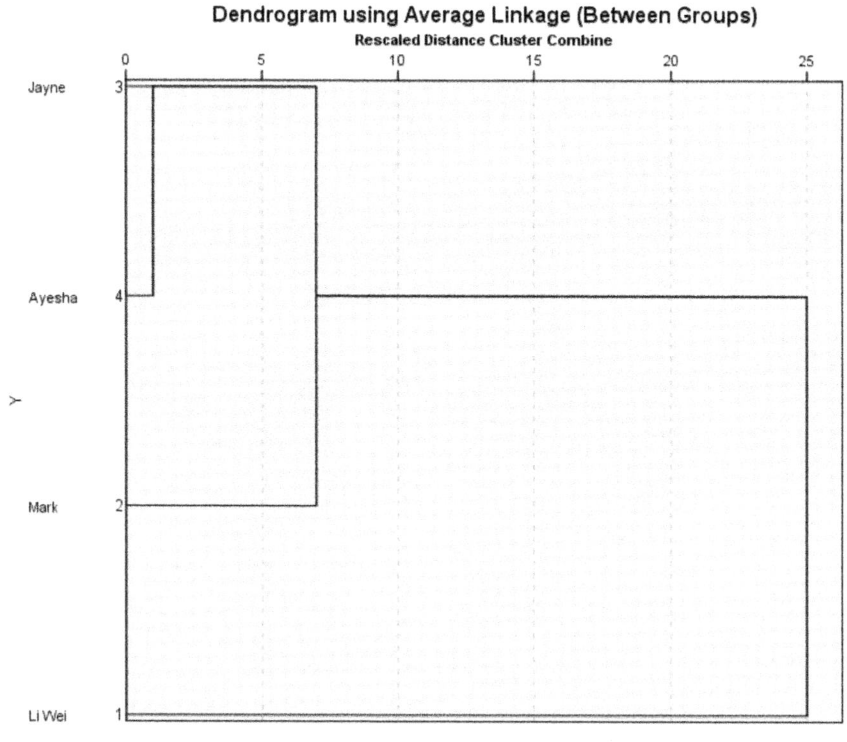

Figure 2.1 An example of a simple dendrogram

becomes as much about a qualitative conceptual decision (based on the substance of the research questions posed and the theory already known) as it is a statistical observation.

Icicle charts

Another common chart used to understand CA results is the icicle chart. The icicle chart reveals how the agglomeration of cases proceeds through the process of CA. Figure 2.2 shows an example of an icicle plot produced from a very simple example dataset comprised of four people who are the inputted cases. The bottom row shows the formation of the first cluster. This is comprised of Jayne and Ayesha. The bold shading in the chart indicates this linkage. At this point of the analysis there are three clusters: Jayne and Ayesha; Mark; Li Wei (Mark and Li Wei remain as individuals). The left-hand scale in the icicle plot in Figure 2.2 shows the number of clusters formed. Moving up the page, the next agglomeration is when two clusters are formed. This happens when Mark joins with Jayne and Ayesha. The bold shading indicated this new linkage. Finally, at the top of the chart, all cases are linked together into a single cluster. Usually this final computation has little

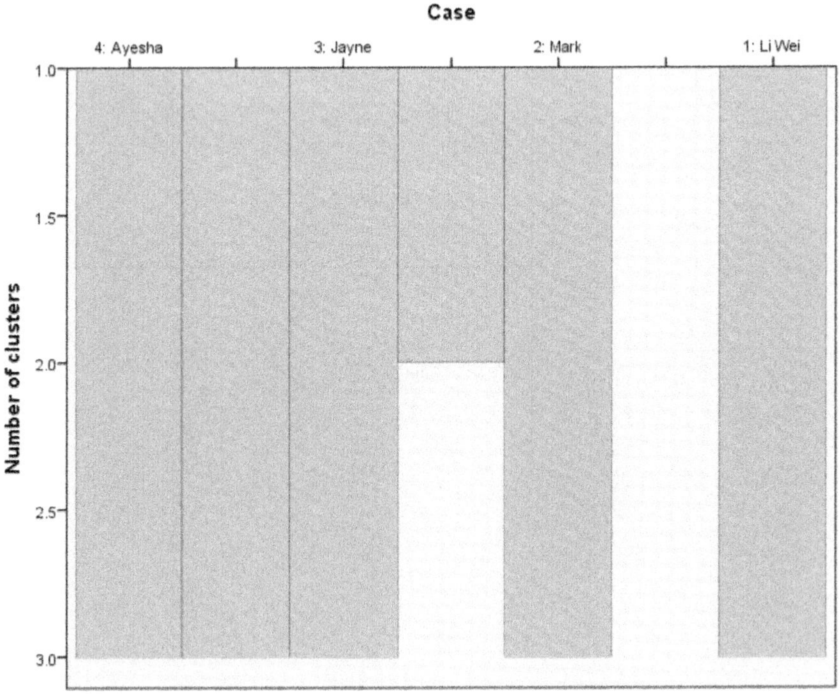

Figure 2.2 Understanding an icicle plot

Table 2.1 Example of an agglomeration schedule: Jayne, Ayesha, Mark and Li Wei

Agglomeration Schedule						
Stage	*Cluster Combined*		*Coefficients*	*Stage Cluster First Appears*		*Next Stage*
	Cluster 1	*Cluster 2*		*Cluster 1*	*Cluster 2*	
1	3	4	2.000	0	0	2
2	2	3	13.000	0	1	3
3	1	2	46.667	0	2	0

substantive value and it merely represents the final mathematical completion of the agglomerative scheduling.

Cluster Analysis also gives some statistical output to assist with the visual and conceptual decision about how clusters are being formed. For example, when using hierarchical CA, SPSS by default produces a table called the agglomeration schedule (Table 2.1). This schedule reveals the mathematical sequence of the selection of cases into clusters where the already selected distance measurement joins the most similar cases together to form the first cluster. The measurement calculation then proceeds to compare this first cluster with other cases to complete the hierarchical agglomeration into further clusters. By examining the coefficient scores in the agglomeration table, it is usually possible to see a point of increased differentiation where there is noticeably less evidence of similarity. In Table 2.1, the differentiation is immediate, as the coefficient has to increase from 2.0 to 13.00 at stage 2 before case 2 (Mark) can be linked with Jayne (case 3). At this point, Ayesha has already been subsumed earlier in stage 1 into case 3, to form a single cluster. Comparing this evidence with the dendrogram in Figure 2.1, the researcher might well decide that there is not enough substantive evidence for arguing that Mark can be linked to the same cluster as Jayne and Ayesha. Notice in the SPSS output that the agglomeration schedule table textual language uses the wording *cluster combine*, as a proxy also for illustrating 'case combine'. Note that the scores of the measurement coefficient will be different in other examples, depending on the type of distance measurement selected in the computer software, but this should not affect the overall principle of judging at what point in each example a major change in differentiation occurs.

Using SPSS to calculate and compare cluster methods

In this next section, SPSS version 24 is used to illustrate the differences that can result in approaches to hierarchical agglomerative cluster analysis, as described above when selecting different clustering algorithms. A simple and fictional data set is used, to maximise understanding of the consequences of different mathematical approaches.

Table 2.2 Fictional dataset for hierarchical CA

City	*GDP 2016 (£m)*	*Percentage of adults in relative poverty*	*Percentage of adults over 65*	*Average temp (C)*	*National university ranking*	*Percentage of jobs in manufacturing*	*Tourist visits per year*
Barchester	2.3	9	17	15	3	2	250,000
Wexton	4.0	21	10	12	12	7	400,000
Morching-ham	4.1	19	11	12	24	10	450,000
Longford	1.7	17	12	14	45	14	150,000
Middling	2.1	11	10	14	1	7	90,000
Seaport	3.4	20	15	12	77	11	85,000
Highborough	2.9	12	14	12	18	8	150,000

The example dataset is defined in Table 2.2 and shows seven cities as defined by seven different variables.

When this data was entered into SPSS version 24, the data and variable windows in Figures 2.3 and 2.4 were produced. All variables are scale variables.

Using SPSS version 24 it is possible to compute a hierarchical CA.

The following SPSS command menus are applied.

Analyse/Classify/Hierarchical Cluster

This presents a sub menu in Figure 2.5.

All seven scale variables are entered into the box to the right of the menu and the city name string variable is entered into 'Label Cases by' box.

In this example, the purpose is to examine the consequence of using different cluster methods. This is demonstrated by examining dendrograms produced by the different methods. The aim is to turn off all other output in the SPSS sub menus and to focus solely on the dendrogram figures. However, some output like the agglomeration schedule is produced by default, and so it is not possible to reduce all output only to the dendrogram.

Nevertheless, Figure 2.6 shows how to turn off the icicle plot option and to turn on the dendrogram.

The default clustering method offered by SPSS hierarchical CA is average linkage (between groups) and this option is run in the first example (Figure 2.7). The result is skewed by the large scaling of values distributed in the tourist visits per year variable, as shown in Figure 2.7. While Barchester is linked with Middling, somewhat inconsistently by the dendrogram, it remains outside the first

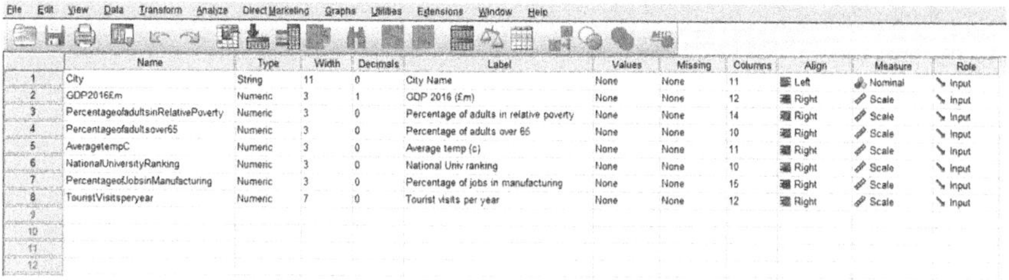

Figure 2.3 City data: SPSS variable definitions view

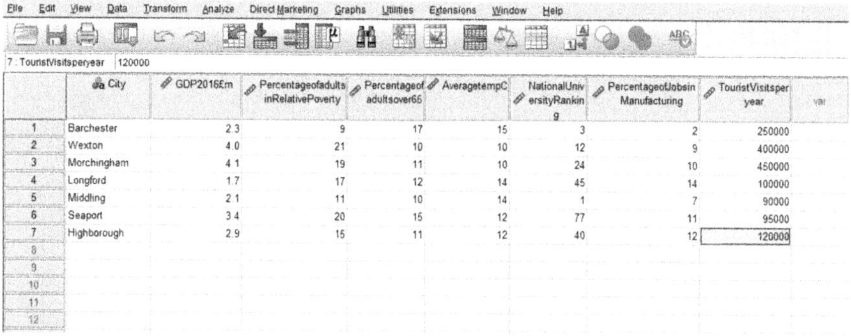

Figure 2.4 City data: SPSS data view

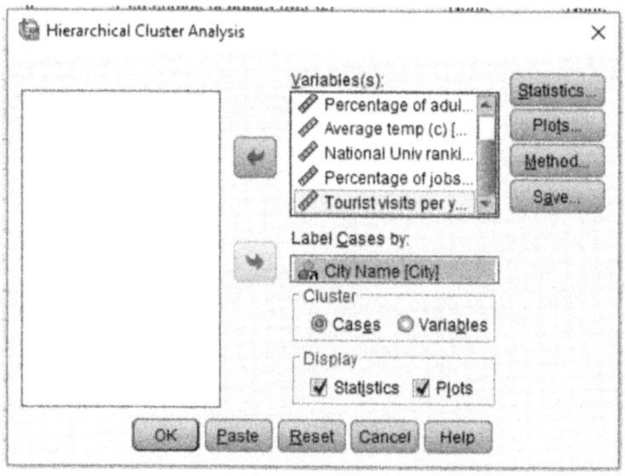

Figure 2.5 Hierarchical cluster sub menu

tight cluster and is given a placement near Wexton and Morchingham. These are two industrial cities that it does not have any real affinity with.

When the same default method is recomputed, but this time using a standardisation to *z* values, Barchester is more decisively aligned with Middling (Figure 2.8).

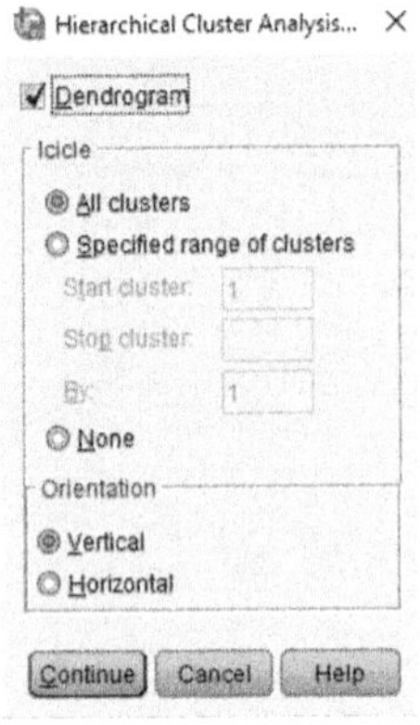

Figure 2.6 Changing the SPSS hierarchical CA plots sub menu

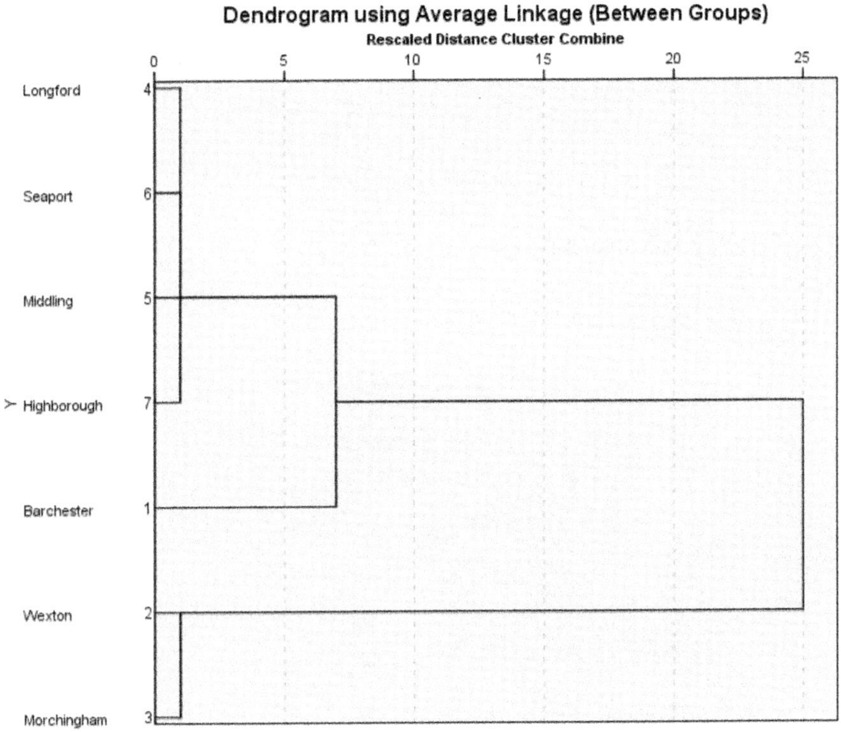

Figure 2.7 Dendrogram using average linkage without standardisation

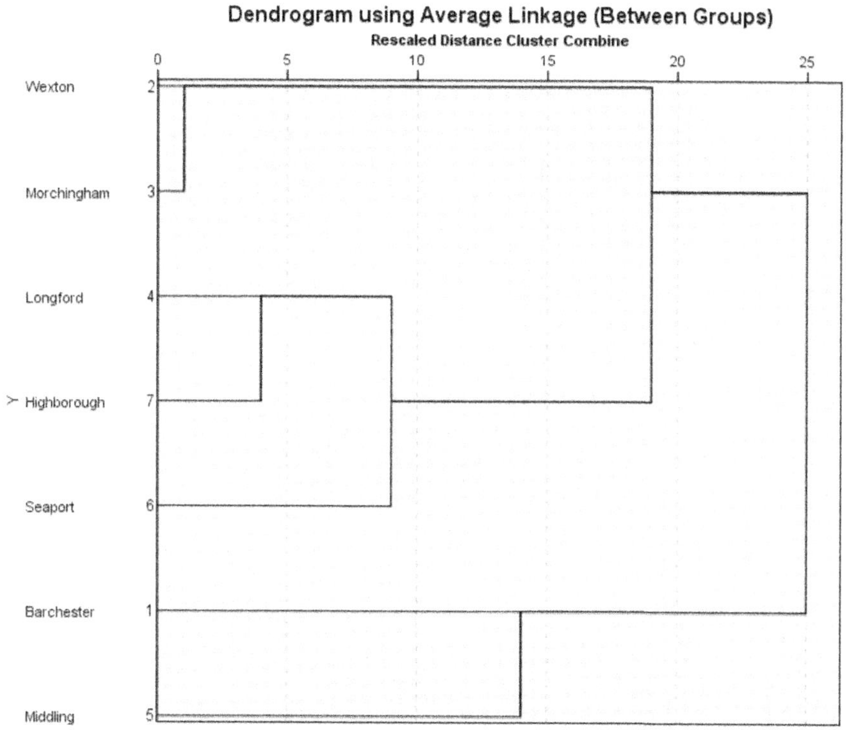

Figure 2.8 Dendrogram using average linkage with standardisation

Further considerations of the effects of clustering algorithms

Having identified that the choice of clustering algorithms can affect the resulting analysis, the next section considers some of the detailed implications of this using the seven cities dataset in Figures 2.3 and 2.4. In all the following examples, z score standardisation is used to mitigate the effect of the extent of the scale variable tourist visits per year.

Ward's method has proved popular with many social science studies in the past. It amalgamates clusters based on calculating the smallest possible increase in the error sum of squares (ESS). It has been argued that this results in the method isolating the optimal number of descriptive clusters for the dataset early in the cluster calculation process. Figure 2.9 shows the resulting dendrogram using Ward's Linkage. Three clusters are formed in the early stages of the analysis, with three clear branches resulting. Cluster 1 is Wexton and Morchingham; cluster 2 is Longford and Highborough and Seaport; and cluster 3 is Barchester and Middling. Any further amalgamation occurs much later in the analysis.

The next example run by the computer uses the clustering algorithm of Complete Linkage (Figure 2.10). The same cluster interpretation results when compared to

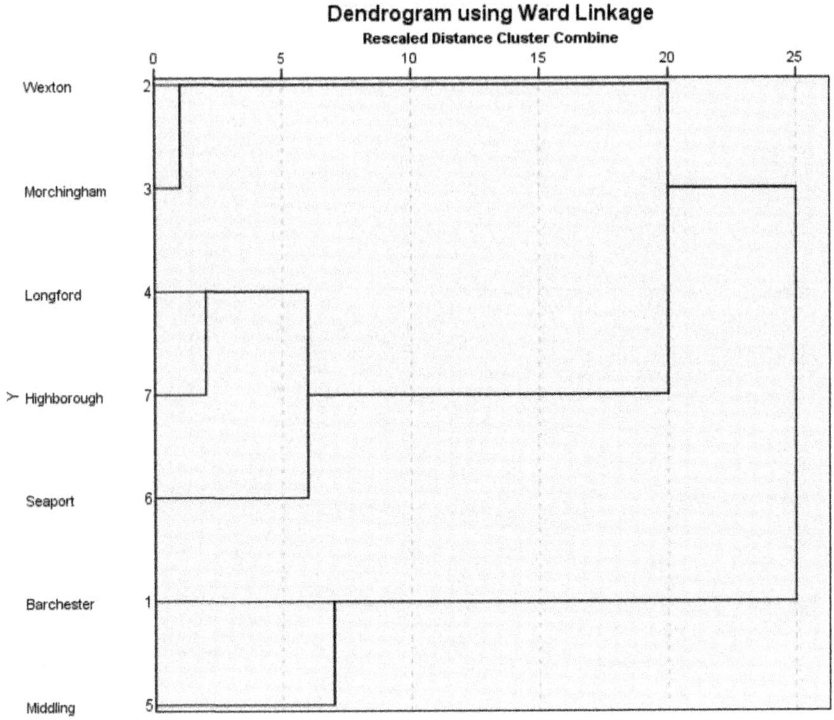

Figure 2.9 Ward's method with standardised data: the city data set

Ward's method in Figure 2.9, but the only difference is that the clusters form slightly later in the analytical process. This is evidenced by the differences in the *rescaled distance cluster combine scale* at the top of the dendrograms in Figures 2.9 and 2.10.

The next clustering algorithm that is used is Median Linkage. This method can mitigate distributional issues where some variables have skewed distributions. The results are shown in Figure 2.11. Again, the same three clusters are demonstrated, but the dendrogram raises issues about the third cluster, as Barchester and Middling are linked late in the analysis on the rescaled cluster combine axis.

The remaining clustering algorithms begin to disrupt the fundamental three cluster model that has been created so far. Figure 2.12 uses the Centroid Linkage method. As a result, as seen in the dendrogram, Barchester is separated from its partnership with Middling and instead kept as an outlier. Late in the computer analysis Middling is joined with the second cluster, so is ultimately judged to be more similar to Longford, Highborough and Seaport than Barchester. This is a conceptual shift when compared to the three clustering methods applied previously.

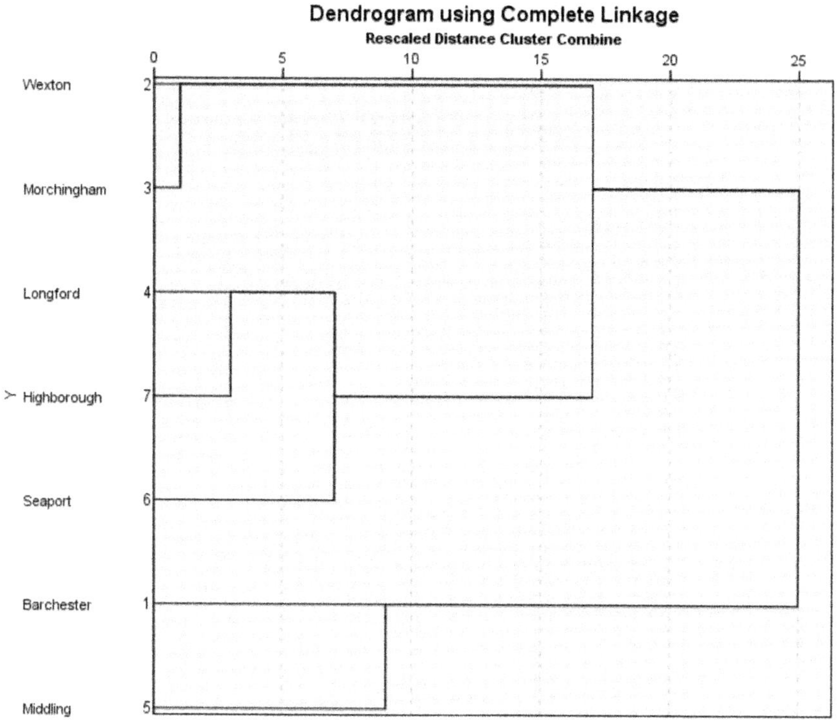

Figure 2.10 Complete linkage method with standardised data: the city data set

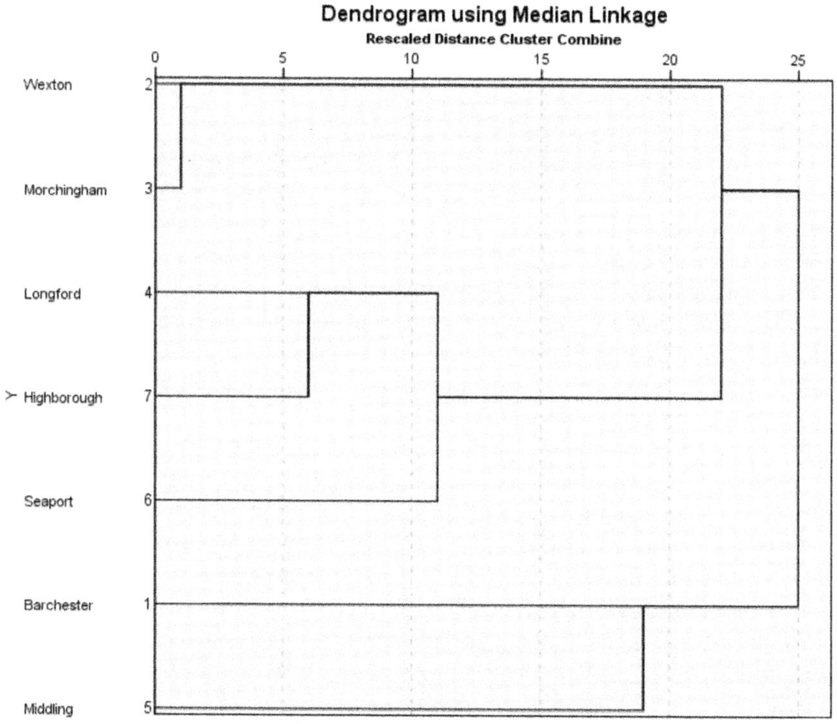

Figure 2.11 Median linkage method with standardised data: the city data set

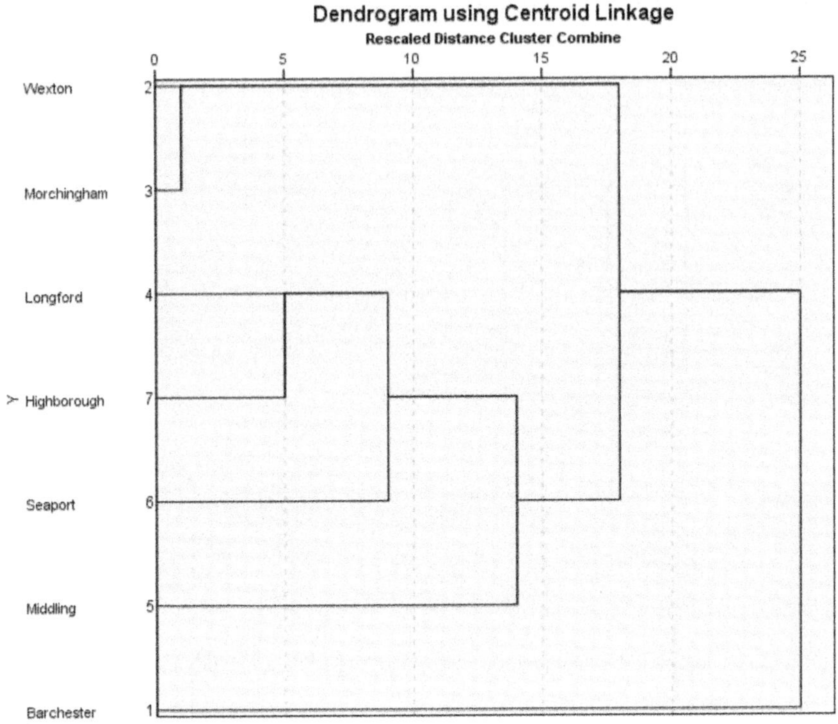

Figure 2.12 Centroid linkage method with standardised data: the city data set

In Figure 2.13, the application of the clustering algorithm Average Linking (Within Groups), reproduces a dendrogram structure that is almost identical to the Centroid Linkage method. Again, Barchester is separated as outlier. The only difference between Figures 2.12 and 2.13 is that the final agglomeration of clusters 1 and 2 happens later in the model, with there being greater distance in the Rescaled Distance Cluster Combine score at this point in the analysis. This has little substantial influence on the conceptual analysis, as arguably the researcher will make a qualitative judgement that cluster 1 and 2 should remain separate entities, regardless of the detail of these differences.

The same principle applies when examining Figure 2.14. This final example demonstrates a computation of a different clustering method, Single Linkage. The distance of cluster combining is slightly higher than when using Average Linking.

Overall, by running all the possible clustering methods available in SPSS v24, while holding the cases and data constant, and standardised as *z* scores, the substantive effects of the different methods have been demonstrated.

The overall effect can be summarised as the effect that different methods have through their use of different calculations of similarity and difference, and this

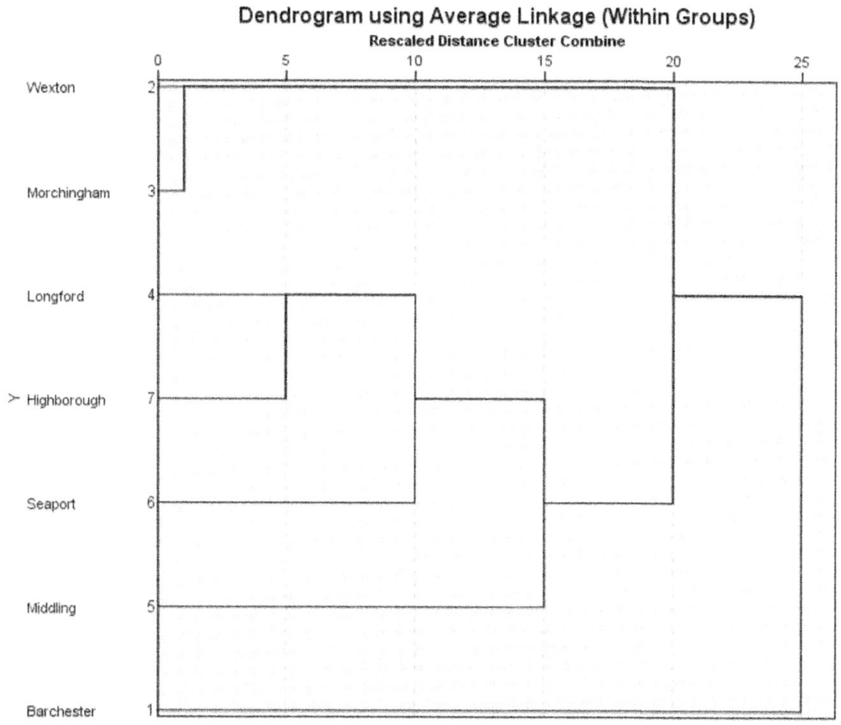

Figure 2.13 Average linkage method with standardised data: the city data set

results in different points in the matrix at which clusters are agglomerated. While the standardisation of scores ensures most of the overall resulting substantive clusters are similar in their shape and appearance, the different methods can result in different judgements about potential outliers. The key case in this respect is Barchester and whether it should be considered as unique, or similar to Middling. An associated decision of categorisation is whether Middling should be considered as similar to cluster 2.

To be more confident about our final substantive research decision with regard to the categorisation of these cities into theoretical clusters, it is necessary to understand more about the variable effects on cluster membership. It is also important to remember that cluster membership is not necessarily mutually exclusive, especially over time. For example, it is quite possible for a city to be partially like one set on some variable aspects and partially like another cluster set on other variable aspects. This is a reality that is realistic and important to conclude in a world of complex systems. Similarly, it is entirely possible that cases can change how similar or dissimilar they look to other cases over time, as the complex systems they inhabit evolve.

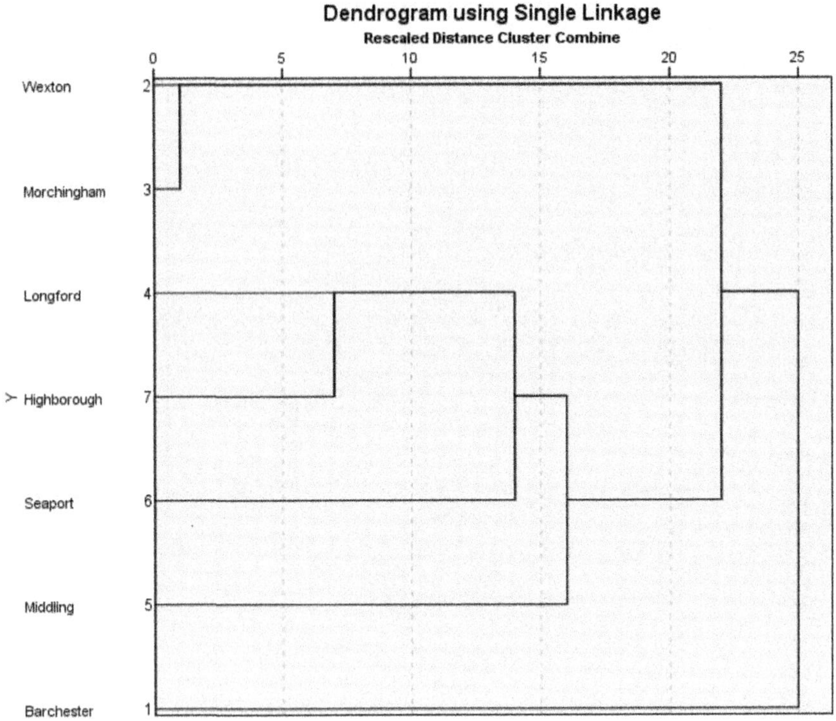

Figure 2.14 Single linkage method with standardised data: the city data set

Understanding variable relationships within cluster formulation

Having created clusters with a range of variables, the researcher needs to know what variables are shaping the definition of clusters. It is possible to explore this using a range of conventional descriptive statistics. Inferential statistics can also be computed, but care is needed in their interpretation. Cluster Analysis is primarily an exploratory approach, often with a sample sub set of data and not necessarily a sample being inferred to a large population. Critical values of probability and significance may therefore have little logical application. Nevertheless, alongside measures of association and effect, significance values can still be computed to give an indication of where association and effect are substantial, and less likely to be noise and random artefacts in the real world. The computation of p values in this way can guard against over interpretation of an effect size with a small dataset. Again, the overriding issue here is that the researcher is using quantitative measures and calculations in an explorative, almost qualitative way, for informed judgements, rather than to make final scientific controlled decisions. Arguably for this reason, the best methods approach when seeking to understand the impact of variables on clusters is to use QCA. This chapter will move to fully assess the concurrent use of QCA with CA, both to validate further clusters identified, but also to understand variable effects on cluster definition. First it is important to make one further point about how CA can help understand dynamic patterns in social life.

Repeating CA over time

Cluster Analysis allows the researcher to explore the relationship of cases by assessing their similarity and difference according to a multiple range of information from different variable scores. Rather than computing a typical case based on aggregate independent variable scores that best predicts a single dependent variable score, CA retains the integrity of the case by seeing how similar or different cases are by putting them into similar groups. Each case is not primarily defined by its dependent variable score, and what caused it to get that score, but instead defined by its characteristics on a wide range of variables and how that compares it to others. For complex case entities like people, cities and countries, this ability to view the case as a multiple collection of information is important. In some research, seeing people according to a major performance variable such as educational score may remain important, but in many other situations having a broader and more complex view of cases is vital if one is to avoid overly simplifying the corresponding assessment of social life.

What adds considerably to our case based understanding in the complex social world, is how cases are changing over time in relation to each other. Arguably such knowledge is much more useful to a practitioner or policymaker than a simple one off cross sectional picture of case similarities.

Therefore, dynamic pattern analysis and having a synthesis based understanding of cases' changing relationships over time, depends on repeating CA over time, with the same cases and ideally the same variable measures. Of particular interest are cases that move between cluster groups over time.

Given the dynamic nature of cases and how they interact, we cannot expect the relationship between variable scores and cases, and variables and clusters to remain stable over time. The researcher will expect these patterns to be a mixture of stability and instability, static and change.

One method that can be used to better inform the construction and imperfection of clusters, in particular with regard to variable influences, is QCA. The next section explains how this method works, before the chapter proceeds to apply a working example to the city dataset.

Qualitative Comparative Analysis

Qualitative Comparative Analysis (QCA) has a background in comparative political sociology as a method to compare countries (Ragin, 1987, 1999). This has been referred to as 'Macro-Comparative' research (Berg-Schlosser, et al., 2009, p. 3). By implication, QCA has become associated with analysing a small sample of cases where the given number of countries (for example, OECD countries) was the sample being studied. The method was never designed to compute statistical inference from a sample to a population. It is fundamentally explorative and qualitative in nature, using numbers and mathematical logic to systematically scrutinise theory and ideas of causation. Berg-Schlosser et al. (2009, p. 5) identify that within a methods typology it lies between a paired comparison and a statistical method. Although it does use mathematical logic, QCA is inherently qualitative in its desire to consider configurational patterns and possible pattern contradictions (Hudson & Kuhner, 2013). In more recent years it has also been used to explore meso level comparisons, for example the social and policy practices of organisations, and also – in some cases – individuals. It is also argued that QCA does have the potential to work with larger sample sizes, although some authors caution against doing this (Ebbinghaus, 2005).

Qualitative Comparative Analysis is a case based method that is interested in how cases compare rather than aggregate variable scores that are supposed to represent archetypal cases. As mentioned in Chapter 1, QCA provides a method for considering what Ragin referred to as 'multiple conjunctural causation', that is, a causation that is not necessarily permanent and subject to different circumstances which result in the same outcome (Ragin, 1997). This makes it ideal for considering the complex and changing combination of patterns associated with the phenomenon of complex social systems.

Qualitative Comparative Analysis is a method that uses the quantitative coding of categories or ordinal scales to systematically compare cases and their degree of similarity or difference to each other. Its innovative contribution to social science methods has been in illustrating real world examples of multiple and complex causal configurations (Ragin, 1987). For example, such differentiated configurations result in cases that might share the same outcome but, as sub groups of cases, have some fundamentally different variable scores. These cases experience different paths to get to the same outcome. Such patterns of configuration, as understood by different sub groups of cases and patterns of cases, are an alternative to statistical models of aggregation where causality is demonstrated by aggregate and average variable scores and cases are related to a central tendency of the distribution of experiences. Qualitative Comparative Analysis has also become known for explaining multiple causality by using the convention of Boolean algebra. By offering a method to consider an outcome variable and routes to outcome, QCA offers something as a case based method that CA cannot. It has been argued that QCA is a method for testing macro theory and that it should usually be used for this purpose, rather than to explore datasets in a less structured manner (Rihoux, et al., 2011).

Crisp set QCA

The earliest version of QCA became known as crisp set QCA often abbreviated as QCA^{cs} . In the crisp set version, the variables used to define the experience of the cases are reduced to two categories. In effect, they become nominal, dichotomous

Table 2.3 A truth table examining pollution in cities

	Car ownership	*Employed*	*Growth*	*Pollution*
City one	1	0	0	1
City two	1	0	0	1
City three	1	1	1	1
City four	0	1	1	0
City five	0	1	1	0

Table 2.4 A simplified truth table examining pollution in cities

	Car ownership	*Employed*	*Growth*	*Pollution*
Cities one/two	1	0	0	1
City three	1	1	1	1
Cities four/five	0	1	1	0

variables. This results in a reduction of variables into two categories that are above or below a set threshold. The crisp set approach also lends itself well to the use of variables that are by their nature – binary constructs, in particular whether a case does, or does not, have a specific characteristic. A key judgement of the researcher is setting these thresholds. For example, a decision might be made to set the threshold at the median point of a scale variable that measures percentage scores. Crisp set allocation is used to generate a so-called 'truth table' (Ragin, 1999). A truth table is simply a presentation of binary scores for each case (or similar groups of cases) on each variable, usually including the identification of an outcome variable also.

Table 2.3 shows an example of a truth table with five cases and four variables. Here the variables were originally measured with intervals (using city percentage scores) and, for the purposes of the truth table, are reduced and separated into dichotomous categorical variables by use of the median average point in the data set. This allows each cell to be expressed as a 0 (below median score) and 1 (above median score). There are four variables and the fourth is used as an outcome variable (average rate of air pollution)

As several individual cities share identical variable scores, the table can be reduced to Table 2.4.

Boolean algebra can be used to explore the table results. The following Boolean convention is used. Lower case letters denote below threshold variable scores and upper case, capital letters, denote above threshold scores. The symbol * means plus, or in addition to. The symbol + means or, as an alternative.

The outcome of lower city pollution levels (using the notation of lower case p) can be expressed as follows:

$$c * E * G = p$$

The outcome of the higher city pollution levels is more complex and has multiple configurations, but can be expressed as:

$$C * e * g + C * E * G = P$$

This shows that P has two different causal configurations. However, there is one factor that is shared by both configurations and that is C, high car ownership. Boolean algebra refers to such shared characteristics in causation as prime implicants. So, C is the prime implicant of P.

Of course, there is another key piece of quantitative evidence in respect of P. Two cities do share the same configuration (cities one and two) compared with one that does not (city three).

It should be noted that Boolean algebra can also use other forms of notation.

Many would argue that QCA is designed to be a theoretical tool, especially in the sense of exploring theoretical explanations. Therefore, with the above result it would certainly make sense to look at the key differences of city three when compared to cities one and two, as city three is effectively an outlier. It would be useful to add further cities with the same data to see if more configurations arise, of if city three continues to be an outlier. Also, it might be possible to add additional variables to explore what effect they have on the configurations and the ability to summarise solutions.

One method for dealing with the concern about dichotomising interval or ordinal variables is to use QCA^{cs} primarily to examine variables with a single degree of freedom. For example, in political studies, QCA^{cs} has been used to compare whether nation states have particular types of institutions or if a specific type of historical event has influenced them. These aspects of consideration are dichotomous.

Another approach has been to develop the QCA method further so that it offers more sensitivity with the explanatory scoring variables (Ragin, 2009). Fuzzy set QCA, abbreviated as QCA^{fs}, allows the researcher to grade the extent that cases are represented by specific variables (Kvist, 1999). The binary of 0 and 1 is still used by the researcher as a starting point to allocate a score, but a decimal fraction is used to indicate the degree and extent to which the variable reflects traces of the case. As an example, if cases are cities, and the researcher is interested in the extent to which a city is historical, the research could allocate a proportionate score where 0 indicates a new city with no history, 0.45 as a limited influence of history, 0.5 as typical history as expected for the country context, and 0.9 as very historical and 1 for an ancient city with protected status and no modern development of any significance. This provides a more 'fine grain' measurement than the simple 'in' or 'out', 0 or 1 dichotomy.

In addition, QCA has also a multivalue method. Here some of the variables can be assigned different values, not just the dichotomy of 0 or 1. Both these methods, while introducing more measurement precision, make clear theoretical statements potentially more difficult to extract.

The use of more fine grain measurements in QCA is a trade-off with the concept of using QCA to simplify and explore theoretical simplifications and summary statements. Of course, if one adds more fine grain measurement, this makes more difficult the task of deducing simplified theoretical statements that follow the logical rules implicit in the method.

This can be considered as a trade-off between simplifications of measurement versus simplification of theory. Any model or theory in the sub domain of complexity theory is a simplification and a simple statement about more complex things.

Accounting for time in case based methods

Various approaches have been proposed as to how to measure and account for the passing of time in QCA models (García-Castro & Ariño, 2013). While some of these have focused on including a time variable, the approach taken in this book is for time to be considered a different dimension to the research rather than as a variable. It is important that time is considered as a further, third dimension and not as a standard independent variable because time is a consistent presence across all cases and variables and cannot be weighted in its influence in a comparative manner when viewed alongside other variables (Gerrits & Verweij, 2013). Therefore, the approach in this book and in the development of the DPS approach is to simply repeat the running of models at different time periods with the same cases. This avoids a time variable in a multivariate model distorting the effect of other variables as an artefact. The purpose is then for the researcher to observe changes in the complete model, in particular with regard to the location of cases in relation to each other, at different time points. Time is, therefore, treated as a consistent dimension, not a variable.

Combining the two methods: CA and QCA

The method presented in this book for the synthesis of dynamic patterns is to use a combined application of CA and QCA and to repeat this over time with the same cases and variables.

The advantages offered by CA are that it can make full benefit of interval and scale variables and their influence of cluster differences. This negates the challenge and judgement of reducing variables in QCA to a limited number of categories, such as thresholds in QCA^{cs} or fuzzy scores in QCA^{fs} or simplified numerical scale scores in QCA^{mv}. Cluster Analysis is also an exploratory tool, whereas QCA has been developed primarily for testing theory.

The challenge, however, presented after finding a useful CA model, is to ascertain what variable scores are most related to cluster definition at a fixed point in time. While conventional statistical descriptives, effect tests and even inferential statistics, have some value in understanding variable effects on cluster definition, they also contain certain dangers, in terms of potentially making statistical assumptions about the actual degree of variable influence.

Given the qualitative nature of the epistemological task that presents the researcher who is interpreting the real meaning of the social existence of the clusters they discover, and that clusters often represent ideal types and summary statements and are rarely evidence of a continuous static state, QCA is entirely appropriate for validating clusters. If hierarchical CA is used to propose a hypothesis about the likely number of substantive clusters, QCA is an appropriate method for testing this theoretical statement. QCA is also suitable for considering variable effects on cluster definition at one time point, and if required, computing an outcome variable at that time point. Further, it is also possible for the researcher to be flexible at the QCA stage in terms of adding additional explanatory categorical variables to the model that were not possible to add to the CA.

The sequence of this combined method is to undertake the CA first, to make informed judgements about the most 'real' clusters to test. These clusters are then considered as an outcome variable against variable definitions using QCA, to see how well this validates the clusters, to consider adding additional explanatory variables to the QCA, and to consider whether an additional outcome variable should be added to the final model. Once a satisfactory combined model has been demonstrated and argued, the same combined method should be replicated, at a later time point. This method, in combination, including both its quantitative and qualitative aspects, construes DPS. Dynamic Pattern Synthesis is the ability of the researcher to interpret the social interaction and changing dynamic of the existence of cases in the context of their social environment, and over time.

Qualitative Comparative Analysis and software packages

There are many different software packages available to perform QCA. A good starting point is to consider what is currently available via the COMPASS website (www.compasss.org). COMPASS represents an international network of scholars and researchers who are interested in systematic logical analysis of cases. It is an abbreviation for Comparative Methods for Systematic cross-case analysis. The website provides an excellent resource and overview of this area of methods. It includes a comprehensive summary of software available to carry out QCA and methods similar to QCA with hyperlinks provided to where the software can be downloaded.

One of the most long standing software products that can be used relatively easily with a Windows PC to compute a QCA is Tosmana, as developed by Dr Lasse Cronqvist at the University of Trier. The software is now in version 1.52 as released in September 2016. The software and details about its copyright and use can be downloaded at www.tosmana.net.

Applying QCA

Table 2.5 shows the process for reducing the seven city data table originally demonstrated in Table 2.1 to a set of binary scores that can be analysed with a crisp set QCA. Each city's score on a variable is converted to a binary score of 0 or 1 according to the relationship with the mean and median averages measures of central tendency for the seven cities. A 0 represents that the case is below threshold for that variable. A score of 1 represents the case is above threshold for that variable.

Table 2.5 QCA: conversion of city data variables to binary scores

City	*GDP 2016 £m*	*Percentage of adults in relative poverty*	*Percentage of adults over 65*	*Average temp (C)*	*National university ranking*	*Percentage of jobs in manufacturing*	*Tourist visits per year*
Barchester	2.30	9.00	17.00	15.00	3	2.00	250,000
Wexton	4.00	21.00	10.00	10.00	12	9.00	400,000
Morchingham	4.10	19.00	11.00	10.00	24	10.00	450,000
Longford	1.70	17.00	12.00	14.00	45	14.00	100,000
Middling	2.10	11.00	10.00	14.00	1	7.00	90,000
Seaport	3.40	20.00	15.00	12.00	77	11.00	95,000
Highborough	2.90	15.00	11.00	12.00	40	12.00	120,000
Mean	*2.93*	*16.00*	*12.29*	*12.43*	*28.86*	*9.29*	*21,5000*
Median	*2.90*	*17.00*	*11.00*	*12.00*	*24.00*	*10.00*	*120,000*
Conversion to binary scores					*(reversed)*		
Barchester	0	0	1	1	1	0	1
Wexton	1	1	0	0	1	0	1
Morchingham	1	1	0	0	1	1	1
Longford	0	1	1	1	0	1	0
Middling	0	0	0	1	1	0	0
Seaport	1	1	1	0	0	1	0
Highborough	1	0	0	0	0	1	0

The national scores for the cities' universities are reversed, so that ranks 1, 3, 12 and 24 are recorded as 1 (above threshold). Where one city's score is identical to the median average, reference is made to the mean average in order for the researcher to decide whether to record it as above or below threshold.

When using Microsoft Excel the following formula can be used to convert scale scores to a binary: =IF(OR(AND(B2>=B$15),), "1",IF(AND(B2<=B$15), "0 ", " ")). In this example, B2 is the cell with the scale variable score to be used for conversion and the constant B$15 is the median average threshold reference point.

Next, in Table 2.6, a cluster outcome variable is created so that the binary patterns can be compared with the cluster definitions. Qualitative Comparative Analysis is now used to test the hypothesis that the three clusters evidenced in the CA methods and the resulting dendrograms in Figures 2.8 through to 2.11 can be justified with reference to the variable patterns.

Table 2.6 is ranked and sorted first by the final column and cluster values and then in order of each of the independent conditions. This forms a table that

Table 2.6 QCA threshold scores with cluster outcome variable added

City	*GDP 2016 £m*	*Percentage of adults in relative poverty*	*Percentage of adults over 65*	*Average temp (C)*	*National university ranking*	*Percentage of jobs in manufacturing*	*Tourist visits per year*	*CLUSTER*
Morchingham	**1**	**1**	**0**	**0**	**1**	1	**1**	1
Wexton	**1**	**1**	**0**	**0**	**1**	0	**1**	1
Highborough	1	0	0	0	**0**	**1**	**0**	2
Seaport	1	1	1	0	**0**	**1**	**0**	2
Longford	0	1	1	1	**0**	**1**	**0**	2
Middling	**0**	**0**	0	**1**	**1**	**0**	0	3
Barchester	**0**	**0**	1	**1**	**1**	**0**	1	3

provides a clear visual pattern of how threshold scores relate, or not, to final cluster membership.

Analysis of Table 2.6 provides good evidence to support the hypothesis that three clusters exist. Threshold scores represented in bold in Table 2.6 are 'prime implicants' for that cluster membership. That is to say that the cases in that cluster share the same variable binary score. Using the capital and lower case notation style popular with QCA, we can summarise the cluster memberships with a number of logical statements. Lower case text indicates below threshold and use of capitals indicates above threshold.

Cluster 1 GDP ∗ ADULTS IN POVERTY ∗ adults over 65 ∗ average temp c ∗ NAT. UNIVERSITY RANKING ∗ TOURIST VISITS PER YEAR

Cluster 2 nat. university ranking ∗ JOBS IN MANUFACTURING ∗ tourist visits per year

Cluster 3 gdp ∗ adults in poverty ∗ AVERAGE TEMP C ∗ NAT. UNIVERSITY RANKING ∗ jobs in manufacturing

The conclusion from this simple QCA is that it provides good evidence for supporting the hypothesis derived from the first CA iterations that there are three cluster groups of cities. The remaining task is to qualitatively summarise the substance of these clusters.

Cluster 1 appears to be larger cities, due to their comparatively high total GDP. They have a strong cultural and historical basis with good universities and many tourist visits per year. Cluster 2 is best summarised as cities that retain an industrial and manufacturing base to their economies. Cluster 3 are smaller cities, as indicated by their lower total GDP, with good temperatures (so probably in the geographical south) and strong universities.

An alternative confirmation method: ANOVA

An alternative method for checking the validity of the clusters produced by CA is to use a conventional Analysis of Variance (ANOVA) with eta squared, where eta squared gives an indication of the strength of association between an independent variable and cluster definition.

Some writers caution against using ANOVA, MANOVA or discriminant function analysis in this way to confirm the existence of clusters, because cluster results are rarely being inferred directly from a sample to a population. Given the separation of cases into clusters, CA is an idealised and associative model rather than a probabilistic separation of cases, and a mixed methods approach with inferential and probability based statistics may overstate the substantive effects of the variables on the cluster formation (Aldenderfer & Blashfield, 1984). It can be a self-fulfilling prophesy to confirm clusters in this way, given that the clusters have already been created by a mathematical method. Similar to the validity problem inherent in factor analysis, computer based mathematical approaches to CA will deliver cluster patterns in their output, even if they have no substantive meaning in social reality. This is why the researcher's qualitative judgement of what the mathematical patterns represent is so important. Nevertheless, conventional statistical approaches to variable relationships in CA can still be of some descriptive value overall, if the prior limitations are considered, and scores of associations like eta squared are used to understand the relative influence of variables rather than to make absolute statements about probability estimations.

It has been argued that a better method for statistical validation of clusters with larger datasets is to use Monte Carlo simulation, where different aspects of a sample, segmentation of a large sample or population data is taken at random to replicate cluster definition (Aldenderfer & Blashfield, 1984). Small samples make this difficult. With small samples, additional variables can be added to the cluster modelling, to see if the established clusters retain their structure and coherence (Pastor, 2010). The latter approach is particularly valuable in macro social, political and economic research where countries are being compared. Samples that have a relatively small number of cases but a large number of variables are prone to being influenced by variables with large scales and so standardisation is often advisable when entering new and additional variables to an existing model.

Table 2.7 shows the mean average score for each variable for each cluster. Some features stand out. For example, in cluster 3, Barchester and Middling are strongly linked by having excellent universities.

Table 2.8 reveals the full ANOVA results. Given that it is unlikely that these city results will be inferred to a larger population of cities, these results are of limited value. Nevertheless, the F scores give some context to the strength of association between variables and cluster definition and this is presented more clearly in Table 2.9, which gives the eta and eta squared scores for each variable. This shows the five variables that seem to be contributing the most to cluster definition. It is important here to remember that variable contribution to cluster definition may be different to variables that best characterise an individual cluster. The mean

Table 2.7 Mean average scores by clusters; city example

Cluster	*GDP 2016 (£m)*	*Percentage of adults in relative poverty*	*Percentage of adults over 65*	*Average temp (C)*	*National university ranking*	*Percentage of jobs in manufacturing*	*Tourist visits per year*
1	4.050	20.00	10.50	10.00	18.00	9.50	425.00
2	2.667	17.33	12.67	12.67	54.00	12.33	105.00
3	2.200	10.00	13.50	14.50	2.00	4.50	170.00
Total	2.929	16.00	12.29	12.43	28.86	9.29	215.00

Table 2.8 ANOVA results for mean average cluster scores

			Sum of squares	*df*	*Mean square*	*F*	*Sig.*
GDP 2016 (£m) * Cluster	Between groups	(Combined)	3.783	2	1.891	4.876	.085
	Within groups		1.552	4	.388		
	Total		5.334	6			
Percentage of adults in relative poverty * Cluster	Between groups	(Combined)	109.333	2	54.667	13.120	.017
	Within groups		16.667	4	4.167		
	Total		126.000	6			
Percentage of adults over 65 * Cluster	Between groups	(Combined)	9.762	2	4.881	.580	.601
	Within groups		33.667	4	8.417		
	Total		43.429	6			
Average temp (C) * Cluster	Between groups	(Combined)	20.548	2	10.274	12.977	.018
	Within groups		3.167	4	.792		
	Total		23.714	6			
National University ranking * Cluster	Between groups	(Combined)	3574.857	2	1787.429	8.125	.039
	Within groups		880.000	4	220.000		
	Total		4454.857	6			
Percentage of jobs in manufacturing * Cluster	Between groups	(Combined)	73.762	2	36.881	8.350	.037
	Within groups		17.667	4	4.417		
	Total		91.429	6			
Tourist visits per year * Cluster	Between groups	(Combined)	128550.000	2	64275.000	17.854	.010
	Within groups		14400.000	4	3600.000		
	Total		142950.000	6			

Table 2.9 Eta and eta squared results for variables explanation of cluster definitions, ranked by largest eta squared score

Measures of Association		
	Eta	*Eta squared*
Tourist visits per year * Cluster	.948	.899
Percentage of adults in relative poverty * Cluster	.932	.868
Average temp (C) * Cluster	.931	.866
Percentage of jobs in manufacturing * Cluster	.898	.807
National university ranking * Cluster	.896	.802
GDP 2016 (£m) * Cluster	.842	.709
Percentage of adults over 65 * Cluster	.474	.225

average scores and the QCA table give a better sense of the latter 'within cluster' influence.

The application of CA and QCA as a combined method

Having explained the fundamental joint uses of CA and QCA in social and economic research, this section examines further issues about how they can be combined to look at complex and changing patterns in society over time. This combined and longitudinal method named and outlined in this book is called DPS.

Chapter 1 explained the development of the application of complexity theory to social science. At the core of this development is the need for methods that can embrace the social realism that the relationship between cases (like people, organisations and countries) is constantly evolving and changing as they interact and feedback to each other over time. One-off research studies, therefore (or what are often referred to as cross sectional studies), are of limited use because one of the central methods for understanding complexity is to understand how interactions are changing social and economic behaviour over time.

Cluster Analysis and QCA when combined give us important information about the dominant patterns of similarity between cases, but this pattern analysis needs to be repeated over time in order to understand the aspects of patterns that are stable over the longer term and which aspects are unstable and changing.

In order to demonstrate this, a second fictional cities dataset is added. It is the same data, measured consistently, but recorded three years later. By computing a similar analysis and comparing the results, it is then possible to conclude on the DPS.

Dynamic Pattern Synthesis: seven cities, three years later

Table 2.10 shows an extension of the seven cities data into an imaginary future. The same variables have been modified to record scores for a second-time period. The resulting appearance of the new and comparable SPSS file is shown in

Table 2.10 Fictional dataset at time point 2 for hierarchical CA

City	*GDP 2019 £m*	*Percentage of adults in relative poverty*	*Percentage of adults over 65*	*Average temp (C)*	*National university ranking*	*Percentage of jobs in manufacturing*	*Tourist visits per year*
Barchester2	2.1	7	19	16	1	1.0	310,000
Wexton2	4.2	23	9	10	11	11.0	410,000
Morchingham2	4.2	19	10	10	22	11.0	460,000
Longford2	1.9	17	12	14	39	10.0	110,000
Middling2	2.5	12	9	13	3	10.0	90,000
Seaport2	3.5	19	14	12	75	12.0	95,000
Highborough2	3.0	14	12	12	44	10.0	110,000
Mean Average	*3.1*	*15.9*	*12.1*	*12.4*	*27.9*	*9.3*	*226,429*
Median Average	*3.0*	*17.0*	*12.0*	*12.0*	*22.0*	*10.0*	*110,000*

Figure 2.15. Cluster Analysis is computed with this new dataset using Ward's method and with variable scores standardised as *z* scores. The dendrogram output option is selected from the plots sub command. The resulting dendrogram is shown in Figure 2.15.

Figure 2.15 shows that the future modified dataset results in a slightly different pattern to that produced when Ward's method was applied to the first dataset in Figure 2.9. Barchester is now an outlier and Middling has been positioned in cluster 2 before the agglomeration of Seaport into the same cluster. This presents a hypothesis of two clusters and one outlier. Crisp set QCA can be used to see whether confirmation of these clusters is appropriate.

Threshold setting for binary crisp set conversion

Table 2.11 demonstrates the process of threshold setting and binary conversion decisions for the QCA process. Given the proximity of several specific variable scores to the median, deciding on binary scores becomes more arbitrary for percentage of the population over aged 65, average temperature (C) and percentage of jobs in manufacturing. The mean average can help inform such decisions, but the researcher needs to note the lack of clear discrimination around the central tendency that the binary scores are making in this research example.

Table 2.12 shows the threshold scores for the second time period matched and sorted against the CA cluster outcomes. Cluster 2, while larger, given the addition

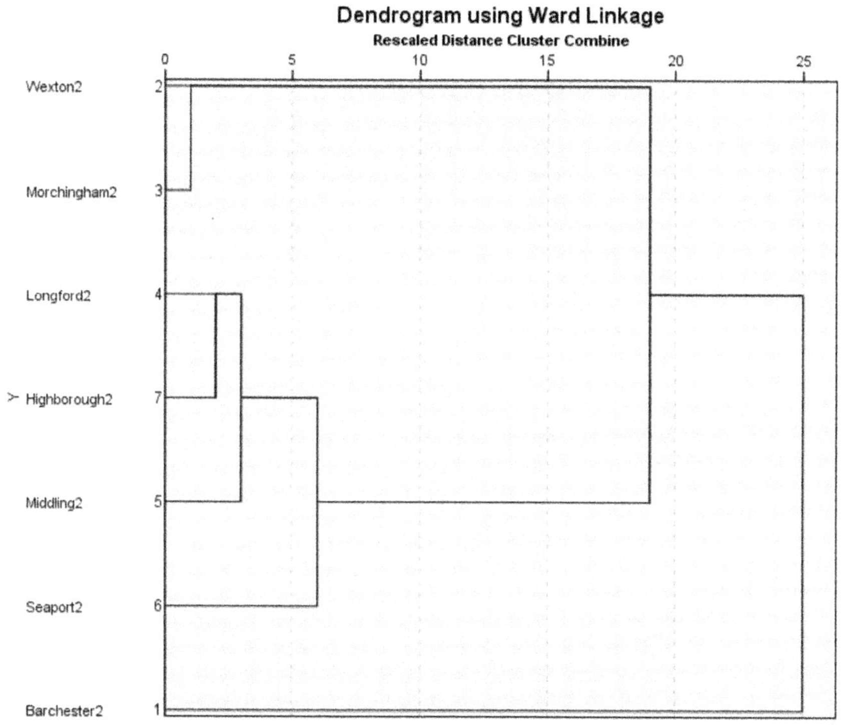

Figure 2.15 Cluster Analysis with Ward's method and standardised data: city dataset 2

of Middling in the second time period, has some important fuzzy elements. The cluster would be more homogeneous if Middling was excluded. This is because Seaport, Highborough and Longford share threshold scores for percentage of adults over 65 and national university rankings. Cluster 1 is unchanged from the first time period and remains homogeneous. Dynamic change over time can be noted in cluster 2 and the separation of Barchester as an outlier.

The prime implicants for the new clusters can be summarised as:

Cluster 1 GDP ∗ ADULTS IN POVERTY ∗ adults over 65 ∗ average temp c ∗ NAT. UNIVERSITY RANKING ∗ TOURIST VISITS PER YEAR

Cluster 2 AVERAGE TEMP C ∗ tourist visits per year

Prime implicant 'near misses'

When specifying the prime implicants for each time period, it can be important to check any 'near misses'. An example of a prime implicant near miss could be a larger cluster where all but one case share the same threshold for a given variable.

Table 2.11 QCA time period 2: conversion of city data variables to binary scores

City	*GDP 2019 £m*	*Percentage of adults in relative poverty*	*Percentage of adults over 65*	*Average temp (C)*	*National university ranking*	*Percentage of jobs in manufacturing*	*Tourist visits per year*
Barchester2	2.1	7	19	16	1	1.0	310,000
Wexton2	4.2	23	9	10	11	11.0	410,000
Morchingham2	4.2	19	10	10	22	11.0	460,000
Longford2	1.9	17	12	14	39	10.0	110,000
Middling2	2.5	12	9	13	3	10.0	90,000
Seaport2	3.5	19	14	12	75	12.0	95,000
Highborough2	3.0	14	12	12	44	10.0	110,000
Mean average	*3.1*	*15.9*	*12.1*	*12.4*	*27.9*	*9.3*	*226,429*
Median average	*3.0*	*17.0*	*12.0*	*12.0*	*22.0*	*10.0*	*110,000*
Conversion to binary scores					*(reversed)*		
Barchester2	0	0	1	1	1	0	1
Wexton2	1	1	0	0	1	1	1
Morchingham2	1	1	0	0	1	1	1
Longford2	0	1	1	1	0	0	0
Middling2	0	0	0	1	1	0	0
Seaport2	1	0	1	0	0	1	0
Highborough2	1	0	1	0	0	0	0

It needs to be remembered that the allocation of scale variables to thresholds associated with the median and influenced by the mean can become arbitrary where scale variable scores have low variance or are not normally distributed. In this situation, it is important to form a final qualitative judgement about whether a variable is a prime implicant for a cluster.

An example of a near miss in Table 2.8 is with cluster 2 and the percentage of adults over 65. This variable is above threshold for three cities: Seaport, Highborough and Longford, but not for one: Middling. If the original scale scores are checked in Table 2.11 for this variable, Middling has a score of 9%, which is well below the median (12) and mean (12.1). In this example, it is not

Table 2.12 QCA time period 2: threshold scores with cluster outcome variable added

City	*GDP 2019 £m*	*Percentage of adults in relative poverty*	*Percentage of adults over 65*	*Average temp (C)*	*National university ranking*	*Percentage of jobs in manufacturing*	*Tourist visits per year*	*CLUSTER*
Wexton2	**1**	**1**	**0**	**0**	**1**	**1**	**1**	1
Morchingham2	**1**	**1**	**0**	**0**	**1**	**1**	**1**	1
Seaport2	1	0	1	**1**	0	1	**0**	2
Highborough2	1	0	1	**1**	0	0	**0**	2
Longford2	0	1	1	**1**	0	0	**0**	2
Middling2	0	0	0	**1**	1	0	**0**	2
Barchester2	0	0	1	1	1	0	1	3

appropriate to make a qualitative judgement to overrule the binary coding and to make this variable a prime implicant for cluster 2. If the Middling score had been very close to the median, a 'threshold overruling' decision might have been appropriate.

Other considerations for the DPS

One key consideration at the end of a DPS is to judge the relative stability of case and variable patterns over the given time period. This can, in part, be done mathematically by calculating the trend changes in variables used and the number of QCA above and below threshold scores that remain the same for each case across the given time period of study. It is also a qualitative exercise, in terms of observing which cases have remained in the same clusters and those that have moved cluster memberships.

The stability of variables in DPS

It is possible to examine the stability of variable scores by examining the changing trends over time of each variable used in a DPS model. Table 2.13 examines the variable trends for the seven cities example.

The variable average trend analysis can inform decisions about how scores close to the threshold should be binary coded in the next time period, given considerations about the longitudinal direction of travel of a variable trend and its impact on patterns of similarity. Other trend statistics can be considered at this point, like changes in the Coefficient of Variance (CoV).

Table 2.13 Variable average trends, the seven cities example

	GDP 2019 £m	*Percentage of adults in relative poverty*	*Percentage of adults over 65*	*Average temp (C)*	*National university ranking*	*Percentage of jobs in manufacturing*	*Tourist visits per year*
t = 1	*2.9*	*16.0*	*12.3*	*12.4*	*28.9*	*9.3*	*215,000*
t = 2	*3.1*	*15.9*	*12.1*	*12.4*	*27.9*	*9.3*	*226,429*
	^	stable	v	stable	v	stable	^

Stability of cases in the chosen sample

In most samples and populations there will be some instability in the case membership. This reflects the dynamic nature of social change as explored in this book. The researcher needs to decide if entirely the same cases will be used at each time point in the DPS. The first consideration is whether records for the chosen variables are available for the same cases over the given time frame. This may not be possible. For example, if studying progression over several years in a given school some of the children will leave and others will join. Likewise, a case based study of the countries in the European single currency, decided to include some new countries joining at the later time stages (Haynes & Haynes, 2016).

If a good percentage of the cases are available at each of the selected time points, it is acceptable to have some other cases exiting and joining, but this feature needs to be addressed and accounted for in the research findings and conclusion. New case memberships in a given system will be a key part of the dynamic that affects the overall synthesis of the model and the resulting qualitative and conceptual conclusions.

The stability of combined case and variable interactions can be examined by computing a table of above and below threshold scores that remain stable between a case and variable over the time period studied. An example, for the seven cities, is shown in Table 2.14. A Microsoft Excel IF statement is created to assess all the given truth tables and to form a new table that identifies all cases that have consistent above and below threshold variable scores because they persist through all the time periods under observation. Box 2.1 illustrates how Microsoft Excel can be used for this task.

The size of the chosen sample

As the examples later in this book demonstrate, it is easier to manage and reflect on the overall synthesis of a DPS with a smaller size sample. The techniques embedded in CAs and QCA quickly become more complex as the sample size grows and

Table 2.14 Longitudinal truth table: the stability of prime implicants over time

City	*GDP 2019 £m*	*Percentage of adults in relative poverty*	*Percentage of adults over 65*	*Average temp (C)*	*National university ranking*	*Percentage of jobs in manufacturing*	*Tourist visits per year*
Barchester	Below	Below	Above	Above	Above	Below	Above
Wexton	Above	Above	Below	Below	Above		Above
Morchingham	Above	Above	Below	Below	Above	Above	Above
Longford	Below	Above	Above	Above	Below		Below
Middling	Below	Below	Below	Above	Above	Below	Below
Seaport	Above		Above	Below	Below	Above	Below
Highborough	Above	Below		Below	Below		Below

Box 2.1 Computation of a longitudinal truth table: the stability in prime implicants over time

Cut and paste the binary threshold conversion scores into an Excel spreadsheet. Do this for each of the time points, putting each time point table underneath the one before it.

	A	*B*	*C*	*D*
1		*Variable a*	*Variable b*	*Variable c*
2	Case i	1	0	1
3	Case ii	0	0	1
4	Case iii	1	1	0
5	Case iv	1	1	0
6	Case v	0	1	1
	A	B	C	D
7		*Variable a*	*Variable b*	*Variable c*
8	Case i	1	0	1
9	Case ii	0	0	1
10	Case iii	1	1	0
11	Case iv	1	1	0
12	Case v	0	1	1

Once the binary threshold scores are included for all time points, create a further table at the bottom that includes the same column and row definitions.

	A	*B*	*C*	*D*
14		*Variable a*	*Variable b*	*Variable c*
15	Case i			
16	Case ii			
17	Case iii			
18	Case iv			
19	Case v			

Use the following Excel formula to compute whether a case has a consistent threshold score over time. The example below relates to the first case i with the first variable a. The IF statement would be located in cell B15.

= IF(OR(AND(B2=1,B8=1),), "ABOVE", IF(AND(B2=0,B8=0), "BELOW", " "))

The above Excel formula assumes the case has a variable threshold score of 1 or 0 at two time periods, represented by B2 for time period one and B8 for time period two. If both these scores are consistently 1 the computer will return the text "ABOVE". If both these scores are consistently 0, the computer will return the text "BELOW". If the computer finds an inconsistency over time, ie: 1 and 0, or 0 and 1, it will return a blank cell as the result.

In the example given, cell B15, using the formula will return the result "ABOVE". This is because of the consistent and repeated above threshold score of 1 for case i when combined with variable a.

If the IF formula is cut and pasted through B15: D19, it will compute a consistency threshold score for each case and variable relationship.

it becomes harder to discern the overall patterns and which patterns have substantive social meaning rather than being chance artefacts. The ideal sample size for DPS is probably between 10 and 20 cases, although this is a judgement based on experience rather than a mathematical rule. It is entirely reasonable to use bigger samples, but one has to be careful not to try and work with larger clusters that have limited heterogeneity. Smaller clusters will have greater homogeneity and more likely reflect the realities of society and social practice. Larger samples can always be broken into sub samples, on the basis of a logic or sample stratification that makes qualitative sense to the research problem and questions being posed. Two step CA provides a slightly different approach to exploring much larger samples than hierarchical CA, although it is not without its substantive challenges. Two step CA can be used to segment a larger sample into clusters that can then be subjected to a DPS.

The number of time points in the DPS

The minimum number of time points needed to undertake a DPS is two, although it is not ideal in terms of having a confident conclusion about time effects. The more time points that can be reasonably managed the better. One option with DPS is to start with a few time points and then to add later years with the same dataset as part of an ongoing longitudinal research project.

Conclusion

Box 2.2 summarises the key steps for carrying out a DPS. Such a form of data synthesis should also be located in the context of previous research and scholarship and inform future research agendas.

Box 2.2 A summary of steps for conducting a Dynamic Pattern Synthesis

- Select a suitable number of comparable cases with a longitudinal dataset that is defined by several scale and interval variables (additional categorical variables can be added at the second QCA stage, if required).
    - If the dataset has a large number of cases (for example above 50), reduce to a logical number of sub samples and proceed to consider each sub sample separately before comparing the results, or consider the first use of two step CA to decide on cluster sub samples.
- Decide on the periodic reference points and check data is consistent and available for each time point.
- Carry out a hierarchical CA on the dataset.
    - Make informed decisions about the clustering method, measures and plots to be used. Use a dendrogram to assist with making the final decision about what is the socially 'real' number of clusters available is highly recommended.
- Make a key decision from the results of the CA and propose a hypothesis about the number of clusters that exist in the data.
- Convert the scale data used in the CA into binary threshold scores, for example, scores above and below the median. Use the mean and median average to help inform the decision and if necessary consider other aspects of the distribution of variable scores.
- Use QCA to test the hypothesis and confirm or not evidence for the existence of clusters with prime implicants. Consider adding additional binary categorical variable at this point, if required to aid the model explanation.
- If no prime implicants exist for one or more clusters, consider reducing the clusters to smaller sub sets, like two smaller clusters. This might

also involve deciding a case is an outlier from a cluster and cannot logically be argued to be a cluster member.

- If necessary, use other statistical methods, like ANOVA, to explore the variable effects on cluster membership. Remember to distinguish between variable effects on the overall cluster model and those that are key effects within specific clusters.
- Specify 'prime implicants' for any clusters discovered. These are threshold scores that are homogenous for all cluster members.
- For 'near miss' prime implicants check for arbitrary proximity scoring at thresholds and consider 'threshold overruling' to clarify further prime implicants that help to clarify and confirm the DPS model.
- Consider variable trend changes over time and which variables remain stable and those that change relatively more.
- Consider case changes over time and identify the cases that stay in stable constant proximity to each other (for example, they remain in the same cluster or hierarchical cluster structure) and those that move clusters or remain as outliers or become outliers.
- Compute a case and variable matrix that identifies case based above or below threshold variable scores that remain stable over time.
- Conclude on relative stability and instability in cluster membership over time and how variable explanations for the existence of clusters changes over time.
- Conclude on the overall key points of change and influence in the DPS model.

3 Macro examples of Dynamic Pattern Synthesis

Introduction

In this chapter, Dynamic Pattern Synthesis (DPS) is used to explore the changing dynamic of the social and economic circumstances of European countries. The macro level focuses on the differences between the selected countries of Europe. The cases in this context are a sample of countries in Europe as made available by a specific dataset. The two case studies examine the aggregate process of change in Europe.

The first case study explores the social care circumstances of older people in Europe and the extent to which there are different pattern relationships for key health and social care variables depending on the country under consideration. The second case study examines the changing economic characteristics of countries using the euro currency after 2002.

Macro case study 1: health and social care in Europe

The longitudinal dataset used for the first case study is the Survey of Health, Ageing and Retirement in Europe (SHARE) (Börsch-Supan, et al., 2016). The aggregate country score variables used are derived from the easySHARE data file release 5.0.0 (Gruber, et al., 2016). Data is taken from people aged 50 and over and country sub samples are weighted to give balanced age profiles.

Longitudinal data is compared for 10 countries over four waves of data collection, wave 1 in 2004, wave 2 in 2006, wave 4 in 2010 and wave 5 in 2013. Wave 3 of the same dataset is not directly comparable in this context, due to it being focused on some different themes and measures when compared to previous versions. The dates selected cover the period of the close collaboration sought by the expansion of the European Union and the establishment of the single currency for some European countries. The selected time period also covers any change through the period of the financial crisis, 2007–08 and its aftermath. The 10 countries included in the first macro case study are: Austria, Germany, Sweden, the Netherlands, Spain, Italy, France, Denmark, Switzerland and Belgium. The 14 variables included are shown in Table 3.1.

The chosen cluster method is Ward's, using linkages measured by the squared Euclidean distance. Variables are standardised using z scores before computation. This follows the method as previously demonstrated in Chapter 2.

Table 3.1 Variables included in macro case study 1

- Country
- Average of household size, persons
- Average number of respondent's siblings alive
- Average number of respondent's children
- Average number of respondent's grandchildren
- Average of respondent's self perceived health score (where high scores indicate poor health)
- Average of respondent's number of chronic diseases
- Average of respondent's CASP score: quality of life and well-being index – where high score is better quality of life and well-being
- Average of respondent's Depression scale EURO-D score – where high score is depressed
- Average times that a respondent has seen or talked to a medical doctor in the last 12 months
- Percentage of respondents in employment
- Percentage of respondents with at least one child who lives in the building
- Percentage of respondents with at least one child who lives less than 1 km away
- Percentage of respondents who have given help to another outside their household in the last 12 months

Macro case study 1, wave 1, 2004

The first wave of data (2004) includes a total sample (all countries) of 10 cases. Table 3.2 shows the resulting agglomeration schedule. The gradient of coefficient score differences between each stage rises rapidly, making a precise estimate of the likely number of clusters quite difficult, but there is a change in gradient after stage 3. An icicle plot in Figure 3.1 provides an alternative visual representation of cluster formation where it is possible to see the most similar pairings that provide the basis for the final hierarchical structure of the clusters.

The icicle plot in Figure 3.1 shows the process of agglomeration of cases. The first two cases to be agglomerated are Denmark and Sweden. Next, France and Belgium are joined. At the third stage Germany and Austria are linked. At the fourth stage of the analysis, Spain and Italy are connected. The fifth stage joins the Netherlands and Switzerland. After this, the cluster agglomeration moves beyond pairings to grouping larger hierarchical clusters. The Netherlands and Switzerland merge with Denmark and Sweden and next France and Belgium merge with Germany and Austria. In the final stages of the Cluster Analysis (CA) these eight countries are merged before they are joined in the last stage by Spain and Italy.

The dendrogram in Figure 3.2 provides more visual clues about how to interpret the cluster agglomerations. This implies either three or five clusters are noteworthy. A key decision is whether to proceed to the conceptualisation of the three clusters or to remain with the first level of pairings.

Qualitative Comparative Analysis (QCA) can be used to test whether there are three clusters. First the data is prepared in Table 3.3. Here the mean and median are used to decide on binary threshold scores for each variable with each case.

Table 3.2 Agglomeration schedule for country aggregates, case study 1, 2004

Stage	*Cluster Combined*		*Coefficients*	*Stage Cluster First Appears*		*Next Stage*
	Cluster 1	*Cluster 2*		*Cluster 1*	*Cluster 2*	
1	3	8	1.458	0	0	6
2	7	10	3.855	0	0	7
3	1	2	8.277	0	0	7
4	5	6	13.536	0	0	8
5	4	9	20.540	0	0	6
6	3	4	31.689	1	5	9
7	1	7	42.931	3	2	8
8	1	5	67.546	7	4	9
9	1	3	117.000	8	6	0

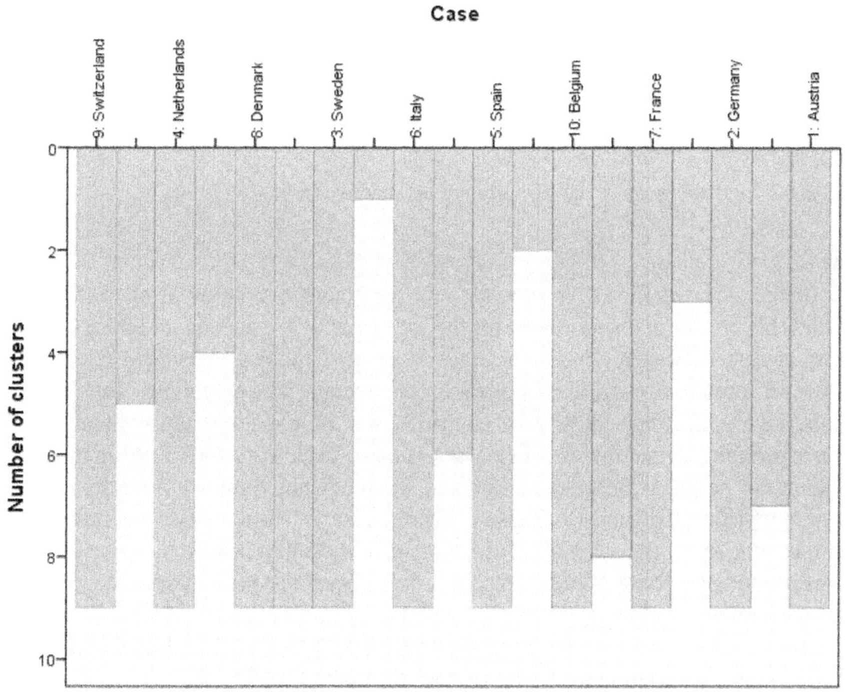

Figure 3.1 Icicle plot of cluster formulation: macro case study 1, 2004

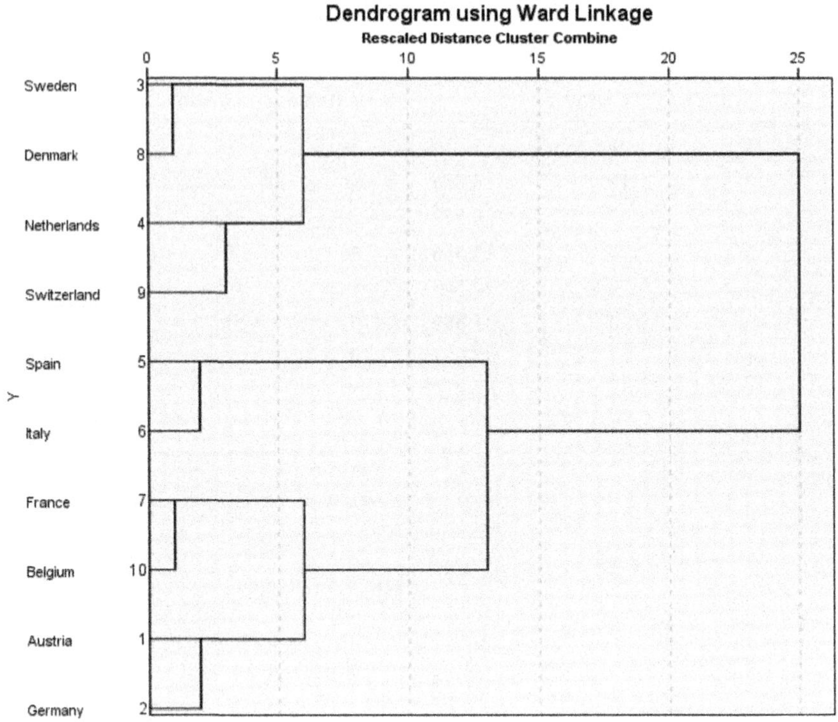

Figure 3.2 Dendrogram of cluster formulation: macro case study 1, 2004

Table 3.4 shows the QCA truth table for the macro case study using the wave 1 data. This confirms the evidence for the existence of the second and third cluster with several prime implicant variables evidenced for those clusters. Cluster 1, however, only has one prime implicant – the average self-perceived health score. This is above average for all four countries, but there is a diversity of scores for other variables. Nevertheless, if cluster 1 is taken back to its derivative, that is two sub cluster pairings (Belgium and France; Germany and Austria), there are a good range of prime implicants for these two sub clusters. Cluster 1 also has three near misses, but given the strength of the pattern in the sub pairings and four of their mirror opposites for the threshold scores, it is decided to present cluster 1 with its two separate pairings.

The sub clusters of cluster 2 are also shown to be robust with much similarity in the binary variable scores, but this is in the context of an overarching cluster 2 that already has six shared prime implicants. In addition, there are five near misses within this relatively large cluster.

Of the five near misses, four are with Switzerland. These all concern the number and location of family members, where Switzerland has the reverse to the

Table 3.3 QCA: data for truth table macro case study 1, 2004

Country	*Household size*	*Number of siblings alive*	*Number of children*	*Number of grandchildren*	*Self-perceived health*	*Number of chronic diseases*	*CASP: quality of life and well-being index*	*Depression scale EURO-D*	*How often seen or talked to medical doctor last 12 months*	*Percentage in employment*	*At least one child lives in the building*	*At least one child lives less than 1 km away*	*Helped someone in the last 12 months*
Austria	1.93	2.20	1.98	2.53	2.98	0.94	38.36	2.02	6.53	17.10	38.10	47.50	24.40
Germany	2.08	2.06	1.96	2.20	3.25	1.16	38.76	2.15	8.42	29.40	34.00	41.90	33.80
Sweden	1.91	2.22	2.35	3.39	2.72	1.09	39.28	1.96	3.38	40.80	16.60	24.50	42.10
The Netherlands	2.06	3.33	2.36	3.04	2.94	0.91	40.45	1.92	5.29	30.40	23.90	35.00	42.00
Spain	2.54	2.68	2.39	2.83	3.42	1.21	35.71	2.78	7.10	19.90	57.00	70.80	13.70
Italy	2.53	2.60	2.03	2.26	3.28	1.11	33.68	2.84	9.00	18.80	63.80	71.40	23.70
France	2.07	2.87	2.27	3.09	3.20	1.04	37.55	2.83	6.88	30.50	30.80	38.20	29.60
Denmark	1.96	2.32	2.26	3.08	2.59	1.02	40.91	1.82	4.79	39.00	17.70	23.70	47.80
Switzerland	2.08	2.60	2.08	2.30	2.67	0.77	40.74	1.92	5.04	40.00	34.20	41.40	34.60
Belgium	2.10	2.76	2.15	2.96	2.99	1.14	37.41	2.50	8.25	25.00	30.00	40.90	41.70
Mean	*2.13*	*2.57*	*2.18*	*2.77*	*3.00*	*1.04*	*38.28*	*2.27*	*6.47*	*29.09*	*34.61*	*43.50*	*33.34*
Median	*2.07*	*2.60*	*2.21*	*2.90*	*2.98*	*1.07*	*38.56*	*2.08*	*6.70*	*29.90*	*32.40*	*41.15*	*34.20*
Conversion to binary scores													
Austria	0	0	0	0	1	0	0	0	0	0	1	1	0
Germany	1	0	0	0	1	1	1	1	1	0	1	1	0
Sweden	0	0	1	1	0	1	1	0	0	1	0	0	1
The Netherlands	0	1	1	1	0	0	1	0	0	1	0	0	1
Spain	1	1	1	1	1	1	0	1	1	0	1	1	0
Italy	1	1	0	0	1	1	0	1	1	0	1	1	0
France	0	1	1	1	1	0	0	1	1	1	0	0	0
Denmark	0	0	1	1	0	0	1	0	0	1	0	0	1
Switzerland	1	1	0	0	0	0	1	0	0	1	1	1	1
Belgium	1	1	0	1	1	1	0	1	1	0	0	0	1

Table 3.4 QCA truth table for macro case study 1, 2004

Country	*Household size*	*Number of siblings alive*	*Number of children*	*Number of grandchildren*	*Self-perceived health*	*Number of chronic diseases*	*CASP: quality of life and well-being index*	*Depression scale EURO-D*	*How often seen or talked to medical doctor last 12 months*	*Percentage in employment*	*At least one child lives in the building*	*At least one child lives less than 1 km away*	*Helped someone in the last 12 months*	*Cluster*
Belgium	1	1	0	1	**1**	1	0	1	1	0	0	0	1	1
France	0	1	1	1	**1**	0	0	1	1	1	0	0	0	1
Germany	1	0	0	0	**1**	1	1	1	1	0	1	1	0	1
Austria	0	0	0	0	**1**	0	0	0	0	0	1	1	0	1
Switzerland	1	1	0	0	**0**	**0**	**1**	**0**	**0**	**1**	1	**1**	1	2
The Netherlands	0	1	1	1	**0**	**0**	**1**	**0**	**0**	**1**	0	**0**	1	2
Sweden	0	0	1	1	**0**	**1**	**1**	**0**	**0**	**1**	0	**0**	1	2
Denmark	0	0	1	1	**0**	**0**	**1**	**0**	**0**	**1**	0	**0**	1	2
Spain	**1**	**1**	1	1	**1**	**1**	**0**	**1**	**1**	**0**	**1**	**1**	**0**	3
Italy	**1**	**1**	0	0	**1**	**1**	**0**	**1**	**1**	**0**	**1**	**1**	**0**	3

other members of its cluster. This is summarised as lower family size, but living in closer proximity. Only on one of these four variables is Switzerland's score so close to the central tendency that an overruling can be justified. This is the variable percentage with at least one child living at least less than 1 km away. This near miss is overruled and the variable becomes an additional prime implicant for cluster 2. The remaining near miss for consideration is Sweden's score for reported average number of chronic diseases, where it is the only country in the cluster above threshold with a score of 1.09 (median = 1.07, mean = 1.04). Given its proximity to the central tendency and the fact it is the first country to be ranked above the median threshold, this score is overruled and the variable becomes a further prime implicant for cluster two.

To conclude on wave 1 (2004), there are advantages with considering four working clusters: Belgium and France; Germany and Austria; Switzerland, the Netherlands, Sweden and Denmark; and Spain and Italy. These can be summarised with the Boolean prime implicant statements in Table 3.5.

Finally, the four clusters can be described qualitatively in the following way. Belgium and France have larger family structures but with less immediate

Table 3.5 Boolean simplification macro case study 1, 2004

Clusters	*Boolean simplification*
Cluster 1 Belgium and France	NUMBER OF SIBLINGS ALIVE * NUMBER OF GRANDCHILDREN * SELF-PERCEIVED HEALTH * quality of life * DEPRESSION * CONTACT WITH DOCTOR * child in building * child near
Cluster 2 Germany and Austria	Number of siblings alive * number of children * number of grandchildren * SELF-PERCEIVED HEALTH * employment * CHILD IN BUILDING * CHILD NEAR * helped someone
Cluster 3 Switzerland, the Netherlands, Sweden and Denmark	Self-perceived health * diseases * QUALITY OF LIFE * depression * contact with doctor * EMPLOYMENT * child near * HELPED SOMEONE
Cluster 4 Spain and Italy	HOUSEHOLD SIZE * SIBLINGS ALIVE * SELF-PERCEIVED HEALTH * DISEASES * quality of life * DEPRESSION * CONTACT WITH DOCTOR * employment * CHILD IN BUILDING * CHILD NEAR * helped someone

residency or geographical location of children. There are numerous health concerns and frequent visits to doctors.

Germany and Austria have smaller family structures but more geographical closeness of children. There are health concerns, but less manifestations of ill health.

The largest cluster, with Switzerland, the Netherlands, Sweden and Denmark, has the highest levels of employment. Self-perceived health tends to be better with corresponding better quality of life and less visits to the doctor. Incidents of helping others are also higher.

Finally, Spain and Italy have large family structures and geographical proximity of children. Incidents of ill health are higher with corresponding increase in likelihood of visits to the doctor and a lower quality of life.

Macro case study 1, wave 2, 2006

Next the macro case study is repeated with the same cases and variables, but using scores for 2006 (SHARE data wave 2). Table 3.6 shows the agglomeration schedule for the wave 2 CA. The coefficient scores gradient changes noticeably between stage 4 and 5, suggesting that 4 clusters might be the optimal number to consider.

The icicle plot in Figure 3.3 provides a visual check as to whether this number of clusters is a viable research decision. It demonstrates the hierarchical process of the agglomeration of cases. First, Belgium and France are joined. This is a change in the first pairing when compared to wave 1 (Figure 3.1). The next pair to be joined are Sweden and Denmark. Then Switzerland and Austria are joined, followed by Italy and Germany. Now the remaining singletons join the existing

Table 3.6 Agglomeration schedule or country aggregates, macro case study 1, 2006

Stage	*Cluster Combined*		*Coefficients*	*Stage Cluster First Appears*		*Next Stage*
	Cluster 1	*Cluster 2*		*Cluster 1*	*Cluster 2*	
1	2	4	2.286	0	0	5
2	3	9	5.240	0	0	6
3	1	10	10.487	0	0	7
4	5	6	18.302	0	0	9
5	2	8	26.199	1	0	8
6	3	7	35.166	2	0	7
7	1	3	50.019	3	6	8
8	1	2	75.794	7	5	9
9	1	5	117.000	8	4	0

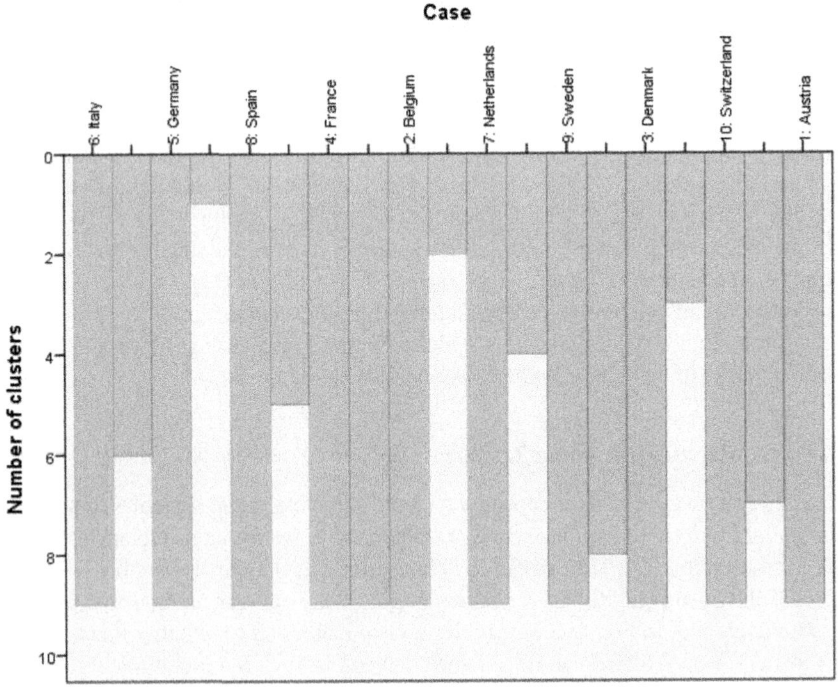

Figure 3.3 Icicle plot of cluster formulation: macro case study 1, 2006

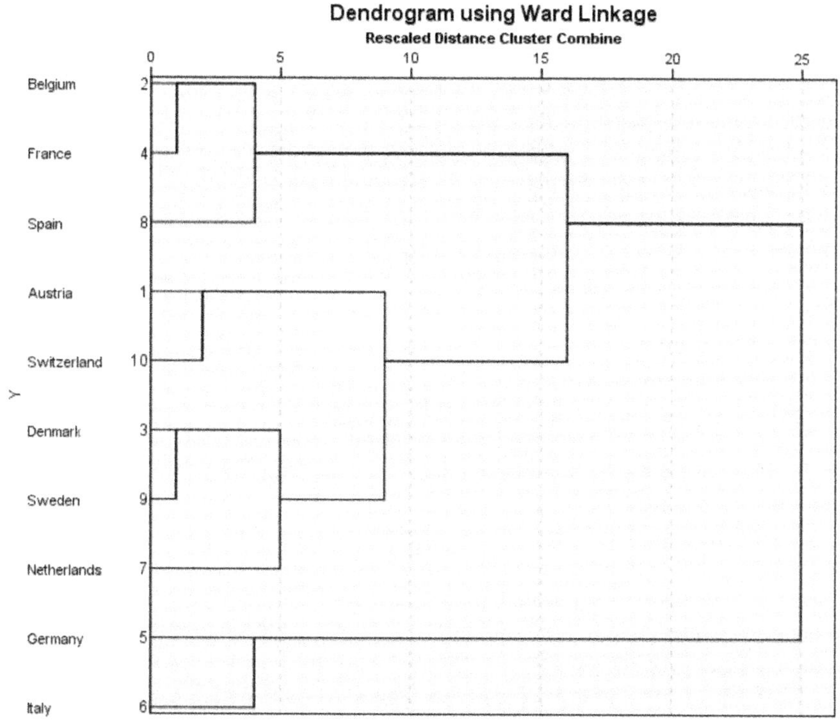

Figure 3.4 Dendrogram of cluster formulation: macro case study 1, 2006

pairings to make larger clusters. Spain joins with France and Belgium and the Netherlands joins with Sweden and Denmark.

The final mergers are better observed in the dendrogram (Figure 3.4). Austria and Switzerland merge with Denmark and Sweden and the Netherlands, this before subsequently the cases all integrate with Belgium, France and Spain. The final agglomeration of the 10 countries brings in the pairing of Germany and Italy.

The key decision at this stage in the analysis is whether to test a three or four cluster model – in other words, whether to merge the pairing of Austria and Switzerland with the triplet of Denmark, Sweden and the Netherlands. It is decided to proceed to the QCA truth table with a three cluster outcome and to see whether any prime implicants can be demonstrated for this larger cluster (tables 3.8 and 3.9).

There are already some substantial changes in the dynamics between countries as they move from wave 1 in 2004 to wave 2 in 2006. Spain and Italy have been separated as a southern European cluster. Austria has moved away from similarity with its neighbour Germany to be more like its other neighbour Switzerland (although Switzerland appears to retain some likenesses to Denmark, Sweden and the Netherlands). Those latter three countries remain consistently together (2004–2006) in both the early wave models, as do Belgium and France.

Table 3.7 shows the process of converting the scale data used in the CA to the binary process for QCA. As in previous examples the decision about the binary scoring is based on both the mean and median and the distribution of the variable scores around the central tendency.

Table 3.8 shows the application of QCA to test the validity of the proposed three clusters. The larger cluster 2 with five countries has four prime implicants: lower household size, higher quality of life scores, lower depression scores and lower number of times that respondents have seen a doctor. Given the relatively large size of this cluster, it is appropriate to consider any near miss scores at the binary thresholds. This method is applied to any variable in cluster 2 where only one country has a different binary score to the other four. Using these criteria, there is one variable with prime implicant near misses where only one country of the five appears to be scoring differently at the threshold. An examination of original scale data in Table 3.7 reveals how close or not these individual case scores are to the threshold and whether they can be reasonably adjusted in the final Boolean simplification model.

The only near miss for cluster 2 is the number of respondent's chronic diseases. On the binary scores in Table 3.8 Sweden is above the threshold and the other countries in cluster 2 are below. An examination of the scale data in Table 3.7 shows that Sweden's score is at the median threshold and only marginally above the mean. Therefore, this individual case score is considered a near miss and the variable is presented as below threshold for cluster 2 in the final Boolean simplification Table 3.9. This results in a total of five prime implicants for cluster 2 in the final model in Table 3.9.

Table 3.9 shows the Boolean simplification for the wave 2 model. The results can be summarised for each cluster. Cluster one has larger families, higher rates of perceived and reported ill health with an associated lower scoring report for quality of life and more contacts and communications with doctors. Cluster 2 has lower family size. It has lower incidents of reported ill health and visits to the doctor and higher quality of life ratings. Finally, cluster 3 has smaller families but with children living near, higher incidents of self-reported and actual ill health and more visits to the doctor.

Macro case study 1, wave 4, 2010

SHARE wave 3 data are not compatible with the longitudinal case study data used here and so is not included (different variables and measures were applied in wave 3). For this reason, the next stage of the application of DPS with the social care and health in Europe macro case study moves to wave 4. Table 3.10 shows the agglomeration schedule for wave 4 data. The coefficient score gradient changes significantly at stage 4 when there is an 8.5 difference in the progression. This suggests that three clusters are the optimal number to consider.

The icicle plot in Figure 3.5 shows that Belgium and France have the closest proximity in scores. Next are the pairing of Germany and Austria, followed by

Table 3.7 QCA: data for truth table, macro case study 1, 2006

Country	*Household size*	*Number of siblings alive*	*Number of children*	*Number of grandchildren*	*Self-perceived health*	*Number of chronic diseases*	*CASP: quality of life and well-being index*	*Depression scale EURO-D*	*How often seen or talked to medical doctor last 12 months*	*Percentage in employment*	*At least one child lives in the building*	*At least one child lives less than 1 km away*	*Helped someone in the last 12 months*
Austria	1.9	2.2	2.0	2.5	3.0	0.9	38.4	2.0	6.5	15.4	37.1	44.9	27.4
Belgium	2.1	2.8	2.2	3.0	3.0	1.1	37.4	2.5	8.2	28.6	32.2	40.6	34.9
Denmark	2.0	2.3	2.3	3.1	2.6	1.0	40.9	1.8	4.8	38.0	14.0	21.9	41.5
France	2.1	2.9	2.3	3.1	3.2	1.0	37.5	2.8	6.9	31.6	21.5	32.7	42.7
Germany	2.1	2.1	2.0	2.2	3.2	1.2	38.8	2.1	8.4	20.2	54.4	67.5	13.5
Italy	2.5	2.6	2.0	2.3	3.3	1.1	33.7	2.8	9.0	18.8	59.2	67.9	25.9
The Netherlands	2.1	3.3	2.4	3.0	2.9	0.9	40.4	1.9	5.3	29.9	28.4	34.8	27.5
Spain	2.5	2.7	2.4	2.8	3.4	1.2	35.7	2.8	7.1	42.3	16.5	22.2	44.7
Sweden	1.9	2.2	2.3	3.4	2.7	1.1	39.3	2.0	3.4	41.8	31.5	37.6	32.7
Switzerland	2.1	2.6	2.1	2.3	2.7	0.8	40.7	1.9	5.0	25.3	27.3	38.3	40.9
Mean	*2.1*	*2.6*	*2.2*	*2.8*	*3.0*	*1.0*	*38.3*	*2.3*	*6.5*	*29.2*	*32.2*	*40.8*	*33.2*
Median	*2.1*	*2.6*	*2.2*	*2.9*	*3.0*	*1.1*	*38.6*	*2.1*	*6.7*	*29.3*	*30.0*	*38.0*	*33.8*
Conversion to binary scores													
Austria	0	0	0	0	1	0	1	0	0	0	1	1	0
Belgium	0	1	0	1	1	1	0	1	1	0	1	1	1
Denmark	0	0	1	1	0	0	1	0	0	1	0	0	1
France	0	1	1	1	1	0	0	1	1	1	0	0	1
Germany	0	0	0	0	1	1	1	0	1	0	1	1	0
Italy	1	1	0	0	1	1	0	1	1	0	1	1	0
The Netherlands	0	1	1	1	0	0	1	0	0	1	0	0	0
Spain	1	1	1	1	1	1	0	1	1	1	0	0	1
Sweden	0	0	1	1	1	1	1	0	0	1	1	0	0
Switzerland	0	1	0	0	0	0	1	0	0	0	0	1	1

Table 3.8 QCA truth table for macro case study 1, 2006

Country	*Household size*	*Number of siblings alive*	*Number of children*	*Number of grandchildren*	*Self-perceived health*	*Number of chronic diseases*	*CASP: quality of life and well-being index*	*Depression scale EURO-Dore is depressed*	*How often seen or talked to medical doctor last 12 months*	*Percentage in employment*	*At least one child lives in the building*	*At least one child lives less than 1km away*	*Helped someone in the last 12 months*	*Cluster*
Spain	1	**1**	1	**1**	**1**	1	**0**	**1**	**1**	1	0	0	**1**	1
France	0	**1**	1	**1**	**1**	0	**0**	**1**	**1**	1	0	0	**1**	1
Belgium	0	**1**	0	**1**	**1**	1	**0**	**1**	**1**	0	1	1	**1**	1
Switzerland	**0**	1	0	0	0	0	**1**	**0**	**0**	0	0	1	1	2
The Netherlands	**0**	1	1	1	0	0	**1**	**0**	**0**	1	0	0	0	2
Denmark	**0**	0	1	1	1	0	**1**	**0**	**0**	1	0	0	1	2
Sweden	**0**	0	1	1	1	1	**1**	**0**	**0**	1	1	0	0	2
Austria	**0**	0	0	0	0	0	**1**	**0**	**0**	0	1	1	0	2
Italy	1	1	**0**	**0**	**1**	**1**	0	1	**1**	**0**	**1**	**1**	**0**	3
Germany	0	0	**0**	**0**	**1**	**1**	1	0	**1**	**0**	**1**	**1**	**0**	3

Table 3.9 Boolean simplification macro case study 1, 2006

Clusters	*Boolean simplification*
Cluster 1 Belgium, France and Spain	SIBLINGS ALIVE * NUMBER OF GRANDCHILDREN * SELF-PERCEIVED HEALTH * quality of life * DEPRESSION * CONTACT WITH DOCTOR * HELPED SOMEONE
Cluster 2 Austria, Switzerland, the Netherlands, Sweden and Denmark	Household size * QUALITY OF LIFE * diseases * depression * contact with doctor
Cluster 3 Germany and Italy	Number of children * number of grandchildren * SELF-PERCEIVED HEALTH * DISEASES * CONTACT WITH DOCTOR * employment * CHILD IN BUILDING * CHILD NEAR * helped someone

Table 3.10 Agglomeration schedule for country aggregates, macro case study 1, 2010

Stage	*Cluster Combined*		*Coefficients*	*Stage Cluster First Appears*		*Next Stage*
	Cluster 1	*Cluster 2*		*Cluster 1*	*Cluster 2*	
1	7	10	1.861	0	0	6
2	1	2	4.825	0	0	6
3	8	9	10.924	0	0	7
4	5	6	18.300	0	0	8
5	3	4	26.160	0	0	7
6	1	7	35.125	2	1	8
7	3	8	46.939	5	3	9
8	1	5	68.756	6	4	9
9	1	3	117.000	8	7	0

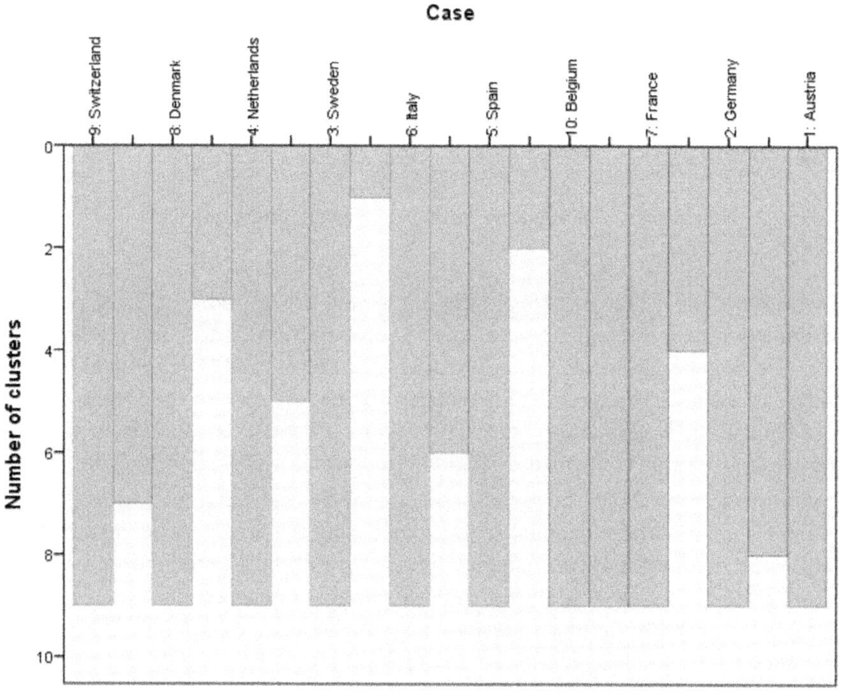

Figure 3.5 Icicle plot of cluster formulation: macro case study 1, 2010

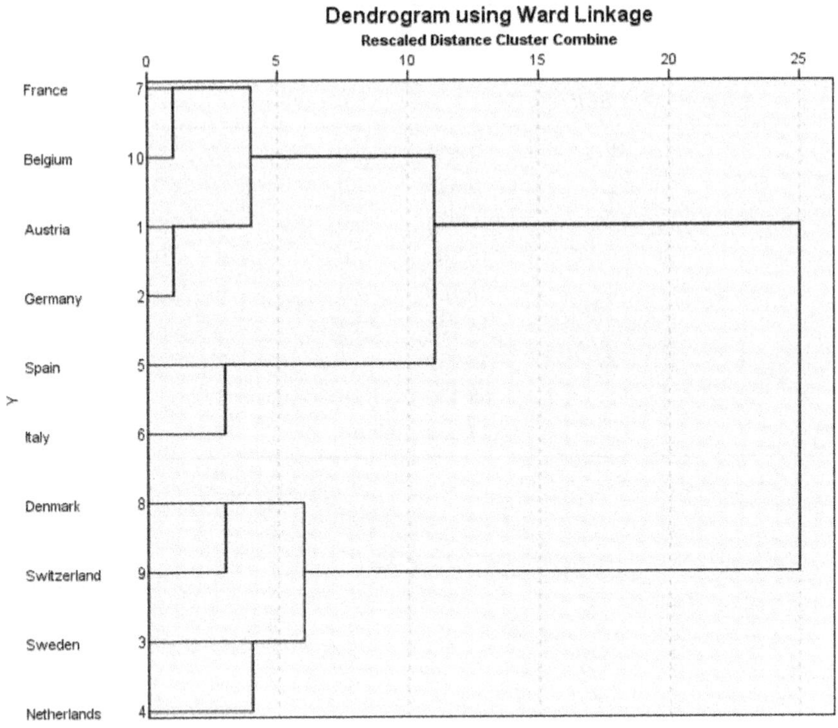

Figure 3.6 Dendrogram plot of cluster formulation: macro case study 1, 2010

Switzerland and Denmark. Next Italy and Spain are paired. The final pairing, before any larger group agglomerations, is between Sweden and the Netherlands. The first larger agglomerations are between the pairings of Belgium and France and Austria and Germany. Next the two pairings of Switzerland and Denmark and Sweden and the Netherlands combine. Further agglomerations look to be of little substantive value as confirmed by the dendrogram in Figure 3.6. Figure 3.6 seems to confirm the existence of three clusters and this is next examined using QCA.

Table 3.11 shows the detailed scale variable scores for each case and variable. This is the raw data that was used by the CA algorithms. For the purpose of performing a crisp set QCA to understand the variable effects on cluster definition, the data is converted to binary scores where the threshold is again set by making reference to the median and mean and distribution of the data. Some variables have distributions close to the central tendency and this makes allocation to binary scores rather arbitrary. Examples are the variables of average self-perceived health and the average number of chronic diseases. It is important to keep in mind the substantive issue that national average differences are not always substantial. This factor influences the issue of prime implicant near misses and some binary overruling at the final stage of the modelling.

Table 3.11 QCA: data for a truth table, case study 1, 2010

Country	*Household size*	*Number of siblings alive*	*Number of children*	*Number of grandchildren*	*Self-perceived health*	*Number of chronic diseases*	*CASP: quality of life and well-being index*	*Depression scale EURO-D*	*How often seen or talked to medical doctor last 12 months*	*Percentage in employment*	*At least one child lives in the building*	*At least one child lives less than 1 km away*	*Helped someone in the last 12 months*
Austria	2.0	2.3	2.1	2.5	2.9	1.1	39.7	2.1	6.9	23.4	34.8	47.2	21.6
Germany	2.0	2.1	2.0	2.4	3.3	1.3	38.7	2.3	8.8	22.9	27.1	38.3	27.8
Sweden	1.8	2.2	2.3	3.8	2.9	1.1	38.8	2.0	3.2	27.4	8.7	19.8	36.6
The Netherlands	2.0	3.3	2.4	3.1	2.9	0.9	40.7	1.9	5.6	29.7	18.0	30.8	34.1
Spain	2.5	2.7	2.5	2.8	3.4	1.3	35.7	2.9	7.2	19.6	48.0	67.9	12.7
Italy	2.5	2.5	2.1	2.3	3.2	1.1	33.8	2.7	9.8	20.1	55.9	66.9	22.7
France	2.0	2.8	2.2	3.0	3.2	1.1	37.7	2.9	6.7	28.3	24.3	34.2	25.7
Denmark	2.0	2.3	2.3	3.1	2.5	1.0	40.7	1.8	4.7	44.2	19.6	28.1	45.0
Switzerland	2.1	2.5	2.1	2.2	2.6	0.8	40.8	2.0	4.8	42.3	31.0	41.4	27.5
Belgium	2.1	2.7	2.2	2.9	3.0	1.2	37.0	2.6	8.0	29.5	27.9	39.6	35.9
Mean	*2.1*	*2.6*	*2.2*	*2.8*	*3.0*	*1.1*	*38.4*	*2.3*	*6.6*	*28.7*	*29.5*	*41.4*	*29.0*
Median	*2.0*	*2.5*	*2.2*	*2.9*	*3.0*	*1.1*	*38.8*	*2.2*	*6.8*	*27.8*	*27.5*	*39.0*	*27.7*
Conversion to binary scores													
Austria	0	0	0	0	0	1	1	0	1	0	1	1	1
Germany	0	0	0	0	1	1	1	1	1	0	0	0	0
Sweden	0	0	1	1	0	1	1	0	0	0	0	0	0
The Netherlands	0	1	1	1	0	0	1	0	0	1	0	0	1
Spain	1	1	1	0	1	1	0	1	1	0	1	1	1
Italy	1	1	0	0	1	1	0	1	1	0	1	1	1
France	1	1	1	1	1	1	0	1	1	1	0	0	0
Denmark	0	0	1	1	0	0	1	0	0	1	0	0	1
Switzerland	1	1	0	0	0	0	1	0	0	1	1	1	0
Belgium	1	1	0	1	1	1	0	1	1	1	1	1	1

Table 3.12 QCA truth table for macro case study 1, 2010

Country	*Household size*	*Number of siblings alive*	*Number of children*	*Number of grandchildren*	*Self-perceived health*	*Number of chronic diseases*	*CASP: quality of life and well-being index*	*Depression scale EURO-D – high is depressed*	*How often seen or talked to medical doctor last 12 months*	*Percentage in employment*	*At least one child lives in the building*	*At least one child lives less than 1km away*	*Helped someone in the last 12 months*	*Cluster*
France	1	1	**1**	1	**1**	**1**	0	1	**1**	1	0	0	1	1
Belgium	1	1	**1**	1	**1**	**1**	0	1	**1**	1	1	1	1	1
Germany	0	0	**0**	0	**1**	**1**	1	1	**1**	0	0	0	1	1
Austria	0	0	**0**	0	**0**	**1**	1	0	**1**	0	1	1	0	1
Spain	**1**	**1**	1	**0**	**1**	**1**	**0**	**1**	**1**	**0**	**1**	**1**	**0**	2
Italy	**1**	**1**	0	**0**	**1**	**1**	**0**	**1**	**1**	**0**	**1**	**1**	**0**	2
Switzerland	**1**	1	0	0	**0**	**0**	**1**	**0**	**0**	**1**	**1**	**1**	0	3
The Netherlands	**0**	1	1	1	**0**	**0**	**1**	**0**	**0**	**1**	**0**	**0**	1	3
Sweden	**0**	0	1	1	**0**	**1**	**1**	**0**	**0**	**0**	**0**	**0**	1	3
Denmark	**0**	0	1	1	**0**	**0**	**1**	**0**	**0**	**1**	**0**	**0**	0	3

Table 3.12 reveals the final QCA model truth table where the binary scores are patterned with the outcomes of the three clusters. Here it is possible to examine binary variable score patterns for each cluster and to consider whether there is enough evidence of similarity to accept the three cluster definitions.

Cluster 1 has two prime implicants. This is above threshold scores for average number of chronic diseases and how often a person has seen and talked to medical doctors. There is also one other variable with a prime implicant near miss. The near miss is the average self-perceived health score where only Austria in cluster 1 is marginally below the threshold, scoring 2.9. Given that the mean and median are 3.0, this score is considered a near miss for the cluster and the variable is included as an above threshold prime implicant.

Cluster 2 is a strong pairing with 12 prime implicants.

Cluster 3 has four prime implicants and seven near misses. One country, Switzerland, is responsible for five of these near misses. The first near miss is household size where only Switzerland is above threshold. Given that its score of 2.1 is on the threshold point, the score is overruled and the variable becomes a below threshold prime implicant for the cluster. Next, number of children, shows that Switzerland is the only country with a below threshold score. Its score is typical in the distribution of other countries below threshold and so this score is not adjusted to allow a new cluster prime implicant. The same decision is reached for the number of grandchildren, where Switzerland is significantly below the threshold in the data distribution. With the number of chronic diseases, Sweden's score is at the central tendency and this permits overruling the score to allow a further prime implicant. Sweden is also the exception causing the near miss with percentage in employment, where it is the only country in the cluster below threshold. It's score of 27.4 is close to the threshold of 28.0 and so this is overruled and the variable is included as a prime implicant. Switzerland is the exception for the two child proximity variables where it is the only country scoring above threshold in the cluster. For having a child living in the same building it is marginally above threshold and close to the mean of 29.5 with a score of 31. For this reason, the score is overruled and the variable is changed to a below threshold prime implicant for the cluster. Similarly, its score for having a child living near is at the threshold and only 1.5 above the mean of 29.5 and so this is also overruled and the variable is recorded as a below threshold prime implicant. The result of these considerations is that cluster 3 has nine prime implicants.

Table 3.13 shows the final simplified model for the wave 4, 2010, data.

Cluster 1 has higher health problems and resulting contact with doctors. Cluster 2 shares these aspects, but also has stronger family contacts. Cluster 3 has higher scores on the more positive social and health outcomes, with less reporting of health problems and disease, higher quality of life scores, less contact with

Table 3.13 Boolean simplification macro case study 1, 2010

Clusters	*Boolean simplification*
Cluster 1 Belgium, France, Germany and Austria	NUMBER OF CHILDREN * SELF-PERCEIVED HEALTH * DISEASES * CONTACT WITH DOCTOR
Cluster 2 Spain and Italy	HOUSEHOLD SIZE * SIBLINGS ALIVE * grandchildren * SELF-PERCEIVED HEALTH * DISEASES * quality of life * DEPRESSION * CONTACT WITH DOCTOR * employment * CHILD IN BUILDING * CHILD NEAR * helped someone
Cluster 3 Switzerland, the Netherlands, Sweden and Denmark	household size * self-perceived health * diseases * QUALITY OF LIFE * depression * contact with doctor * EMPLOYMENT * child in building * child near

doctors and with employment being more likely to continue post age 50. Household structures and contacts are weaker.

Macro case study 1, wave 5, 2013

The final stage for the first macro case study uses wave 5 of the SHARE as collected in 2013. Table 3.14 shows the agglomeration schedule for country aggregates. A noticeable increase in the gradient between the coefficients occurs after stage 4, implying that 4 clusters may be the optimal solution. The icicle plot in Figure 3.7 indicates that Belgium and France are the first pair to be joined together, followed closely by Denmark and Sweden. The Netherlands then soon joins these pairings. Next Germany joins with Austria and Italy joins with Spain. Further, Switzerland joins with Germany and Austria. This seems to reach the optimal point suggested by the coefficient score changes in the agglomeration schedule. After this, Switzerland, Germany and Austria merge with France, Germany and the Netherlands to form a six country cluster. The dendrogram in Figure 3.8 confirms the hierarchical ordering and shows that in the last few agglomerations Spain and Italy remain as a different pair, this until the final agglomeration of all cases.

Table 3.15 shows the process of binary scoring. This, as in the earlier models, uses the scale data already inputted into the CA. These values are displayed in the top section of Table 3.15. Threshold setting is applied using the median and mean scores for each variable and while also considering the distribution of variables across the cases. The resulting binary score pattern is then displayed in rows for each country.

Table 3.16 applies the binary scores to an explanation of the cluster memberships, using a four cluster structure as suggested in the CA process. Near misses are considered for the household and family size variables in the three country

Table 3.14 Agglomeration schedule for country aggregates, macro case study 1, 2013

Stage	*Cluster Combined*		*Coefficients*	*Stage Cluster First Appears*		*Next Stage*
	Cluster 1	*Cluster 2*		*Cluster 1*	*Cluster 2*	
1	7	10	2.802	0	0	3
2	3	8	6.003	0	0	8
3	4	7	11.856	0	1	7
4	1	2	17.931	0	0	6
5	5	6	24.264	0	0	9
6	1	9	37.010	4	0	7
7	1	4	52.466	6	3	8
8	1	3	73.997	7	2	9
9	1	5	117.000	8	5	0

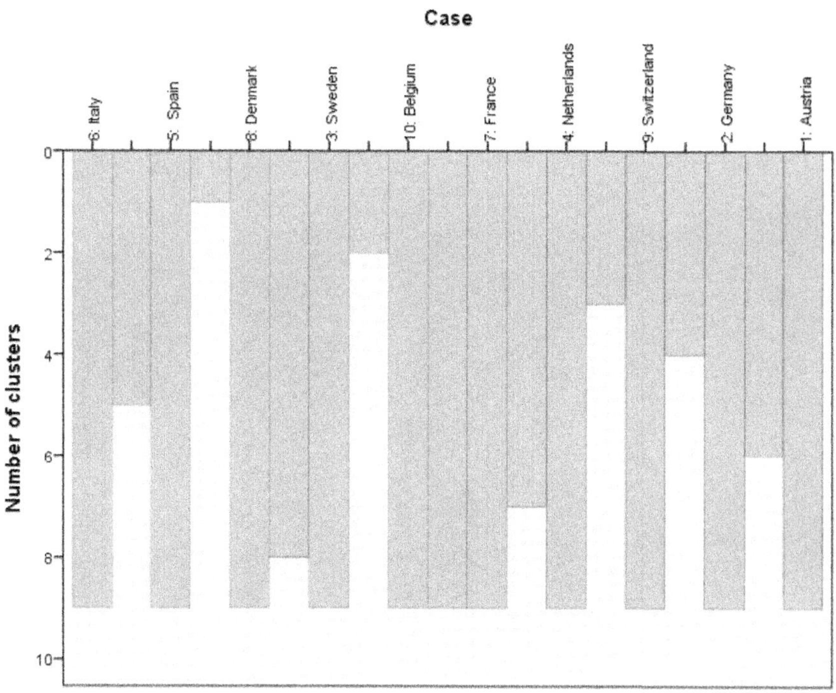

Figure 3.7 Icicle plot of cluster formulation: macro case study 1, 2013

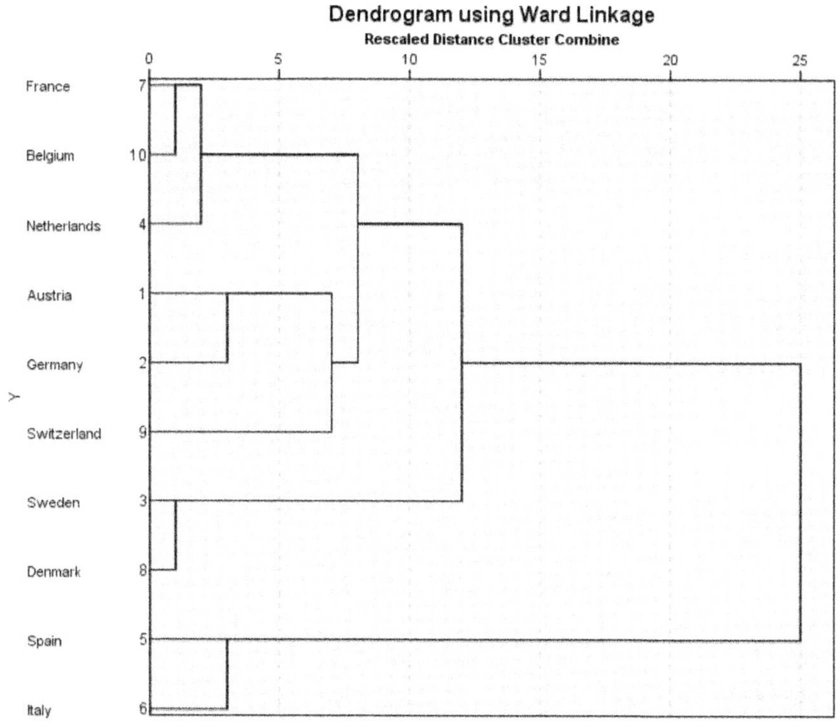

Figure 3.8 Dendrogram of cluster formulation: macro case study 1, 2013

Table 3.15 QCA: data for truth table, macro case study 1, 2013

Country	*Household size*	*Number of siblings alive*	*Number of children*	*Number of grandchildren*	*Self-perceived health*	*Number of chronic diseases*	*CASP: quality of life and well-being index*	*Depression scale EURO-D*	*How often seen or talked to medical doctor last 12 months*	*Percentage in employment*	*At least one child lives in the building*	*At least one child lives less than 1km away*	*Helped someone in the last 12 months*
Austria	2.0	2.4	2.1	2.7	3.0	1.1	40.2	1.9	7.9	19.6	30.8	42.9	25.6
Germany	2.1	2.1	2.0	2.1	3.2	1.3	39.1	2.3	9.1	36.9	34.0	43.1	34.2
Sweden	1.9	2.2	2.4	3.5	2.7	1.1	39.8	2.0	3.9	32.4	12.1	20.6	39.0
The Netherlands	2.0	3.2	2.3	3.2	2.9	1.0	40.8	1.9	6.0	30.0	18.7	30.9	34.2
Spain	2.4	2.6	2.3	2.7	3.3	1.2	35.9	2.6	5.9	22.6	41.9	60.1	12.3
Italy	2.5	2.5	2.0	2.3	3.3	1.1	33.6	3.0	8.4	22.0	54.3	64.5	23.0
France	2.0	2.9	2.3	3.3	3.2	1.1	38.2	2.8	7.0	24.4	18.8	28.4	26.5
Denmark	2.0	2.3	2.3	3.1	2.5	1.1	41.5	1.8	5.4	42.5	17.3	24.9	48.1
Switzerland	2.1	2.6	2.1	2.4	2.7	0.8	40.9	1.9	5.7	38.6	24.2	34.6	26.4
Belgium	2.1	2.8	2.2	3.0	3.0	1.1	37.8	2.5	8.4	28.4	26.0	37.1	35.4
Mean	*2.1*	*2.6*	*2.2*	*2.8*	*3.0*	*1.1*	*38.8*	*2.3*	*6.8*	*29.7*	*27.8*	*38.7*	*30.5*
Median	*2.0*	*2.6*	*2.2*	*2.9*	*3.0*	*1.1*	*39.4*	*2.2*	*6.5*	*29.2*	*25.1*	*35.9*	*30.4*
Conversion to binary scores													
Austria	0	0	0	0	1	0	1	0	1	0	1	1	0
Germany	1	0	0	0	1	1	1	1	1	1	1	1	1
Sweden	0	0	1	1	0	0	1	0	0	1	0	0	1
The Netherlands	0	0	1	1	0	0	1	0	0	1	0	0	1
Spain	1	1	1	0	1	1	0	1	0	0	1	1	0
Italy	1	1	0	0	1	0	0	1	1	0	1	1	0
France	0	1	1	1	1	0	0	1	1	0	0	0	0
Denmark	0	0	1	1	0	0	1	0	0	1	0	0	1
Switzerland	1	1	0	0	0	0	1	0	0	1	0	0	0
Belgium	1	1	0	1	0	0	0	1	1	0	1	1	1

Table 3.16 QCA truth table for macro case study 1, 2013

Country	*Household size*	*Number of siblings alive*	*Number of children*	*Number of grandchildren*	*Self-perceived health*	*Number of chronic diseases*	*CASP: quality of life and well-being index*	*Depression scale EURO-D*	*How often seen or talked to medical doctor last 12 months*	*Percentage in employment*	*At least one child lives in the building*	*At least one child lives less than 1km away*	*Helped someone in the last 12 months*	*Cluster*
Belgium	1	1	0	1	0	0	0	1	1	0	1	1	1	1
France	0	1	1	1	1	0	0	1	1	0	0	0	0	1
The Netherlands	0	1	1	1	0	0	1	0	0	1	0	0	1	1
Switzerland	1	1	0	0	0	0	1	0	0	1	0	0	0	2
Germany	1	0	0	0	1	1	1	1	1	1	1	1	1	2
Austria	0	0	0	0	1	0	1	0	1	0	1	1	0	2
Sweden	0	0	1	1	0	1	1	0	0	1	0	0	1	3
Denmark	0	0	1	1	0	0	1	0	0	1	0	0	1	3
Spain	1	1	1	0	1	1	0	1	0	0	1	1	0	4
Italy	1	1	0	0	1	0	0	1	1	0	1	1	0	4

clusters, because of the limited distribution of these variables. These over-rulings of scale variables in cluster 1 and cluster 2 are shown separately in Table 3.17.

Table 3.17 examines the specific possibilities for threshold overruling due to a case scoring at the mean or median in each variable distribution for clusters 1 and 2 (both these clusters contain three countries). It is decided to overrule in two variables, household size and number of children. Both these variables are promoted to become prime implicants in their respective clusters with the weighting skewed towards the dominant binary scores in each cluster.

Table 3.18 shows the Boolean simplification for the final 2013 wave of the macro case study. Cluster 1 has a tendency towards more external family links, with above threshold scores for the number of siblings alive, number of children and number of grandchildren. Rates of disease are below threshold. Cluster 2

Table 3.17 Considerations for threshold overruling: clusters 1 and 2, 2013

Country	*Household size*	*Number of siblings alive*	*Number of children*	*Number of grandchildren*	*Self-perceived health*	*Number of chronic diseases*	*CASP: quality of life and well-being index*	*Depression scale EURO-D*	*How often seen or talked to medical doctor last 12 months*	*Percentage in employment*	*At least one child lives in the building*	*At least one child lives less than 1km away*	*Helped someone in the last 12 months*
Belgium	2.1	2.8	2.2	3.0	3.0	1.1	37.8	2.5	8.4	28.4	26.0	37.1	35.4
France	2.0	2.9	2.3	3.3	3.2	1.1	38.2	2.8	7.0	24.4	18.8	28.4	26.5
The Netherlands	2.0	3.2	2.3	3.2	2.9	1.0	40.8	1.9	6.0	30.0	18.7	30.9	34.2
Switzerland	2.1	2.6	2.1	2.4	2.7	0.8	40.9	1.9	5.7	38.6	24.2	34.6	26.4
Germany	2.1	2.1	2.0	2.1	3.2	1.3	39.1	2.3	9.1	36.9	34.0	43.1	34.2
Austria	2.0	2.4	2.1	2.7	3.0	1.1	40.2	1.9	7.9	19.6	30.8	42.9	25.6
Mean	*2.1*	*2.6*	*2.2*	*2.8*	*3.0*	*1.1*	*38.8*	*2.3*	*6.8*	*29.7*	*27.8*	*38.7*	*30.5*
Median	*2.0*	*2.6*	*2.2*	*2.9*	*3.0*	*1.1*	*39.4*	*2.2*	*6.5*	*29.2*	*25.1*	*35.9*	*30.4*

Table 3.18 Boolean simplification, macro case study 1, 2013

Clusters	*Boolean simplification*
Cluster 1 Belgium, France and the Netherlands	Household * SIBLINGS * CHILDREN * GRANDCHILDREN * chronic diseases
Cluster 2 Switzerland, Germany and Austria	HOUSEHOLD * children * grandchildren * QUALTY OF LIFE
Cluster 3 Sweden and Denmark	Household * siblings alive * CHILDREN * GRANDCHILDREN * self-perceived health * QUALITY OF LIFE * depression * contact with doctor * EMPLOYMENT * child in building * child near home * HELPED SOMEONE
Cluster 4 Spain and Italy	HOUSEHOLD * SIBLINGS * grandchildren * SELF-PERCEIVED HEALTH * quality of life * DEPRESSION * employment * CHILD IN BUILDING * CHILD NEAR HOME * helped someone

has larger households, but below threshold scores for number of children and grandchildren. It shares above threshold quality of life scores. The Scandinavian countries in cluster 3 (Sweden and Denmark) share above threshold family links, but below threshold scores for children at home and nearby. Similarly, the household size is below threshold. Self-perceived health scores, quality of life and depression scores are all below threshold. There seems to be an above threshold sense of neighbourliness in terms of above threshold scores for helping someone in the last 12 months. Employment is above threshold. The southern European prime implicants for Spain and Italy in cluster 4 are very close to being a mirror reversal of the Scandinavian pattern. Household size and the number of siblings alive are above threshold. Both the variables having children living in the same building and living close by are also above threshold. Together this suggests a major influence of family and the likelihood of access to family support and care. Self-perceived health problems are above threshold, as is depression, but quality of life scores is below threshold. Employment is below threshold. There are some strong similarities here to the previous periods of time modelled, and the synthesis now moves to summarise the overall model.

Macro case study 1: conclusions

The final consideration for the macro case study is to discern the overall changes in case dynamics and resulting patterns. At its simplest, this involves identifying stable case patterns and unstable ones. The former will be cases that remain in a similar location to each other, perhaps remaining in the same cluster across the time period covered.

More complex is the consideration of longitudinal variable effects. While some cases may stay near each other and often appear in the same cluster, this does not necessarily mean their mutual memberships are defined and driven by the same variable influences. It is possible for cases to remain in the same clusters, or to be in cluster proximity, but for these bonds of similarity to be influenced by different variable influences over time. Cases may remain similar because they experience similar change dynamics in the variable influences over time. There is, then, a difference between case stability and variable stability.

Cases

Over the four time periods studied, 2004, 2006, 2010 and 2013, the following country case cluster similarities remain. Sweden and Denmark are always located together. France and Belgium are always located in the same cluster. Spain and Italy are located together in every year apart from 2006. Austria and Germany are located together in every year apart form 2006. This is evidence of relative stability in case based patterns. Switzerland and the Netherlands are the countries that are most likely to change cluster memberships.

Geographical location is an important aspect of DPS, as convergence over time is more likely between geographical neighbours. This spatial feature is demonstrated in macro case study 1. At the end of the current time period, the final clusters reflect geographical location.

France, Belgium and the Netherlands are connected in Northern Europe.

Switzerland, Germany and Austria are interconnected in central Western Europe.

Sweden and Denmark are only separated by the Oresund Sea in Northern Europe, but possess strong social, economic and cultural links, including a bridge.

Spain and Italy are not directly connected, but are close neighbours via France, and are only separated by the Mediterranean Sea.

In the main, macro case study 1 demonstrates a high occurrence of case stability where cases remain in similar clusters. Next the task is to explore whether cluster movement is related to changes in variable trends.

Variables

Table 3.19 shows the underlying variable trends in the DPS across the four different time points. The average household and family structure variables remain very stable. The average scores for self-perception of health and depression are also stable. The average number of chronic diseases rises marginally and might be explained by older people in Europe living longer. Similarly, there is a small rise in the average number of times a person sees a doctor. Despite these changes over time, the average quality of life index rises marginally, as does the percentage in employment. A key trend is that children are less likely to be living in the same household with their older parent/s, or living very close by, with declines in both these variables. There is also an average decline in the reported 'neighbourliness' activities from the older people interviewed. All these trends are aggregates taken from the European sample level and there will be differences at the national country level. It is these accumulations of national case differences that may account for changes in similarity and difference between countries. Overall there is a strong element of variable stability in macro case study 1 over the time period studied – some of this is the nature of the variables used – with indicators about extended family structure that includes the number of family members being expected to be constant over time.

Patterns

The variables that remain stable over time are also more likely to be linked to the same cluster groupings over time, as illustrated in Table 3.20. Table 3.20 shows the mix of case and variable stability over time, recording the QCA, above and below threshold scores that remain consistent for individual cases over the time period studied. This stability matrix, to a larger extent, reflects the dominant clusters over the time scale as previously discussed above.

Given that Switzerland and the Netherlands are the cases that have been identified to be the most likely to change clusters, the remainder of the commentary focused on the experience of these two cases.

Table 3.19 Variable trends, 2004–2013, macro case study 1

	Household size	*Number of siblings alive*	*Number of children*	*Number of grandchildren*	*Self-perceived health*	*Number of chronic diseases*	*CASP: quality of life and well-being index*	*Depression scale EURO-D*	*How often seen or talked to medical doctor last 12 months*	*Percentage in employment*	*At least one child lives in the building*	*At least one child lives less than 1km away*	*Cared for a sick or disabled adult in the last year*
2004	2.1	2.6	2.2	2.8	3.0	1.0	38.3	2.3	6.5	29.1	34.6	43.5	33.3
2006	2.1	2.6	2.2	2.8	3.0	1.0	38.3	2.3	6.5	29.2	32.2	40.8	33.2
2010	2.1	2.6	2.2	2.8	3.0	1.1	38.4	2.3	6.6	28.7	29.5	41.4	29
2013	2.1	2.6	2.2	2.8	3.0	1.1	38.8	2.3	6.8	29.7	27.8	38.7	30.5
	stable	**stable**	**stable**	**stable**	**stable**	∧	∧	**stable**	∧	∧	∨	∨	∨

Switzerland ends the case study in 2013 with its geographical neighbours, Germany and Austria. It shares smaller family size with above average scores for quality of life. In 2010, it clustered with Sweden and Denmark because of shared below threshold scores for less chronic illness and a positive self-assessment perception of health. Similarly, in 2006, it is in a larger cluster that includes Sweden, Denmark, Austria and the Netherlands where chronic illness scores are below threshold. Likewise, in 2004, it also shares this profile with the Netherlands, Sweden and Denmark. The main reason for Switzerland's movement of clusters is its relatively small family size that outweighs morbidity factors in the modelling, at certain points of calculation within the comparisons. This can be seen in the combined case and variable stability plot, in Table 3.20, where Switzerland retains below threshold scores for depression and chronic diseases – across all time points. (That makes Switzerland more similar to Sweden, Denmark and the Netherlands than its geographical neighbours, for these morbidity characteristics.) But the constant factors of lower numbers of children and grandchildren keep Switzerland more similar to German and Austria in some periodic comparisons.

The path taken by the Netherlands shows the reverse aspect regarding the nuclear family structure for the post age 50 generation. The Netherlands has more

Table 3.20 Longitudinal truth table: macro case study 1

OVERALL threshold stability	*Household size*	*Number of siblings alive*	*Number of children*	*Number of grandchildren*	*Self-perceived health*	*Number of chronic diseases*	*CASP: quality of life and well-being index*	*Depression scale EURO-D*	*How often seen or talked to medical doctor last 12 months*	*Percentage in employment*	*At least one child lives in the building*	*At least one child lives less than 1km away*	*Helped someone in the last 12 months*
Belgium		Above		Above			Below	Above	Above				Above
France		Above	Above	Above	Above		Below	Above	Above		Below	Below	
Spain	Above	Above	Above		Above	Above	Below	Above					
Italy	Above	Above	Below	Below	Above		Below	Above	Above	Below	Above	Above	Below
Sweden	Below	Below	Above	Above			Above	Below	Below	Above		Below	
Denmark	Below	Below	Above	Above		Below	Above	Below	Below	Above	Below	Below	
The Netherlands	Below	Above	Above	Above	Below	Below	Above	Below	Below	Above	Below	Below	
Germany		Below	Below	Below		Above	Above		Above				
Austria		Below	Below	Below				Below		Below	Above	Above	Below
Switzerland		Above	Below	Below	Below	Below	Above	Below	Below				

similar family size threshold scores to Sweden and Denmark, while still sharing the good quality of life aspect and lower morbidity scores. In the final CA, 2013, the reason the Netherlands ends up with Belgium and France is because of a closeness in larger family structures to those countries: above threshold for number of siblings (where it is different to Sweden and Denmark). While some differences in comparative variable scores and peculiarities of the cluster agglomeration put Switzerland and the Netherlands away from the Scandinavian cluster in the final CA, the overall weight of the DPS suggests that on the issue of quality of life (and with less experiences in those countries of chronic illness) they are more similar to Denmark and Sweden and this is the more important theme over time to take from the DPS. This, again, illustrates the importance of using qualitative reflection to examine clusters and their usefulness, and why social and economic cluster membership is as much a qualitative judgement as a quantitative one.

For both variable trends and case based patterns, macro case study 1 shows relative stability in the patterns observed.

Macro case study 2: the evolution of the euro based economies

The second macro case study in this chapter explores the evolution of the euro currency after 2000 in terms of its implications on the similarity and differences of the member countries. The data is taken predominantly from Eurostat sources and supplemented by data from the European Central Bank (ECB), European Commission (EU) and OECD. The same longitudinal dataset is used to construct cluster membership at three different time points, 2004, 2006 and 2013. The 12 countries who joined the single currency at its onset are included, but not the European countries that joined later in the period under study. The thirteen variables selected for cluster definition and their statistical sources are shown in Table 3.21. As with the previous case study in this chapter, the chosen cluster method is Ward's method, using linkages measured by the squared Euclidean distance. Like the first case study in this chapter, variables are standardised using z scores to prevent differences in scale or distribution variable from having a dominant effect on cluster definition.

Macro case study 2, wave 1, 2002

Table 3.22 shows the agglomeration schedule for the first-time point, 2002. The largest increase in the gradient of the coefficients occurs at stage 9, suggesting eight or nine clusters for an optimal mathematical solution. But this would only set the countries into pairings at best. Subsequent consideration of the dendrogram in Figure 3.10 suggests that some of the triplets are also worthy of consideration, especially as some are geographical neighbours, or near neighbours, in substantive terms.

The icicle plot in Figure 3.9 shows that the first pairing to be selected as most similar in the hierarchical CA is Germany and France. These are the two largest economies in the group of 12. They are neighbours, and political leaders in the negotiations of the European currency ideal. The next pair to be selected is Finland and Austria, two smaller economies. At the next stage, the Netherlands joins with

Table 3.21 Variables in macro case study 2

- Harmonised Indices of Consumer Prices (HICP), annual percentage change (Eurostat)
- Long term interest rates (ECB)
- Government current account as a percentage of GDP (Eurostat)
- GDP purchasing power standard per inhabitant (Eurostat)
- Total government gross debt as a percentage of GDP (Eurostat)
- Percentage of the working age population in employment (Eurostat)
- Import to export ratio, (Eurostat)
- EU employment migration (Eurostat)
- GDP per person (Eurostat)
- Labour productivity per hour worked (Eurostat)
- Average annual indices of consumer confidence (European Commission)
- Total investment all sectors, percentage of GDP invested (Eurostat)
- State control of business regulation, annual score (OECD)

Table 3.22 Agglomeration schedule for country aggregates case study 2, 2002

Stage	*Cluster Combined*		*Coefficients*	*Stage Cluster First Appears*		*Next Stage*
	Cluster 1	*Cluster 2*		*Cluster 1*	*Cluster 2*	
1	4	5	1.852	0	0	3
2	1	3	5.121	0	0	4
3	4	10	9.980	1	0	7
4	1	2	15.524	2	0	7
5	6	11	21.978	0	0	8
6	7	12	29.151	0	0	9
7	1	4	38.989	4	3	9
8	6	8	49.529	5	0	11
9	1	7	67.223	7	6	10
10	1	9	97.069	9	0	11
11	1	6	143.000	10	8	0

Germany and France. Likewise, Belgium then joins with Finland and Austria. The next stage in the analysis combines Greece and Portugal, followed by the separate pairing of Spain and Ireland. Finally, Italy connects with Greece and Portugal. Luxembourg is best considered as an outlier.

The dendrogram in Figure 3.10 gives the best visual view for deciding on the likely optimal number of clusters that can be proposed for a subsequent QCA. Based on this perspective, it is decided to propose four clusters and one outlier. These are:

Cluster 1	France, Germany and the Netherlands
Cluster 2	Austria, Finland, and Belgium
Cluster 3	Ireland and Spain

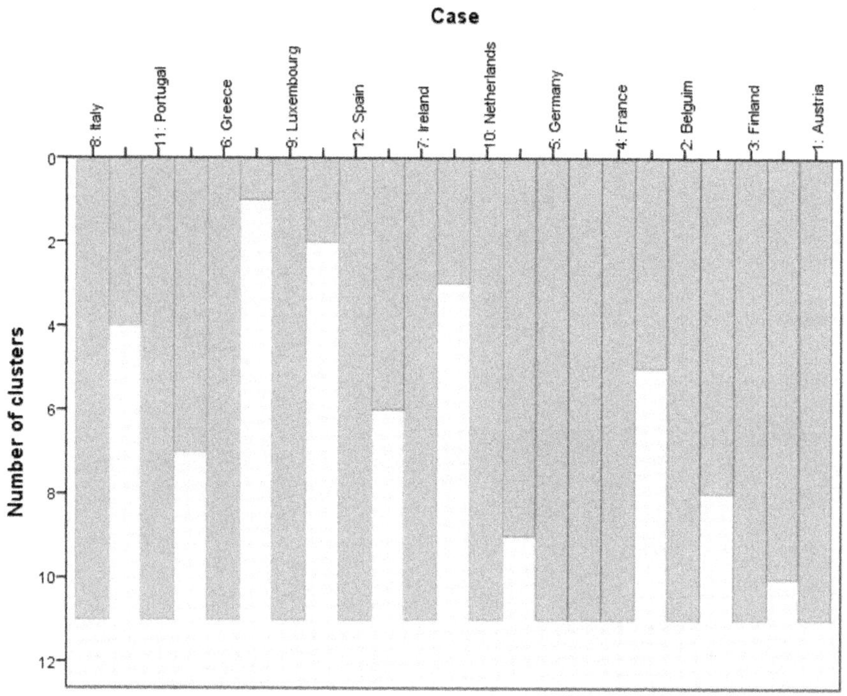

Figure 3.9 Icicle plot of cluster formulation: macro case study 2, 2002

Cluster 4	Greece, Portugal, and Italy
Cluster 5	the outlier, Luxembourg.

Table 3.23 shows the process used for converting the scale variable scores inputted in the CA into binary threshold scores for the QCA. Table 3.24 shows the QCA truth table where the outcome variable is the designated cluster membership.

All clusters in Table 3.24 have prime implicants. As none of the proposed clusters have more than three members, near misses are not considered. As in the previous examples in the book, prime implicants are indicated where the threshold scores are the same for all cluster members and are indicated in bold text in Table 3.24.

Cluster 1 has six prime implicants. Cluster 2 has four. Cluster 3 is a pairing and they share five prime implicants. Lastly, cluster 4 has nine prime implicants.

Table 3.25 shows the process of Boolean simplification of the prime implicants as constructed from the threshold setting process described in Table 3.24. This enables the research to suggest substantive qualitative features for the four clusters. A threshold of 0 for the government current account deficit (this would be a negative scale score in Table 3.22) indicates a higher relative deficit, while a 1 score indicates a lower deficit.

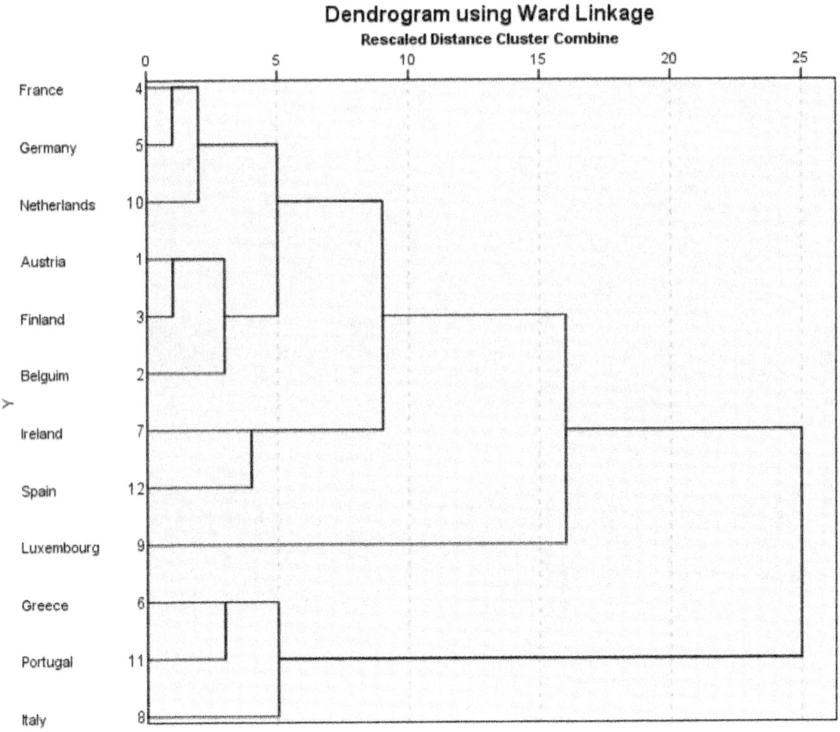

Figure 3.10 Dendrogram of cluster formulation: macro case study 2, 2002

Cluster 1 has low annual GDP growth, a high government current account deficit, high productivity, a higher European Union migrant working population, low investment, and low long term interest rates. This reflects that the largest and strongest economies of the founding European countries are coming out of a mild recession as they move into the new phase of the single currency. Nevertheless, arguably the fundamentals of these economies are sound, especially with regard to high productivity and relatively low long term borrowing costs. In cluster 2, the countries share good economic fundamentals: low inflation, lower government current account deficits, higher consumer confidence and lower levels of state regulatory control of business. Cluster 3 share higher GDP and higher inflation. They also share lower deficits and lower total government debt. Investment is relatively high. Finally, cluster 4, the remaining southern European countries, share higher inflation, a balance of trade towards imports, relatively low GDP purchasing power, higher government deficits, lower European workforce migration, lower productivity, lower consumer confidence, but higher state regulation and long term interest rates. These countries look like the economies that are struggling more as the euro currency is first implemented.

Table 3.23 QCA: data for truth table, macro case study 2, 2002

Country	*Employ 2002*	*GDP 2002*	*HICP 2002*	*Exports 2002*	*GDP PPSI 2002*	*Gov CA 2002*	*Gov Debt 2002*	*Productivity 2002*	*EU15 Workforce 2002*	*Investment GDP 2002 Ratio*	*Customer Confidence 2002*	*State Control of Regulation 2003*	*LTIR 2002*
Austria	71.80	1.70	1.70	1.11	26000.00	−0.70	66.20	113.40	0.01	23.56	−7.70	2.33	4.96
Belgium	65.00	1.40	1.50	1.08	25600.00	−0.10	103.40	145.20	0.06	20.66	1.70	2.35	4.99
Finland	72.60	1.80	2.00	1.30	23500.00	4.20	41.50	109.20	0.00	21.63	2.70	2.26	4.98
France	68.70	0.90	1.90	1.06	23600.00	−3.10	58.80	136.70	0.02	20.87	−12.00	2.83	4.86
Germany	68.80	0.00	1.40	1.14	23400.00	−3.80	60.70	123.60	0.03	20.04	−24.60	2.15	4.78
Greece	62.50	3.40	3.90	0.61	18400.00	−4.80	101.70	79.80	0.00	24.50	−44.00	3.81	5.12
Ireland	70.70	5.40	4.70	1.22	28200.00	−0.40	31.80	118.90	0.03	23.60	8.20	2.50	5.01
Italy	59.40	0.50	2.60	1.04	23000.00	−3.10	105.40	109.20	0.00	21.19	−41.60	3.15	5.03
Luxembourg	68.20	4.10	2.10	1.16	49000.00	2.10	6.30	171.80	0.38	21.72	−10.90	2.69	4.70
The Netherlands	75.80	0.10	3.90	1.11	27200.00	−2.10	50.50	135.90	0.02	21.35	−22.60	2.28	4.89
Portugal	73.60	0.80	3.70	0.77	16300.00	−3.40	56.80	61.40	0.00	25.84	−48.60	3.42	5.01
Spain	62.70	2.70	3.60	0.93	20600.00	−0.30	52.60	102.00	0.01	26.62	−19.50	2.49	4.96
Mean	*68.32*	*1.90*	*2.75*	*1.04*	*25400.00*	*−1.29*	*61.31*	*117.26*	*0.05*	*22.63*	*−18.24*	*2.69*	*4.94*
Median	*68.75*	*1.55*	*2.35*	*1.10*	*23550.00*	*−1.40*	*57.80*	*116.15*	*0.01*	*21.68*	*−15.75*	*2.50*	*4.97*

(*Continued*)

Table 3.23 continued

Country	*Employ 2002*	*GDP 2002*	*HICP 2002*	*Exports 2002*	*GDP PPSI 2002*	*Gov CA 2002*	*Gov Debt 2002*	*Productivity 2002*	*EU15 Workforce 2002*	*Investment GDP 2002 Ratio*	*Customer Confidence 2002*	*State Control of Regulation 2003*	*LTIR 2002*
Conversion to binary scores													
Austria	1	1	0	1	1	1	1	0	0	1	1	0	0
Belgium	0	0	0	0	1	1	1	1	1	0	1	0	1
Finland	1	1	0	1	0	1	0	0	0	0	1	0	1
France	0	0	0	0	1	0	1	1	1	0	1	1	0
Germany	1	0	0	1	0	0	1	1	1	0	0	0	0
Greece	0	1	1	0	0	0	1	0	0	1	0	1	1
Ireland	1	1	1	1	1	1	0	1	1	1	1	1	1
Italy	0	0	1	0	0	0	1	0	0	0	0	1	1
Luxembourg	0	1	0	1	1	1	0	1	1	1	1	1	0
The Netherlands	1	0	1	1	1	0	0	1	1	0	0	0	0
Portugal	1	0	1	0	0	0	0	0	0	1	0	1	1
Spain	0	1	1	0	0	1	0	0	0	1	0	0	0

Table 3.24 QCA truth table for macro case study 2, 2002

	Employ 2002	*GDP 2002*	*HICP 2002*	*Exports 2002*	*GDP PPSI 2002*	*Gov CA 2002*	*Gov Debt 2002*	*Productivity 2002*	*EU15 Workforce 2002*	*Investment GDP 2002 Ratio*	*Customer Confidence 2002*	*State Control of Regulation 2003*	*LTIR 2002*	*Cluster*
The Netherlands	1	**0**	1	1	1	**0**	0	**1**	**1**	**0**	0	0	**0**	1
Germany	1	**0**	0	1	0	**0**	1	**1**	**1**	**0**	0	0	**0**	1
France	0	**0**	0	0	1	**0**	1	**1**	**1**	**0**	1	1	**0**	1
Austria	1	1	**0**	1	1	**1**	1	0	0	1	**1**	**0**	0	2
Finland	1	1	**0**	1	0	**1**	0	0	0	0	**1**	**0**	1	2
Belgium	0	0	**0**	0	1	**1**	1	1	1	0	**1**	**0**	1	2
Ireland	1	**1**	**1**	1	1	**1**	**0**	1	1	**1**	1	1	1	3
Spain	0	**1**	**1**	0	0	**1**	**0**	0	0	**1**	0	0	0	3
Portugal	1	0	**1**	**0**	**0**	**0**	0	**0**	**0**	1	**0**	**1**	**1**	4
Greece	0	1	**1**	**0**	**0**	**0**	1	**0**	**0**	1	**0**	**1**	**1**	4
Italy	0	0	**1**	**0**	**0**	**0**	1	**0**	**0**	0	**0**	**1**	**1**	4
Luxembourg	0	1	0	1	1	1	0	1	1	1	1	1	0	5

Table 3.25 Boolean simplification: macro case study 2, 2002

Clusters	*Boolean simplification*
Cluster 1 The Netherlands, Germany and France	gdp * gov ca * PRODUCTIVITY * EU15 WORKFORCE * investment * ltir
Cluster 2 Austria, Finland and Belgium	hicp * GOV CA * CONSUMER CONFIDENCE * state control
Cluster 3 Ireland and Spain	GDP * HICP * GOV CA * gov debt *INVESTMENT
Cluster 4 Portugal, Greece and Italy	HICP * exports * gdp pps * gov ca * productivity * eu15 workforce * consumer confidence * STATE CONTROL * LTIR

Table 3.26 Agglomeration schedule for country aggregates, macro case study 2, 2006

Stage	*Cluster Combined*		*Coefficients*	*Stage Cluster First Appears*		*Next Stage*
	Cluster 1	*Cluster 2*		*Cluster 1*	*Cluster 2*	
1	1	5	.721	0	0	3
2	2	4	2.816	0	0	6
3	1	10	5.412	1	0	4
4	1	3	9.543	3	0	8
5	7	12	15.758	0	0	9
6	2	8	22.057	2	0	8
7	6	11	30.880	0	0	10
8	1	2	46.520	4	6	9
9	1	7	67.561	8	5	10
10	1	6	100.902	9	7	11
11	1	9	143.000	10	0	0

Macro case study 2, wave 2, 2006

Moving to the second period, 2006, Table 3.26 shows the agglomeration schedule for the same variables, but as recorded with 2006 indicators. The key change in the coefficients' gradient occurs at stage 8. This puts the emphasis on the difference of triplets and pairings, rather than larger clusters, as in the first model for 2002. In contrast, the dendrogram in Figure 3.12 suggests four clusters of interest, plus one outlier (Luxembourg). Figure 3.11 shows the icicle plot for the CA in 2006. The first pairing of similarity is Germany and Austria, followed by France and Belgium. Next, the Netherlands and Finland join with Germany and Austria. Spain then pairs with Ireland, followed by Italy joining France and Belgium. Finally, Greece links with Portugal.

The dendrogram in Figure 3.12 suggests four clusters with Luxembourg as an outlier. In summary, the clusters are:

Cluster 1	Austria, Germany, the Netherlands and Finland
Cluster 2	Belgium, France and Italy
Cluster 3	Ireland and Spain
Cluster 4	Greece and Portugal
Outlier	Luxembourg

Table 3.27 demonstrates the process for converting the scale data used in the CA to binary scores for the crisp set QCA.

Table 3.28 shows the QCA truth table to demonstrate the cluster outcomes proposed.

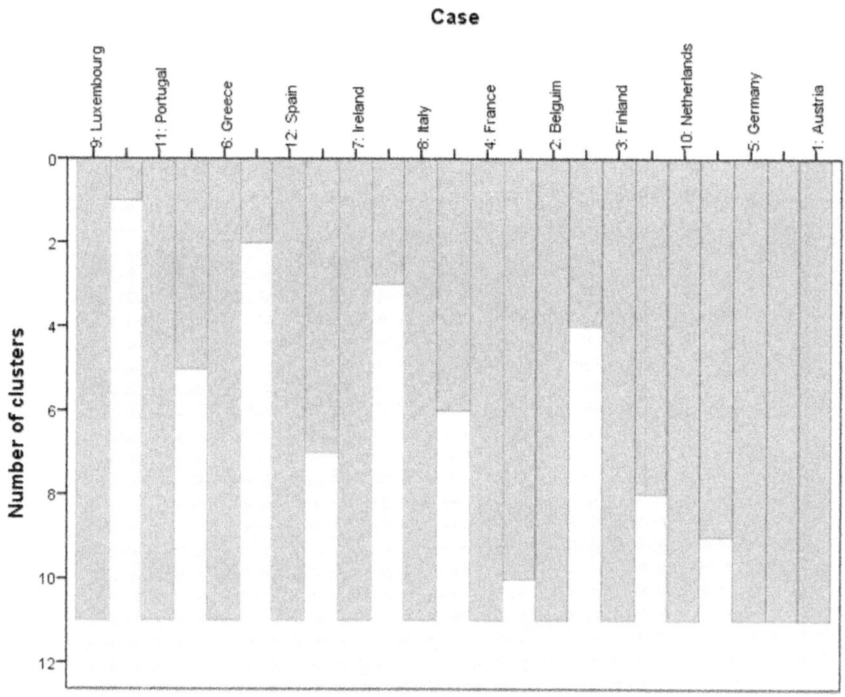

Figure 3.11 Icicle plot of cluster formulation: macro case study 2, 2006

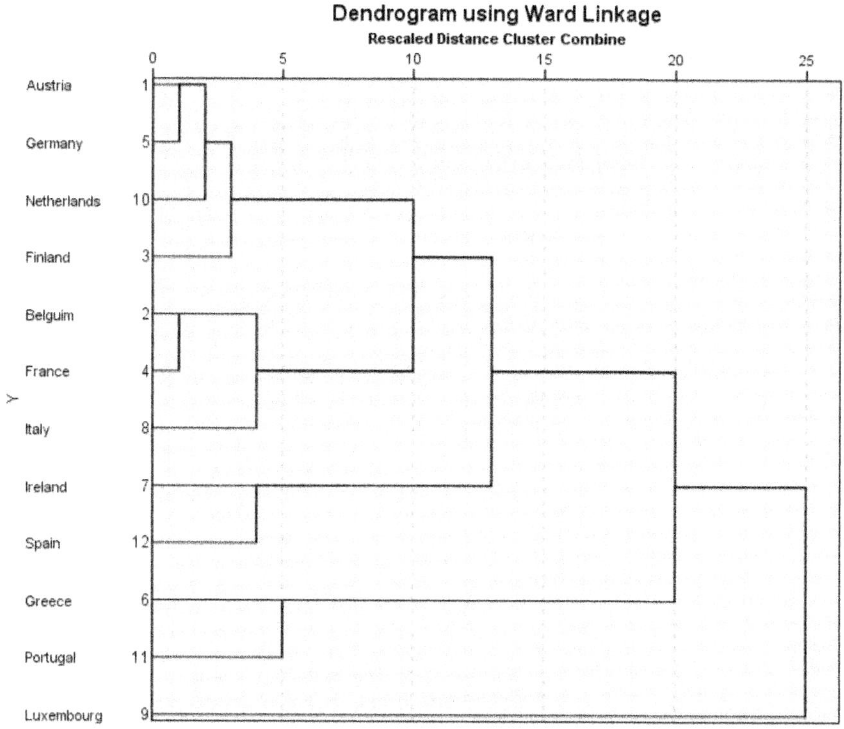

Figure 3.12 Dendrogram of cluster formulation: macro case study 2, 2006

Table 3.27 QCA: data for truth table, macro case study 2, 2006

Country	*Employ 2006*	*GDP 2006*	*HICP 2006*	*Exports 2006*	*GDP PPSI 2006*	*Gov CA 2006*	*Gov Debt 2006*	*Productivity 2006*	*EU29 workforce 2006*	*Investment GDP 2006 Ratio*	*Customer Confidence 2006*	*State Control of Regulation 2006*	*LTIR 2006*
Austria	73.20	3.70	1.70	1.10	29700.00	−1.50	62.30	114.10	4.40	22.67	2.60	1.95	3.80
Belgium	66.50	2.70	2.30	1.05	27800.00	0.40	87.90	136.50	5.90	22.35	19.20	2.15	3.81
Finland	73.90	4.40	1.30	1.12	26900.00	4.20	39.60	108.00	0.70	22.79	23.80	2.18	3.78
France	69.30	2.50	1.90	0.96	25500.00	−2.30	63.70	130.60	2.20	22.39	−14.00	2.41	3.80
Germany	71.10	3.70	1.80	1.14	27300.00	−1.60	68.00	127.40	4.00	19.82	17.10	1.99	3.76
Greece	65.70	5.50	3.30	0.67	21800.00	−5.70	106.10	78.40	1.30	23.69	−42.60	3.33	4.07
Ireland	73.40	5.50	2.70	1.14	34400.00	2.90	24.60	120.30	9.80	30.99	18.90	1.84	3.77
Italy	62.50	2.20	2.20	0.97	24700.00	−3.40	106.30	102.10	1.40	21.48	−46.50	2.58	4.05
Luxembourg	69.10	4.90	3.00	1.22	63800.00	1.40	6.70	192.10	42.20	18.85	−7.50	2.34	3.30
The Netherlands	76.30	3.40	1.70	1.12	31000.00	0.50	47.40	137.10	1.70	21.27	−10.80	1.44	3.78
Portugal	72.70	1.40	3.00	0.78	18700.00	−4.60	69.40	63.20	0.60	22.50	−65.50	2.89	3.91
Spain	69.00	4.10	3.60	0.81	24800.00	2.40	39.70	102.50	3.60	31.05	−31.30	2.16	3.78
Mean	70.23	*3.67*	*2.38*	*1.01*	*29700.00*	*−0.61*	*60.14*	*117.69*	*6.48*	*23.32*	*−11.38*	*2.27*	*3.80*
Median	70.20	*3.70*	*2.25*	*1.08*	*27100.00*	*−0.55*	*63.00*	*117.20*	*2.90*	*22.45*	*−9.15*	*2.17*	*3.79*

Conversion to binary scores													
Austria	1	1	0	1	1	0	0	0	1	1	1	0	1
Belgium	0	0	1	0	1	1	1	1	1	0	1	0	1
Finland	1	1	0	1	0	1	0	0	0	1	1	1	0
France	0	0	0	0	0	0	1	1	0	0	0	1	1
Germany	1	1	0	1	1	0	1	1	1	0	1	0	0
Greece	0	1	1	0	0	0	1	0	0	1	0	1	1
Ireland	1	1	1	1	1	1	0	1	1	1	1	0	0
Italy	0	0	0	0	0	0	1	0	0	0	0	1	1
Luxembourg	0	1	1	1	1	1	0	1	1	0	1	1	0
The Netherlands	1	0	0	1	1	1	0	1	0	0	0	0	0
Portugal	1	0	1	0	0	0	1	0	0	1	0	1	1
Spain	0	1	1	0	0	1	0	0	1	1	0	0	0

Table 3.28 QCA truth table for macro case study 2, 2006

Country	*Employ 2006*	*GDP 2006*	*HICP 2006*	*Exports 2006*	*GDP PPSI 2006*	*Gov CA 2006*	*Gov Debt 2006*	*Productivity 2006*	*EU29 workforce 2006*	*Investment GDP 2006 Ratio*	*Customer Confidence 2006*	*State Control of Regulation 2006*	*LTIR 2006*	*Cluster*
Germany	**1**	**1**	**0**	**1**	**1**	0	1	1	1	0	1	**0**	**0**	1
Austria	**1**	**1**	**0**	**1**	**1**	0	0	0	1	1	1	**0**	**1**	1
Finland	**1**	**1**	**0**	**1**	**0**	1	0	0	0	1	1	**1**	**0**	1
The Netherlands	**1**	**0**	**0**	**1**	**1**	1	0	1	0	0	0	**0**	**0**	1
Belgium	**0**	**0**	1	**0**	1	1	**1**	1	1	**0**	1	0	**1**	2
France	**0**	**0**	0	**0**	0	0	**1**	1	0	**0**	0	1	**1**	2
Italy	**0**	**0**	0	**0**	0	0	**1**	0	0	**0**	0	1	**1**	2
Ireland	1	**1**	**1**	1	1	**1**	**0**	1	**1**	**1**	1	**0**	**0**	3
Spain	0	**1**	**1**	0	0	**1**	**0**	0	**1**	**1**	0	**0**	**0**	3
Portugal	1	0	**1**	**0**	**0**	**0**	**1**	**0**	**0**	**1**	**0**	**1**	**1**	4
Greece	0	1	**1**	**0**	**0**	**0**	**1**	**0**	**0**	**1**	**0**	**1**	**1**	4
Luxembourg	0	1	1	1	1	1	0	1	1	0	1	1	0	5

Cluster 1 is the largest cluster in the sample with four countries and it shares three prime implicants. There are five near misses and these are each considered.

The first near miss is annual change in GDP. Only the Netherlands is below threshold. Examination of the scale data in Table 3.26 reveals that it scores 3.40% and is only marginally below the threshold mean average of 3.67 (median = 3.70%). Given that the Netherlands is the first country in the ranked distribution to be below the average, it is decided to overrule the below threshold score and to make this variable a prime implicant for the cluster.

The second near miss is GDP purchasing power standards per inhabitant. Finland is the only country to be scored below threshold. Its score in Table 3.26 is €26900 where the mean is €27900 and the median €27300. Given that Finland is the first country in the cluster ranked distribution to be below average, it is decided to overrule the below threshold score and to make this variable a prime implicant for the cluster.

The third near miss is government gross debt as a percentage of GDP. Here only Germany is above threshold in the cluster scoring with a score of 68.00% where the sample mean is 60.14% and the median 63.00%. Germany is not the nearest above threshold country to the average in the ranked distribution of scores and so the score is not overruled.

The fourth near miss is state control of regulation where only Finland scores above threshold in this cluster with a score of 2.18. This score is in the threshold setting zone between the mean of 2.27 and the median of 2.17. Finland is the first score on the ranked distribution to be placed above threshold and so the score is overruled and this variable becomes a below threshold prime implicant for this cluster.

The fifth near miss is long term interest rates where only Austria is above threshold with a score of 3.80. This score is in the threshold setting zone, being identical to the mean, where the median is 3.79 and scores are distributed close to the central tendency. It is decided to overrule this score and long term interest rates becomes a below threshold prime implicant for this cluster. Near miss overrules are shown in Table 3.28.

Table 3.29 shows the Boolean simplification statements that result from the QCA truth table (Table 3.28). As with the data used in 2002, care is needed when interpreting the government current account, as above threshold scores indicate a higher level of real deficit which is often a negative score in the original scale data.

Cluster 1 has a relatively strong liberal market economic performance with high employment, GDP, and exports and low regulation and long term interest rates. In contrast, cluster 2 has lower employment, GDP, trade balance and investment and higher relative government gross debt and long term interest rates.

The remaining smaller clusters are noticeably different to the first two as both have higher inflation. In addition, cluster 3 has higher GDP and government deficit, but also higher European labour migration and investment in an environment of lower regulation and long term interest rates.

Finally, cluster 4 has a challenging set of indicators. This includes higher gross government debt, lower productivity, labour migration and consumer confidence. There is also higher state regulation and long term interest rates.

Table 3.29 Boolean simplification: macro case study 2, 2006

Clusters	*Boolean simplification*
Cluster 1 Germany, Austria, Finland and the Netherlands	EMPLOY * GDP * hicp *EXPORTS *GDPPPSI * state control * ltir
Cluster 2 Belgium, France and Italy	Employ * gdp * exports * GOV DEBT * investment * LTIR
Cluster 3 Ireland and Spain	GDP * HICP * GOV CA * gov debt * EU WORKFORCE * INVESTMENT * state control * ltir
Cluster 4 Portugal, Greece and Italy	HICP * exports * gdppps * govca * GOV DEBT * productivity * eu workforce * INVESTMENT *consumer confidence * STATE CONTROL * LTIR

Table 3.30 Agglomeration schedule for country aggregates, case study 2, 2013

Stage	*Cluster Combined*		*Coefficients*	*Stage Cluster First Appears*		*Next Stage*
	Cluster 1	*Cluster 2*		*Cluster 1*	*Cluster 2*	
1	1	5	.956	0	0	4
2	2	4	1.915	0	0	8
3	8	12	3.748	0	0	6
4	1	3	6.830	1	0	5
5	1	10	10.504	4	0	8
6	8	11	14.874	3	0	7
7	7	8	22.798	0	6	9
8	1	2	32.348	5	2	10
9	6	7	56.848	0	7	11
10	1	9	91.911	8	0	11
11	1	6	143.000	10	9	0

Macro case study 2, wave 3, 2013

The third and final part of macro case study 2 examines the same countries and data variable relationships for the time point 2013. This is after the financial crisis of 2007–08.

Table 3.30 shows the agglomeration schedule for the CA. The gradient of coefficients changes substantially after stage 8. There is also a marginal incline after stage 6. The dendrogram presented in Figure 3.14 suggests that a structure with six clusters is logical, but this includes three outliers: Luxembourg, Ireland and Greece, so with three substantive clusters remaining.

The icicle plot in Figure 3.13 shows the hierarchy of the selection of similarity. The first pair to be joined are Germany and Austria, followed by France and Belgium. After this, Spain and Italy are paired, followed by Finland attaching to Germany and Austria.

The dendrogram in Figure 3.14 suggests the following cluster structure:

Cluster 1	Austria, Germany, Finland, the Netherlands
Cluster 2	Belgium, France
Outlier	Luxembourg
Cluster 3	Italy, Spain, Portugal, Ireland
Outlier	Greece

The QCA analysis will be helpful for considering the similarity of Ireland with cluster 3 and whether it should be considered as an outlier from this cluster, and also as to whether there are any substantive similarities between clusters 1 and 2.

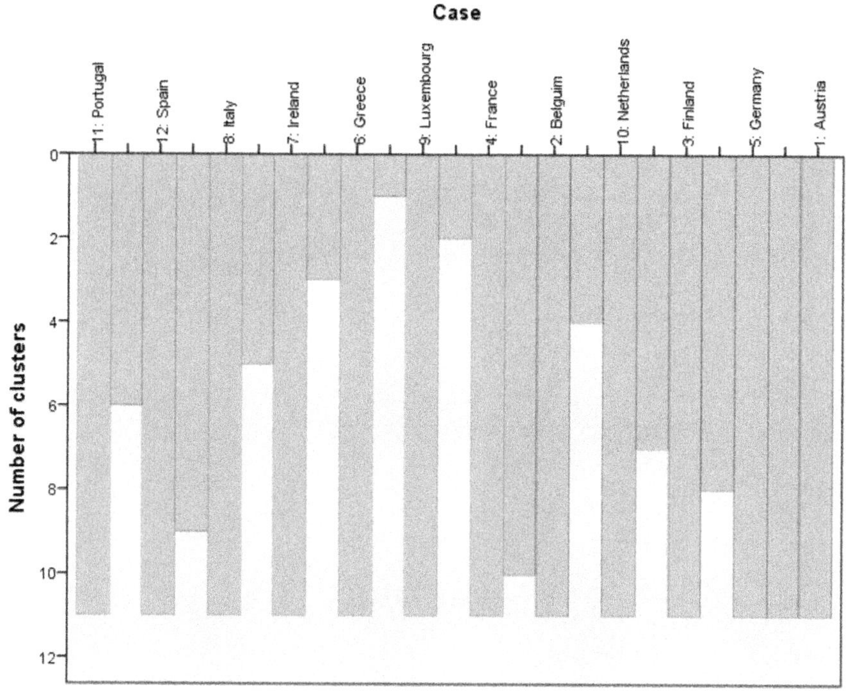

Figure 3.13 Icicle plot of cluster formulation: macro case study 2, 2013

Table 3.31 shows the process of converting the data from the scale variables used in the CA to the QCA binary thresholds. The mean and median provide the reference point for the binary division.

Table 3.32 reveals the resulting QCA truth table following the binary conversion. Cluster 1 has six prime implicants and five near misses.

The first three near misses are all related to Finland that can be seen to be on the proximity of the cluster in Figure 3.12. For three of these variables, exports (balance of trade), gross domestic product per standard inhabitant and productivity, Finland scores below threshold whereas the rest of the cluster are above. An examination of Finland's scores in Table 3.31 shows that there is insufficient evidence to change Finland's threshold score for exports and productivity, but given Finland's proximity to the threshold mean (€31150) and median (€30050) for the variable GDP per standard inhabitant with a score of €29400, it is decided to overrule this result and make this variable an above threshold prime implicant for the cluster.

The other two near misses concern the Netherlands, with it being the only country in the cluster with below threshold scores for investment, as a percentage of GDP (mean = 18.67%) and consumer confidence score (mean = −22.73). For both

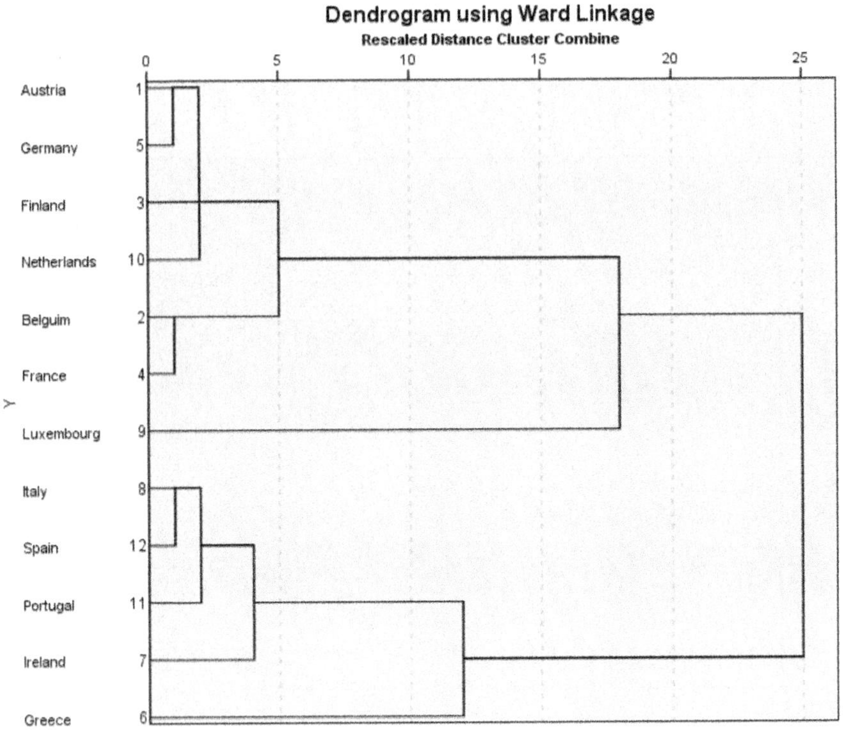

Figure 3.14 Dendrogram of cluster formulation: macro case study 2, 2013

these variables, the Netherlands is next to the threshold point or in the threshold setting zone between the mean and median. Therefore, these two scores are overruled and these variables become above threshold prime thresholds for this cluster.

Cluster 2 has six prime implicants. Cluster 3 has four prime implicants and seven near misses.

The first near miss is the annual percentage change in national GDP where Ireland is the only country that scores above threshold. An examination of the scale scores in Table 3.30 reveals that Ireland's score of −0.30% is close to the mean −0.64% and the only country with a negative score to be recorded above threshold growth. For this reason, the score is overruled and having a below threshold growth becomes a prime implicant for this cluster.

The second near miss is the annual percentage change in inflation (measured by HICP). The only country in the cluster with an above threshold score is Spain (1.5%) where the mean is 1.27% and median 1.40%. Spain is the first country in the ranking distribution to be recorded above threshold and the score is near to the central tendency. For this reason, the score is overruled and this variable becomes a below threshold prime implicant for cluster 3.

Table 3.31 QCA: data for truth table, macro case study 2, 2013

Country	*Employ 2013*	*GDP 2013*	*HICP 2013*	*Exports 2013*	*GDP PPSI 2013*	*Gov CA 2013*	*Gov Debt 2013*	*Productivity 2013*	*EU29 workforce 2013*	*Investment GDP 2013 Ratio*	*Customer Confidence 2013*	*State Control of Regulation 2013*	*LTIR 2013*
Austria	75.50	0.30	2.10	1.09	33100.00	−1.50	74.50	115.10	6.60	22.50	12.80	1.67	2.01
Belgium	67.20	0.20	1.20	1.02	30700.00	−2.60	101.50	132.90	7.00	22.12	−13.10	2.19	2.41
Finland	73.30	−1.40	2.20	1.00	29400.00	−2.10	57.00	105.40	1.30	21.11	2.50	2.13	1.86
France	69.50	0.20	1.00	0.93	27700.00	−4.30	93.50	128.70	2.30	22.11	−30.40	2.37	2.20
Germany	77.10	0.40	1.60	1.14	31500.00	0.00	78.40	126.40	4.40	19.76	12.60	1.86	1.57
Greece	53.20	−3.90	−0.90	0.92	19500.00	−12.70	175.10	74.70	1.50	12.02	−58.20	2.82	10.05
Ireland	65.50	−0.30	0.50	1.28	32900.00	−7.20	123.70	122.40	11.10	17.64	−0.70	2.12	3.79
Italy	59.80	−1.90	1.30	1.09	25600.00	−3.00	132.60	101.80	3.20	17.29	−50.60	2.14	4.32
Luxembourg	71.10	2.10	1.70	1.23	67100.00	0.10	23.10	0.00	46.10	17.65	−9.40	2.45	1.85
The Netherlands	76.50	−0.80	2.60	1.13	32500.00	−2.50	73.50	129.20	2.10	17.92	−21.80	1.43	1.96
Portugal	65.60	−1.40	0.40	1.09	19400.00	−4.90	129.00	65.30	0.60	14.75	−76.50	2.18	6.29
Spain	58.60	−1.20	1.50	1.08	24400.00	−7.10	93.90	109.50	4.20	19.21	−39.90	1.86	4.56
Mean	*67.74*	*−0.64*	*1.27*	*1.08*	*31150.00*	*−3.98*	*96.32*	*100.95*	*7.53*	*18.67*	*−22.73*	*2.10*	*3.57*
Median	*68.35*	*−0.55*	*1.40*	*1.09*	*30050.00*	*−2.80*	*93.70*	*112.30*	*3.70*	*18.57*	*−17.45*	*2.14*	*2.31*

(*Continued*)

Table 3.31 continued

Country	*Employ 2013*	*GDP 2013*	*HICP 2013*	*Exports 2013*	*GDP PPSI 2013*	*Gov CA 2013*	*Gov Debt 2013*	*Productivity 2013*	*EU29 workforce 2013*	*Investment GDP 2013 Ratio*	*Customer Confidence 2013*	*State Control of Regulation 2013*	*LTIR 2013*
Conversion to Binary Scores													
Austria	1	1	1	1	1	1	0	1	1	1	1	0	0
Belgium	0	1	0	0	1	1	1	1	1	1	1	1	1
Finland	1	0	1	0	0	1	0	0	0	1	1	0	0
France	1	1	0	0	0	0	0	1	0	1	0	1	0
Germany	1	1	1	1	1	1	0	1	1	1	1	0	0
Greece	0	0	0	0	0	0	1	0	0	0	0	1	1
Ireland	0	1	0	1	1	0	1	1	1	0	1	0	1
Italy	0	0	0	1	0	0	1	0	0	0	0	1	1
Luxembourg	1	1	1	1	1	1	0	0	1	0	1	1	0
The Netherlands	1	0	1	1	1	1	0	1	0	0	0	0	0
Portugal	0	0	0	1	0	0	1	0	0	0	0	1	1
Spain	0	0	1	0	0	0	1	0	1	1	0	0	1

Table 3.32 QCA truth table for macro case study 2, 2013

	Employ 2013	*GDP 2013*	*HICP 2013*	*Exports 2013*	*GDP PPSI 2013*	*Gov CA 2013*	*Gov Debt 2013*	*Productivity 2013*	*EU29 workforce 2013*	*Investment GDP 2013 Ratio*	*Customer Confidence 2013*	*State Control of Regulation 2013*	*LTIR 2013*	*Cluster*
Austria	**1**	1	**1**	1	**1**	**1**	**0**	1	1	**1**	**1**	**0**	**0**	1
Germany	**1**	1	**1**	1	**1**	**1**	**0**	1	1	**1**	**1**	**0**	**0**	1
The Netherlands	**1**	0	**1**	1	**1**	**1**	**0**	1	0	**0**	**0**	**0**	**0**	1
Finland	**1**	0	**1**	0	**0**	**1**	**0**	0	0	**1**	**1**	**0**	**0**	1
France	1	**1**	**0**	**0**	0	0	0	**1**	0	**1**	0	**1**	0	2
Belgium	0	**1**	**0**	**0**	1	1	1	**1**	1	**1**	1	**1**	1	2
Ireland	**0**	**1**	**0**	**1**	1	**0**	**1**	**1**	1	**0**	1	0	**1**	3
Spain	**0**	**0**	**1**	**0**	0	**0**	**1**	**0**	1	**1**	0	0	**1**	3
Italy	**0**	**0**	**0**	**1**	0	**0**	**1**	**0**	0	**0**	0	1	**1**	3
Portugal	**0**	**0**	**0**	**1**	0	**0**	**1**	**0**	0	**0**	0	1	**1**	3
Luxembourg	1	1	1	1	1	1	0	0	1	0	1	1	0	4
Greece	0	0	0	0	0	0	1	0	0	0	0	1	1	5

The third near miss also relates to the score for Spain with regard to exports (1.08) where the mean is 1.08 and the median 1.09. Given the close proximity to the mean and median the score can be overruled and this variable becomes an above threshold prime implicant for this cluster.

The fourth near miss is for the variable GDP per person standard inhabitant. Here Ireland is the only country in the cluster to score above threshold. The score is not sufficiently close to the threshold to be overruled.

The fifth near miss again relates to Ireland, as it is the only country in the cluster to be recorded above threshold for productivity. The score is not sufficiently close to the mean or median to be overruled.

Next, the sixth near miss is the percentage of GDP spent on investment. Only Spain is above threshold in this cluster. Spain is the first country in the ranked distribution to be recorded above threshold (19.21%) where the mean is 18.67% and the median 18.57%. For this reason, the score is overruled and this variable becomes a below threshold prime implicant for this cluster.

Table 3.33 Boolean simplification: macro case study 2, 2013

Clusters	*Boolean simplification*
Cluster 1 Austria, Germany, the Netherlands, Finland	EMPLOY * HICP * GDPPPSI * GOV CA * gov debt * INVESTMENT * CONSUMER CONFIDENCE * state control * ltir
Cluster 2 France, Belgium	GDP * hicp * exports * PRODUCTIVITY * INVESTMENT * STATE CONTROL
Cluster 3 Ireland, Spain, Italy, Portugal	employ * gdp * hicp * EXPORTS * gov ca * GOV DEBT * productivity *investment * LTIR

The final near miss is the above threshold score for consumer confidence for Ireland that contrasts with the below threshold confidence scores for the rest of the cluster. However, an examination of Table 3.31 shows that Ireland's score is not in close proximity to the mean or median. The score is not overruled.

Table 3.33 shows the process of Boolean simplification for the resulting prime implicants, including the near misses that have overruled the first threshold setting exercise. This enables the summary of clusters and their substantive identity and variable influences.

Cluster 1 has higher employment, GDP purchasing power parity per standard inhabitant, investment and consumer confidence and lower gross government debt, state control of regulation and long term interest rates. Nevertheless, inflation is relatively high, as is the government's current account deficit.

Cluster 2 also has some relatively strong economic performance in comparative terms. GDP is higher, inflation is lower, productivity and investment are relatively high, but exports are lower and state control of regulation is higher.

Cluster 3 has some formidable economic challenges. Employment, GDP, productivity and investment are relatively low, while gross government debt is higher as is long term interest rates. Given the post financial crisis challenges, inflation is relatively low. Taking into account the number of prime implicants shared by the cluster, Ireland appears a clear member despite its slight distance away from the other three countries in the dendrogram in Figure 3.14.

Macro case study 2: conclusions

This section concludes the second macro case study.

Cases

There is a considerable feature of case stability in macro case study 2. Many countries stay in similar cluster formations across the three time points. This pattern stability is based on the following time consistent pairings of: Italy and Portugal,

Table 3.34 Variable trends, 2002–2013, macro case study 2

	Employment	*GDP*	*HICP*	*Exports*	*GDP PPSI*	*Gov CA*	*Gov Debt*	*Productivity*	*EU29 workforce movement*	*Investment GDP*	*Customer Confidence*	*State Control of Regulation*	*LTIR*
2002	68.32	1.90	2.75	1.04	25400.00	−1.29	61.31	117.26	0.05	22.63	−18.24	2.69	4.94
2006	70.23	3.67	2.38	1.01	29700.00	−0.61	60.14	117.69	6.48	23.32	−11.38	2.27	3.80
2013	67.74	−0.64	1.27	1.08	31150.00	−3.98	96.32	100.95	7.53	18.67	−22.73	2.10	3.57
	∨	∨	∨	∧	∧	∨	∧	∧	∧	∨	∨	∨	∨

Spain and Ireland, Austria and Finland, and Germany and the Netherlands. In addition, the two other countries, France and Belgium are located together in both 2006 and 2013 and can be argued to be in a mutually overlapping hierarchical cluster in 2002 (Figure 3.10). Luxembourg is always an outlier. Case patterns between 2002 and 2013 are argued to be relatively stable.

Variables

The final task is to integrate the analysis over the three years. Table 3.34 examines the average variable trends over the three year period for the whole sample. The key features are some decline in employment after the financial crisis, similarly a decline in GDP after a peak in 2006. Inflation also declines. The overall export balance shifts marginally upwards. GDP purchasing power per standard inhabitant increases, but slows after the crisis. The government current accounts and especially gross government debts deteriorate quite markedly. Productivity declines quite markedly after the crisis. The EU migrant workforce increases, but slows in growth after the crisis. Investment as a percentage of GDP declines after the crisis. Consumer confidence improves initially after the establishment of the single currency, but then declines substantially. State control of regulation declines slowly and average long term interest rates are marginally reduced (although the average figures do not reveal the important country variances in long term interest rates shown in Table 3.30). The aggregate variable trend data suggests instability through the time period studied.

Patterns

Table 3.35 indicates the points of case and variable stability in the truth table plot over time. This shows the consistent above and below threshold scores across the three year period. The countries are ranked in Table 3.35 into patterned clusters, based on the data in this table alone, and not linked to any other separate time point CA. A clear Southern European grouping is evidenced (Portugal, Spain, Italy, Greece). As regards the Northern and Central euro based economics, it is notable that France and Belgium have a slightly different profile to their other neighbours and Ireland looks more similar to the above threshold grouping.

This case study illustrates the considerable difficulties with using the euro project to converge European countries towards greater shared economic similarity and it shows the negative impact on convergence of the financial crisis of 2007–08. While economic trends are changing and rather unstable, the cases tended to remain similar to particular pairings and small groups, over the time, rather than shifting chaotically between groupings.

This concludes the macro case study chapter. Chapter 4 focuses on a single meso level case study.

Table 3.35 Longitudinal truth table: macro case study 2

Country	*Employ*	*GDP*	*HICP*	*Exports*	*GDP PPSI*	*Gov CA*	*Gov Debt*	*Productivity*	*EU15 workforce*	*Investment GDP*	*Customer Confidence*	*State Control of Regulation*	*LTIR*
Portugal		Below			Below	Below		Below	Below		Below	Above	Above
Spain	Below				Below			Below			Below	Below	
Italy	Below	Below			Below	Below	Above	Below	Below	Below	Below	Above	Above
Greece	Below			Below	Below	Below	Above	Below	Below		Below	Above	Above
Belgium	Below			Below	Above	Above	Above	Above	Above		Above		Above
France			Below	Below		Below		Above				Above	
Finland	Above					Above	Below	Below	Below		Above	Below	
The Netherlands	Above			Above	Above		Below	Above		Below		Below	Below
Austria	Above	Above		Above	Above					Above	Above	Below	
Germany	Above			Above				Above	Above			Below	Below
Ireland				Above	Above				Above		Above		
Luxembourg		Above		Above	Above	Above	Below		Above		Above	Above	Below

4 A meso case study example

London boroughs

Introduction

Meso level case studies are typically concerned with comparisons of organisations. These could be government organisations, like regional or local governments, or private companies. This often presents the researcher with the challenge of having slightly larger samples than for macro country studies. As a result, one first consideration is whether to break a meso case study into sub samples, where it is then possible to use a classification variable to allocate the cases into sub groups. For example, the first case study in this chapter examines local authorities in England, but rather than including all authorities it focuses on the sub sample of London boroughs, of which there are 32. So, a geographical sub classification is applied to reduce the sample. If the DPS proves interesting, the same process could later be scaled up, with several other geographical sub samples, to include all England local authorities, including those outside of London. One of the London boroughs is, however, excluded from the sample as it is an outlier that has missing data on the chosen secondary datasets. This outlier is the City of London, a business district at the heart of London with an unusually small residential population.

The first case study in this chapter examines social and health care for older people in London boroughs. The first year applied to the case study is 2010. The variables used in this stage of the analysis are listed in Table 4.1

Table 4.1 List of variables for meso case study, 2010: London boroughs and health and social care indicators

- Percentage of London borough population aged 65 and over
- Female life expectancy at age 65
- Male life expectancy at age 65
- Early winter deaths, as estimated from standard mortality ratios
- Percentage of those aged 65 and over who have had an influenza inoculation
- Percentage of those needing or receiving social care who are satisfied with the amount of care they are receiving.
- Early readmissions to hospital following a recent discharge, ratio
- Rate of falls, in relation to local older population
- Ratio of older adults who are residents in care homes supported by the local authorities

Meso case study, 2010

The availability of more cases in this hierarchical CA, when compared to the macro example in Chapter 3, makes it more difficult to decide where to apply the judgement about the optimal point of agglomeration and cluster membership. In Table 4.2, the differential on the stages in the agglomeration schedule reveals that there is a marginal increase in the gradient of the coefficients between stages 6 and 7. It is also important to check that mathematical agglomerations are not artefacts, and whether the resulting clusters are likely to have some real basis in social and economic reality (Everitt, 1993).

In Figure 4.1, the icicle plot for the cluster agglomeration shows that the first two cases to be joined are Havering and Bromley. The next pairing is Hounslow and Ealing, followed by Richmond and Barnet.

Given the number of cases and the relative complexity of the agglomerations, it is easier to get a visual sense of the clustering by examining Figure 4.2. This shows the cluster dendrogram. The dendrogram gives a clear visual basis for where the boundaries can best be drawn around a possible cluster structure hypothesis. This suggests a five cluster structure to case similarity, with the possibility that cluster 3 should be considered for a sub division into two separate homogeneous sets.

Cluster 1	Bromley, Havering, Bexley, Camden, Haringey, Enfield and Kingston upon Thames
Cluster 2	Barnet, Richmond upon Thames, Brent, Harrow and Westminster
Cluster 3	Kensington and Chelsea, Redbridge, Merton, Sutton, Croydon, Ealing, Hounslow, Hillingdon and Waltham Forest
Cluster 4	Greenwich, Tower Hamlets, Hackney, Newham
Cluster 5	Lewisham, Southwark, Lambeth, Hammersmith and Fulham, Islington, Wandsworth and Barking and Dagenham

Given the structures of the icicle plot and the dendrogram it is expected that in the detailed QCA analysis each cluster is likely to have a core with shared prime implicants and a periphery that is less clearly aligned with its cluster.

The method now progresses to the QCA with this five cluster hypothesis.

Table 4.3 shows the process for using the scale data to set up the truth table in Table 4.4. As in the previous examples of DPS, a judgement is made about whether a case should be scored 1 or 0 on each variable, where the binary allocation represents above or below the threshold. The threshold setting decisions are according to the cell score in relation to the mean average and median (as calculated in Table 4.3). For the variable, the percentage of the borough population who are aged 65 and over, eight boroughs record a score of 11% and these are all treated as above threshold in this instance.

Table 4.4 shows the resulting truth table for cluster outcome. All five clusters have at least one prime implicant before considering any stronger sub groupings or near misses.

Table 4.2 Agglomeration schedule for meso case study, 2010

Stage	*Cluster Combined*		*Coefficients*	*Stage Cluster First Appears*		*Next Stage*
	Cluster 1	*Cluster 2*		*Cluster 1*	*Cluster 2*	
1	5	15	.875	0	0	7
2	22	27	2.132	0	0	9
3	8	17	3.595	0	0	11
4	2	26	5.244	0	0	17
5	6	13	7.048	0	0	18
6	23	28	8.923	0	0	10
7	3	5	11.125	0	1	23
8	10	29	13.409	0	0	15
9	21	22	15.741	0	2	21
10	7	23	18.683	0	6	22
11	8	16	22.011	3	0	16
12	4	14	25.428	0	0	17
13	12	18	28.860	0	0	21
14	9	20	32.451	0	0	18
15	10	11	36.404	8	0	19
16	8	30	40.377	11	0	22
17	2	4	46.045	4	12	24
18	6	9	51.880	5	14	23
19	10	24	58.225	15	0	29
20	19	25	65.059	0	0	27
21	12	21	71.956	13	9	25
22	7	8	80.508	10	16	27
23	3	6	90.562	7	18	28
24	2	32	101.622	17	0	28
25	12	31	112.947	21	0	26
26	1	12	125.607	0	25	29
27	7	19	139.658	22	20	30
28	2	3	159.579	24	23	30
29	1	10	183.530	26	19	31
30	2	7	208.945	28	27	31
31	1	2	279.000	29	30	0

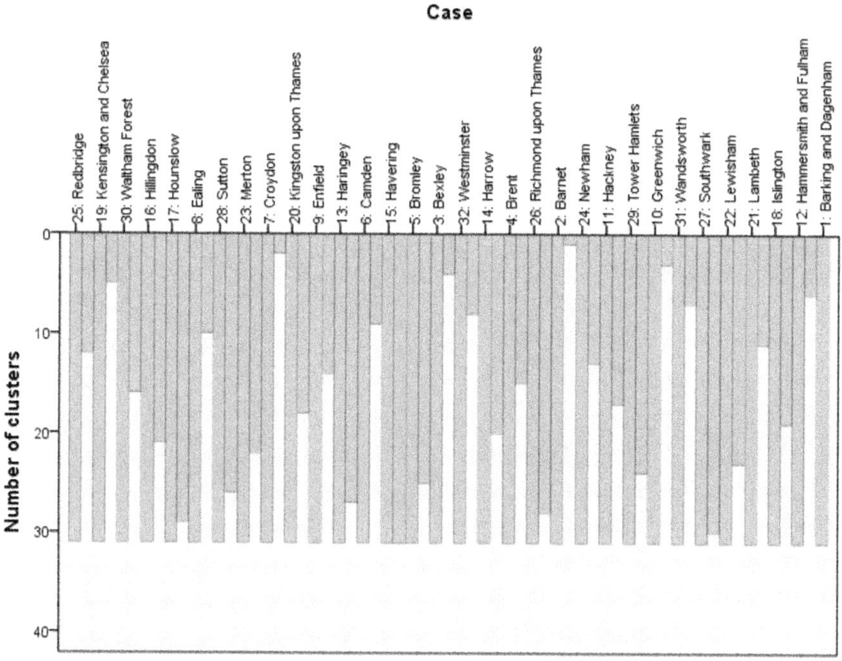

Figure 4.1 Icicle plot of cluster formulation, meso case study, 2010

Cluster 1 is a larger cluster with seven members. It has four variables where one case is a near miss and this prevents a prime implicant for that variable. These near misses are now considered in turn below.

For the variable of female life expectancy at 65, all boroughs in cluster 1 are above threshold except Enfield. An examination of the scale date in Table 4.2 shows that Enfield is only 0.1 of a life year below the median and 0.2 below the mean. For this reason, is it is decided to overrule the threshold scoring and to make female life expectancy an above threshold prime implicant for cluster 1.

Next, the variable of male life expectancy at 65 is considered. This shows all boroughs in cluster 1 are above threshold except Havering. An examination of the scale data in Table 4.2 shows that Havering's score is 18.1 years, compared to the mean and median scores of 18.4. While this is close to threshold, the scores for all boroughs are distributed tightly to the mean with the standard deviation being 1.0. The difference for men's life expectancy here is not as close as the difference in score for female life expectancies between this cluster, and so it is decided not to overrule in this situation.

The third variable for consideration in cluster 1 is early winter deaths. All boroughs in the cluster are above threshold, apart from Bexley. An examination of the scale data in Table 4.2 from which the threshold scores are derived shows that Bexley's score is 16.9 compared with the London borough sample mean and

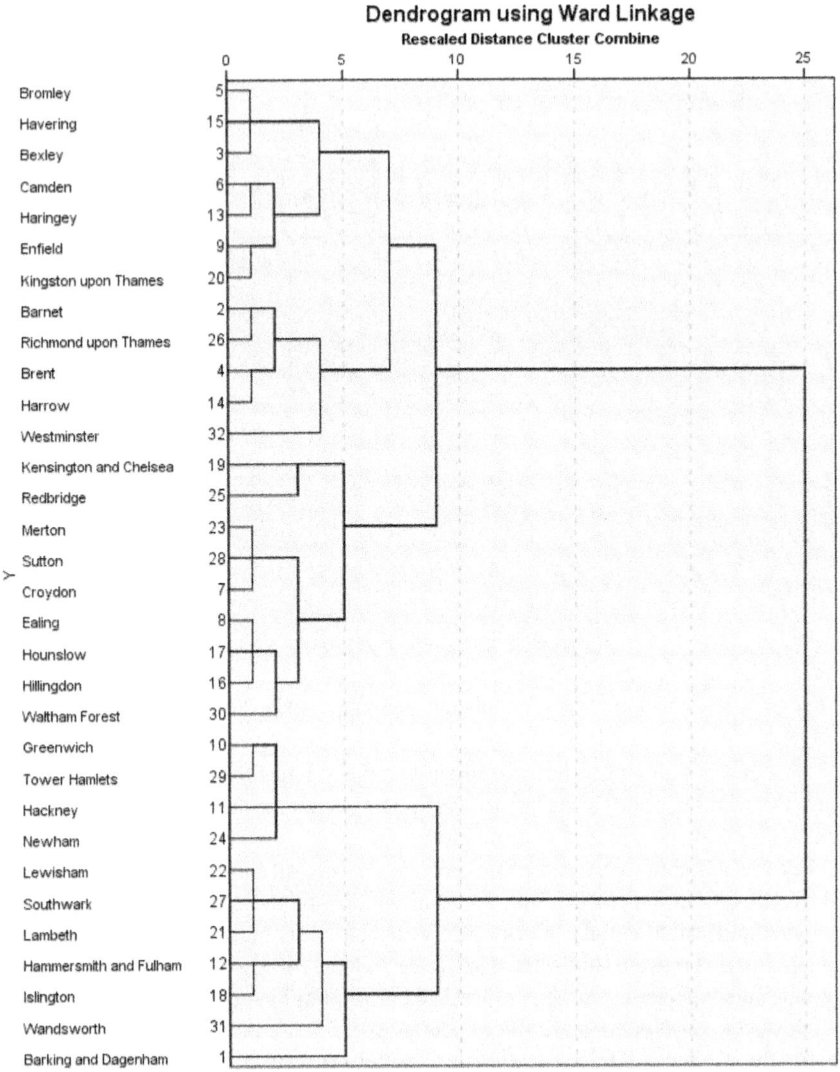

Figure 4.2 Dendrogram of cluster formulation: meso case study, 2010

median of 17.2. In this data distribution, the standard deviation is 6.0 and Bexley is the first case below the mean in the ranking of all below threshold scores. For this reason, it is decided to overrule the threshold score for Bexley and to make early winter deaths above threshold for cluster 1.

The fourth variable for consideration in cluster 1 is the percentage of the borough population aged 65 and over. All the London boroughs in cluster 1, except Haringey, are above threshold for this variable. An examination of Haringey's score in Table 4.2 shows that it is 9%, two percent below the mean and median threshold

Table 4.3 QCA meso case study, 2010: conversion of meso data variables to binary scores

London borough	*Female life ex 65*	*Male life ex 65*	*Early winter deaths*	*Flu jab 65+*	*Care satisfaction*	*Early readmissions*	*Falls*	*Supported residents ratio*	*Percentage pop over 65*
Barking and Dagenham	19.5	17.0	17.6	64.9	50.7	12.9	2363.0	894.3	0.11
Barnet	21.8	19.1	12.1	74.1	39.7	11.8	1994.4	530.7	0.13
Bexley	21.5	18.5	16.9	69.7	35.8	10.9	1952.9	693.9	0.16
Brent	22.0	19.0	8.2	69.6	35.0	11.1	1920.8	525.3	0.11
Bromley	21.7	19.0	23.4	71.9	38.0	11.5	1895.9	581.5	0.17
Camden	23.2	18.6	22.1	70.1	32.3	12.1	1916.3	719.1	0.11
Croydon	20.7	18.4	10.4	67.8	42.9	12.1	2289.4	429.3	0.12
Ealing	21.1	18.5	16.6	68.0	33.5	11.8	2518.1	337.6	0.11
Enfield	21.1	18.5	25.9	72.7	34.0	10.6	1664.7	511.3	0.13
Greenwich	19.9	17.1	14.6	73.5	37.7	10.7	1971.0	706.3	0.11
Hackney	20.6	18.1	9.2	71.0	42.2	11.0	1813.5	675.3	0.07
Hammersmith and Fulham	21.4	18.1	15.8	71.3	39.2	12.7	3100.3	789.4	0.09
Haringey	22.0	18.4	17.7	69.7	34.1	11.8	2039.9	526.7	0.09
Harrow	22.8	20.5	13.2	72.5	33.7	11.7	1803.3	366.6	0.14
Havering	21.4	18.1	20.2	72.6	39.6	11.5	2050.6	489.2	0.18
Hillingdon	21.4	18.6	22.4	70.9	39.8	12.3	2327.0	574.1	0.13
Hounslow	21.1	18.2	24.0	70.8	34.5	11.5	2422.0	398.5	0.11
Islington	20.4	17.4	9.5	70.7	38.9	11.7	2643.8	1069.1	0.09
Kensington and Chelsea	23.9	20.6	18.8	70.8	41.2	12.9	2548.6	139.9	0.12
Kingston upon Thames	21.7	19.3	24.1	67.7	37.2	11.7	1445.4	488.3	0.13
Lambeth	20.3	17.3	13.3	66.7	36.8	11.2	2305.5	807.2	0.08
Lewisham	20.3	16.8	19.2	68.4	37.8	12.1	2222.6	852.1	0.10
Merton	21.5	18.9	15.2	69.0	38.0	10.6	2413.1	624.0	0.11
Newham	20.0	16.7	18.2	73.8	39.8	9.3	2248.2	394.5	0.07
Redbridge	21.2	18.8	14.6	73.4	45.8	11.8	2646.1	101.7	0.12
Richmond upon Thames	23.2	19.6	12.1	75.8	40.9	12.1	1792.4	682.0	0.13
Southwark	20.9	17.1	21.0	68.2	42.1	12.0	2400.4	736.5	0.08
Sutton	21.0	18.7	13.0	69.0	37.0	11.6	2486.0	406.2	0.14
Tower Hamlets	19.5	16.6	13.1	74.5	39.4	10.7	2071.6	982.2	0.06
Waltham Forest	20.7	18.0	28.1	73.2	36.0	12.4	2832.3	362.0	0.10
Wandsworth	20.6	17.3	33.8	68.4	41.3	10.2	2335.7	805.7	0.09
Westminster	23.1	20.8	5.8	75.0	32.4	13.2	2630.6	758.2	0.11
Mean	*21.3*	*18.4*	*17.2*	*70.8*	*38.4*	*11.6*	*2220.8*	*592.5*	*0.11*
Median	*21.2*	*18.4*	*17.2*	*71.0*	*38.0*	*11.6*	*2216.3*	*583.0*	*0.11*

(*Continued*)

Table 4.3 continued

London borough	*Female life ex 65*	*Male life ex 65*	*Early winter deaths*	*Flu jab 65+*	*Care satisfaction*	*Early readmissions*	*Falls*	*Supported residents ratio*	*Percentage pop over 65*
Conversion to binary scores									
Barking and Dagenham	0	0	1	0	1	1	1	1	1
Barnet	1	1	0	1	1	1	0	0	1
Bexley	1	1	0	0	0	0	0	1	1
Brent	1	1	0	0	0	0	0	0	1
Bromley	1	1	1	1	0	0	0	0	1
Camden	1	1	1	1	0	1	0	1	1
Croydon	0	0	0	0	1	1	1	0	1
Ealing	0	1	0	0	0	1	1	0	1
Enfield	0	1	1	1	0	0	0	0	1
Greenwich	0	0	0	1	1	0	0	1	1
Hackney	0	0	0	1	1	0	0	1	0
Hammersmith and Fulham	1	0	0	1	1	1	1	1	0
Haringey	1	1	1	0	0	1	0	0	0
Harrow	1	1	0	1	0	1	0	0	1
Havering	1	0	1	1	1	0	0	0	1
Hillingdon	1	1	1	1	1	1	1	0	1
Hounslow	0	0	1	1	0	0	1	0	1
Islington	0	0	0	1	1	1	1	1	0
Kensington and Chelsea	1	1	1	1	1	1	1	0	1
Kingston upon Thames	1	1	1	0	0	1	0	0	1
Lambeth	0	0	0	0	0	0	1	1	0
Lewisham	0	0	1	0	0	1	1	1	0
Merton	0	1	0	0	1	0	1	1	1
Newham	0	0	1	1	1	0	1	0	0
Redbridge	0	0	0	1	1	1	1	0	1
Richmond upon Thames	1	1	0	1	1	1	0	1	1
Southwark	0	0	1	0	1	1	1	1	0
Sutton	0	1	0	0	0	1	1	0	0
Tower Hamlets	0	0	0	1	1	0	0	1	0
Waltham Forest	0	0	1	1	0	1	1	0	0
Wandsworth	0	0	1	0	1	0	1	1	0
Westminster	1	1	0	1	0	1	1	1	1

Table 4.4 QCA truth table for meso case study, 2010

London borough	*Female life ex 65*	*Male life ex 65*	*Early winter deaths*	*Flu jab 65+*	*Care satisfaction*	*Early readmissions*	*Falls*	*Supported residents ratio*	*Percentage pop over 65*	*Cluster*
Camden	1	1	1	1	0	1	**0**	1	1	1
Bromley	1	1	1	1	0	0	**0**	0	1	1
Kingston upon Thames	1	1	1	0	0	1	**0**	0	1	1
Haringey	1	1	1	0	0	1	**0**	0	0	1
Bexley	1	1	0	0	0	0	**0**	1	1	1
Havering	1	0	1	1	1	0	**0**	0	1	1
Enfield	0	1	1	1	0	0	**0**	0	1	1
Richmond upon Thames	**1**	**1**	**0**	1	1	1	0	1	**1**	2
Barnet	**1**	**1**	**0**	1	1	1	0	0	**1**	2
Westminster	**1**	**1**	**0**	1	0	1	1	1	**1**	2
Harrow	**1**	**1**	**0**	1	0	1	0	0	**1**	2
Brent	**1**	**1**	**0**	0	0	0	0	0	**1**	2
Hillingdon	1	1	1	1	1	1	**1**	0	1	3
Kensington and Chelsea	1	1	1	1	1	1	**1**	0	1	3
Merton	0	1	0	0	1	0	**1**	1	1	3
Ealing	0	1	0	0	0	1	**1**	0	1	3
Sutton	0	1	0	0	0	1	**1**	0	0	3
Waltham Forest	0	0	1	1	0	1	**1**	0	0	3
Hounslow	0	0	1	1	0	0	**1**	0	1	3
Redbridge	0	0	0	1	1	1	**1**	0	1	3
Croydon	0	0	0	0	1	1	**1**	0	1	3
Newham	**0**	**0**	1	**1**	**1**	**0**	1	0	**0**	4
Greenwich	**0**	**0**	0	**1**	**1**	**0**	0	1	**1**	4
Hackney	**0**	**0**	0	**1**	**1**	**0**	0	1	**0**	4
Tower Hamlets	**0**	**0**	0	**1**	**1**	**0**	0	1	**0**	4
Hammersmith and Fulham	1	**0**	0	1	1	1	**1**	**1**	0	5
Barking and Dagenham	0	**0**	1	0	1	1	**1**	**1**	1	5
Southwark	0	**0**	1	0	1	1	**1**	**1**	0	5
Wandsworth	0	**0**	1	0	1	0	**1**	**1**	0	5
Lewisham	0	**0**	1	0	0	1	**1**	**1**	0	5
Islington	0	**0**	0	1	1	1	**1**	**1**	0	5
Lambeth	0	**0**	0	0	0	0	**1**	**1**	0	5

setting score of 11%. Given the tight distribution of data for this variable, with a standard deviation less than 1, it is not appropriate to overrule the scoring.

Cluster 2 has good evidence of homogeneity with four prime implicants and two near misses. The prime implicants are that both female and male life expectancy at aged 65 are above threshold. Also, early winter deaths are below threshold. The cluster is also above threshold for the percentage of the population who are aged 65 and over.

The first of the near misses is the variable showing the percentage of those aged 65 and over in the borough who have had a flu jab. Only Brent has been scored below threshold. An examination of the scale data in Table 4.2 shows the Brent score to be 69.6% where the mean for all boroughs is 70.8% and the median 71%. The standard deviation for this data distribution is 2.5 and there are other below threshold boroughs with marginally higher scores than Brent. For this reason, the score is not overruled.

The second near miss is for the variable early readmissions to hospital following discharge. Only Brent is below threshold with the other boroughs in cluster 2 scoring above threshold. Table 4.2 reveals Brent's score to be 11.1 where the mean and median are 11.6 and the standard deviation is 0.8. Given the tight distribution that is close to the mean and the fact there is one other borough with a below threshold score scoring higher than Brent, this score is not overruled.

Cluster 3 is the largest cluster with nine boroughs. It has one prime implicant and this is above threshold for the ratio of falls in the population. There is one variable with a near miss, this is the ratio of older adults who are residents in care homes supported by the local authority. Merton is the only borough to score above threshold for this variable. An examination of Table 4.2 shows that Merton scores 624 where the mean for all boroughs is 592.5 and the median is 583. The standard deviation is 217.8 indicating a data set that is not distributed too closely to the mean. Merton's score is the lowest rank score for all those boroughs scoring above the threshold. For this reason, it is decided to overrule this near miss and to make the ratio of older adults who are residents in care homes supported by the local authority a below threshold prime implicant for this cluster.

This cluster does display some other possible sub cluster structures. Most importantly there is a sub sample threshold divide for the variable male life expectancy at aged 65, where five boroughs are above threshold and four below. However, when these are checked against the original cluster dendrogram in Figure 4.2 this single variable threshold allocation does not correlate with the multivariate scale calculations influencing cluster allocations, and so there is not consistent evidence for a sub cluster divide.

Cluster 4 is a small four borough cluster with homogeneity. There are five prime implicants and all other variables are near misses. Given the cluster is relatively small compared to the sample, near misses should be at mean and median threshold zone for any over-ruling. Of the near misses in Table 4.2 only one threshold meets this criterion. Greenwich is at the exact threshold point for percentage of the population aged 65 and over (mean and median = 11.0%). For this reason, the Greenwich score is overruled and is included as a prime implicant for cluster 4 as being below threshold for this variable.

Table 4.5 Boolean simplification, meso case study, 2010

Clusters	*Boolean simplification*
Cluster 1	FEMALE LIFE EX * EARLY WINTER DEATHS * falls
Cluster 2	FEMALE LIFE EX * MALE LIFE EX * early winter deaths * POP OVER 65
Cluster 3	FALLS * supported residents
Cluster 4	Female life ex * male life ex * FLU JAB * CARE SATISFACTION *early readmissions * pop over 65
Cluster 5	female life ex * male life ex * FALLS * SUPPORTED RESIDENTS * pop over 65

Cluster 5 has seven boroughs and three prime implicants. There are two near misses. The first near miss is Hammersmith and Fulham's score for the variable female life expectancy at aged 65. The score for Hammersmith and Fulham is 21.4 and the mean for the sample is 21.3 and the median 21.2. The standard deviation is 1.0. Given that Hammersmith and Fulham are only 0.1 above the threshold, their score is overruled and the prime implicant for the cluster becomes below threshold.

The second near miss is Barking and Dagenham's score for the variable the percentage of the population aged 65 and over. The borough score is at the threshold mean and median point of 11.0%. For this reason, the score is overruled and the prime implicant of below threshold is recorded for cluster 5.

Following the process of these data threshold overrules and the creation of additional prime implicants, Table 4.5 shows the final classification of prime implicants and Boolean simplification with regard to the variable influences on cluster definition.

At the end of this first time period for the meso case study, the next task before continuing with the DPS in subsequent years is to attempt a qualitative summary of what has been found in the cluster classifications so far.

The most interesting theme developing is the possible patterning of three key areas: life expectancy, service activities and health outcomes. Clusters 1 and 2 have above threshold life expectancies, although this is more marked in cluster 2 than 1, where it is for both genders. Conversely, clusters 4 and 5 have below threshold scores for life expectancy and lower than average proportions of their population as older.

Cluster 2 has a below threshold for the negative health outcome of early winter deaths. Cluster 1 achieves reduced comparative levels of falls, but not for early winter deaths (that are above threshold).

Cluster 4 is of interest because, while it has below threshold life expectancy, it has some positive service activities. It has a pleasing uptake of flu jabs, satisfaction with the availability of social services and an outcome of low levels of rapid readmissions to hospital following discharge. All this implies some quite strong service approaches overall.

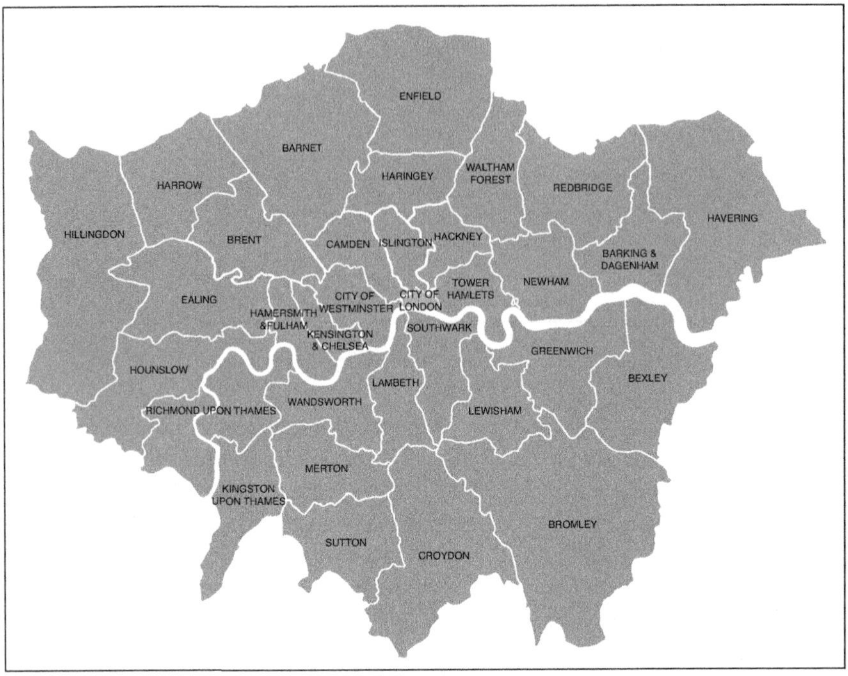

Figure 4.3 Map of the location of London boroughs

Cluster 5, on the other hand, has more falls in its older population and applies more funding to care home placements. Cluster 3 also has an above threshold ratio of falls but no other pattern associated with it.

Figure 4.3 shows a map of the location of the London boroughs being studied. There would appear to be some association between cluster membership and geographical location, although this is not a dominant feature for all borough's health and social care profiles. The most evident geographical pattern is in cluster 4 where the cluster members are all located in the east of London and most are direct neighbours (Newham, Tower Hamlets, Hackney) with only Greenwich divided from them by being south of the river Thames. Similarly, cluster 2 shares a geographical strip north of the river running from Westminster, Brent, leading to Harrow and Barnet on the edge of the capital city. But Richmond upon Thames, also in this cluster, is not joined geographically, and is south of the river.

The larger clusters have some significant pairings of geographically colocated boroughs within their structures, but do not share geographical homogeneity across the whole cluster. For example, cluster 1 has the geographical pairings of Bromley and Bexley, also with Havering being separated from Bexley by the Thames. Cluster 3 has the separated pairings of Redbridge and Waltham Forest, Ealing and Hillingdon, and also the triplet of Croydon, Sutton and Merton.

Cluster 5 includes three boroughs that are located adjacent to each other: Lambeth, Southwark and Wandsworth.

One reason for the importance of geography on data patterns is the reality that London boroughs increasingly share health and social care services with adjacent neighbours and so it is expected that there will be some geographical patterns resulting. Geographic location is also an important and well established cause of convergence when examining social and economic patterns over time (Montfort, 2008; Haynes & Haynes, 2016).

Meso case study, 2011

The same DPS process is repeated with the equivalent cases and variables one year later in 2011, to examine evidence of change.

Table 4.6 shows the resulting agglomeration schedule. The coefficients' gradient begins to increase between stages 5 and 6, although the gradient of increase is not steep. This gradual gradient increase was also observed in the first example for this case study in 2010 (Table 4.1). It suggests caution is needed when deciding on the optimal number of clusters and that the qualitative reflection on what number of clusters best represents social reality is very important.

Figure 4.4 reveals the icicle plot for the 2011 data, as related to the agglomeration schedule. It shows the strongest pairings that emerge in the early stages of the cluster combinations. In order of appearance, these are: Waltham Forest and Hounslow, Merton and Haringey (soon joined by Hillingdon), Islington and Southwark, Brent and Barnet and Lambeth and Lewisham. Given the complexity of the sample and its clustering, the dendrogram in Figure 4.5 offers the best visual method for examining the possible interpretation of cluster structure. The following five cluster structure is suggested for further examination with the QCA confirmatory method.

Cluster 1	Hounslow, Waltham Forest, Redbridge, Greenwich, Wandsworth and Bexley
Cluster 2	Bromley, Kingston upon Thames, Enfield, Havering, Sutton, Haringey, Merton, Hillingdon, Barnet, Brent
Cluster 3	Richmond upon Thames, Westminster, Camden, Kensington and Chelsea, Harrow
Cluster 4	Ealing, Hammersmith and Fulham, Islington, Southwark, Lambeth, Lewisham, Croydon, Barking and Dagenham.
Cluster 5	Hackney, Tower Hamlets, Newham

Cluster 2 is a large cluster with 10 boroughs. The analysis process that follows will reflect on whether there is evidence that it should be sub divided into two sets. Cluster 4 is a large cluster with nine boroughs. The analysis process will also consider whether Ealing and Hammersmith and Fulham are a sub set of cluster 4.

Table 4.8 shows the truth table to examine the proposed five clusters. Cluster 1 has three prime implicants. There is one near miss. This is Redbridge's score for early winter deaths where it is the only borough scoring below threshold.

Table 4.6 Agglomeration schedule for meso case study, 2011

Stage	*Cluster Combined*		*Coefficients*	*Stage Cluster First Appears*		*Next Stage*
	Cluster 1	*Cluster 2*		*Cluster 1*	*Cluster 2*	
1	17	30	.301	0	0	8
2	13	23	1.207	0	0	4
3	18	27	2.614	0	0	18
4	13	16	4.049	2	0	13
5	2	4	5.495	0	0	13
6	21	22	7.277	0	0	7
7	7	21	9.980	0	6	18
8	17	25	12.756	1	0	26
9	5	20	15.727	0	0	19
10	6	19	18.863	0	0	17
11	15	28	22.174	0	0	23
12	11	29	25.558	0	0	27
13	2	13	29.134	5	4	23
14	26	32	32.746	0	0	21
15	10	31	37.082	0	0	22
16	8	12	41.445	0	0	24
17	6	14	46.345	10	0	21
18	7	18	51.314	7	3	20
19	5	9	56.580	9	0	25
20	1	7	63.673	0	18	24
21	6	26	70.893	17	14	29
22	3	10	78.298	0	15	26
23	2	15	86.606	13	11	25
24	1	8	95.704	20	16	30
25	2	5	106.133	23	19	28
26	3	17	120.299	22	8	28
27	11	24	138.213	12	0	30
28	2	3	160.984	25	26	29
29	2	6	192.782	28	21	31
30	1	11	225.127	24	27	31
31	1	2	279.000	30	29	0

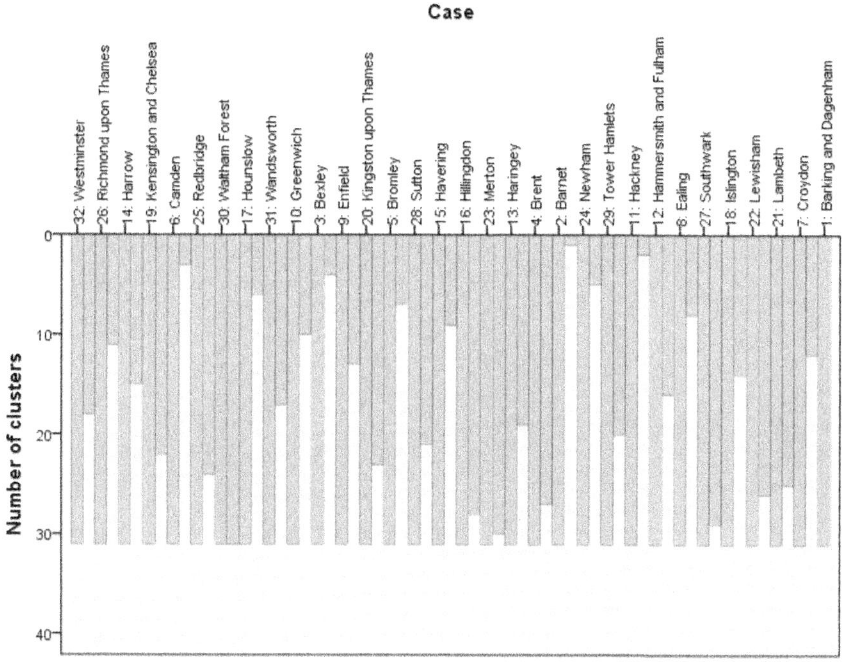

Figure 4.4 Icicle plot of cluster formulation: meso case study, 2011

Examination of the data in Table 4.7 shows that there is insufficient evidence to overrule this score. Bexley and Redbridge are a sub set of cluster 1, as defined by above threshold life expectancy for both men and women, whereas the other boroughs in the cluster have below threshold life expectancy for their older population.

At first glance cluster 2 is not well defined with no prime implicants recorded, although there are two near misses that need consideration. The first of these is male life expectancy at aged 65. Only Havering scores below threshold with 18.4. While this is close to the mean (18.7) and median average (18.8) for all boroughs, the distribution is close to the mean (standard deviation = 1.0) and several other authorities recorded below threshold have similar scores to Havering. For this reason, the score is not overruled.

The second near miss is the percentage of the boroughs population aged 65 and over. Haringey scores 9% of its population as being aged 65 and is below the median and mean scores of 11% for this variable. Haringey's below threshold score cannot be overruled.

The hypothesis that cluster 2 exists is not well supported by the QCA data. A re-examination of the cluster structure for cluster 2 in the Figure 4.4 dendrogram shows that there are three sub sets, Bromley, Kingston upon Thames and Enfield;

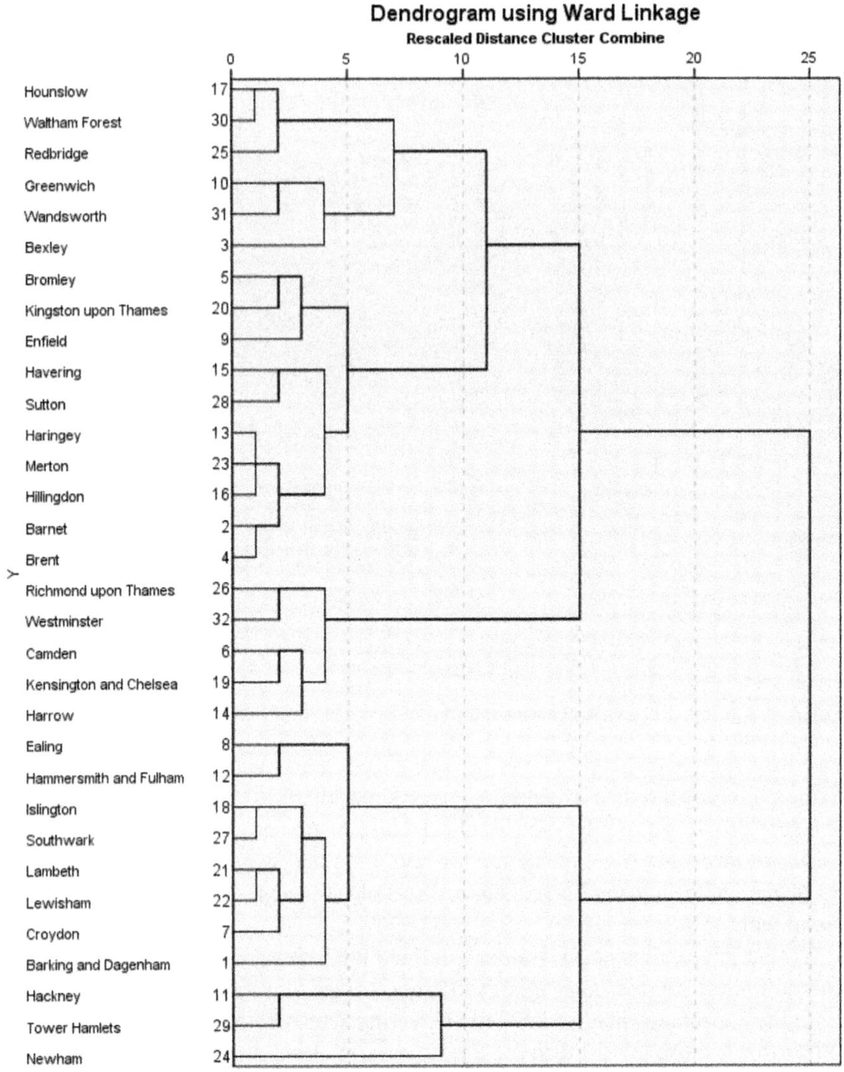

Figure 4.5 Dendrogram of cluster formulation: meso case study, 2011

the pairing of Havering and Sutton and Haringey, Merton, Hillingdon, Barnet and Brent. Table 4.9 reorders the QCA truth table for cluster 2, to allow close inspection of these sub sets against variable thresholds.

Table 4.9 shows strong evidence for three sub sets within cluster 2. Cluster 2A has four prime implicants. Cluster 2B is a pairing with six prime implicants. Cluster 2C has two prime implicants. These sub structures have more internal coherent than the larger cluster 2.

Cluster 3 is a homogeneous group with four prime implicants.

Table 4.7 QCA meso case study, 2011: conversion of meso data variables to binary scores

London borough	*Female life ex 65*	*Male life ex 65*	*Early winter deaths*	*Flu jab 65+*	*Care satisfaction*	*Early readmissions*	*Falls*	*Supported residents ratio*	*Percentage pop over 65*
Barking and Dagenham	20.1	17.1	26.8	69.4	35.9	12.9	2614.6	1044.5	0.10
Barnet	22.1	19.5	22.3	73.8	37.8	11.3	2204.8	534.5	0.13
Bexley	21.7	18.8	20.3	69.0	48.9	12.2	1941.4	677.2	0.16
Brent	22.5	19.4	22.5	72.2	40.5	11.9	2246.4	548.1	0.11
Bromley	22.0	19.3	21.7	72.0	40.6	12.2	1806.1	549.6	0.17
Camden	23.5	19.5	11.5	72.2	39.1	12.7	2417.7	529.6	0.11
Croydon	21.1	18.6	16.4	67.2	37.6	12.3	2418.3	547.7	0.12
Ealing	21.5	18.7	26.4	68.6	33.7	12.4	2736.8	359.3	0.11
Enfield	21.7	18.9	30.7	73.3	39.4	10.4	1530.3	514.6	0.12
Greenwich	20.4	17.4	26.0	72.6	44.7	12.5	1644.3	617.6	0.10
Hackney	20.6	18.3	8.9	73.7	41.9	11.3	2256.8	665.7	0.07
Hammersmith and Fulham	21.5	18.4	17.1	69.3	34.9	13.3	3257.4	671.8	0.09
Haringey	22.0	18.9	18.7	71.0	37.4	11.8	2230.1	497.9	0.09
Harrow	23.2	20.8	18.1	72.2	32.2	11.7	2252.8	404.3	0.14
Havering	21.8	18.4	11.2	70.4	38.2	11.6	2167.9	538.1	0.18
Hillingdon	21.6	18.9	18.7	70.4	34.6	12.3	2306.9	553.8	0.13
Hounslow	21.5	18.6	19.8	71.4	41.4	12.6	2604.8	344.3	0.11
Islington	20.8	17.6	14.9	72.5	39.8	11.9	2685.1	889.7	0.09
Kensington and Chelsea	23.7	20.7	17.0	70.3	38.7	12.5	2457.9	176.0	0.12
Kingston upon Thames	22.0	19.5	21.7	69.4	38.9	11.2	1653.1	404.8	0.13
Lambeth	21.0	17.9	22.1	68.5	38.7	12.4	2496.8	805.1	0.08
Lewisham	20.8	17.4	18.2	69.6	37.6	12.0	2295.4	560.7	0.09
Merton	22.0	19.3	15.9	70.6	37.1	11.8	2244.6	638.3	0.12
Newham	20.5	17.5	28.4	73.8	41.0	9.4	2229.0	246.4	0.07
Redbridge	21.6	18.9	15.0	74.0	45.8	12.5	2536.7	323.0	0.12
Richmond upon Thames	23.4	19.8	11.8	76.7	40.9	12.6	2024.6	407.8	0.14
Southwark	21.2	17.6	13.8	70.7	38.3	12.4	2752.7	664.5	0.08
Sutton	21.6	18.8	15.8	70.6	40.9	11.8	2392.4	170.6	0.14
Tower Hamlets	20.2	16.9	4.3	76.6	38.3	11.2	2458.1	877.8	0.06
Waltham Forest	21.3	18.4	19.1	72.2	40.3	12.8	2760.6	316.6	0.10
Wandsworth	21.0	17.8	26.7	70.1	45.8	12.2	2546.2	709.0	0.09
Westminster	23.0	20.7	16.9	75.8	37.0	12.8	2353.8	735.1	0.11
Mean	*21.7*	*18.7*	*18.7*	*71.6*	*39.3*	*12.0*	*2328.9*	*547.6*	*0.1*
Median	*21.6*	*18.8*	*18.5*	*71.2*	*38.8*	*12.2*	*2330.3*	*547.9*	*0.1*

(*Continued*)

Table 4.7 continued

London borough	*Female life ex 65*	*Male life ex 65*	*Early winter deaths*	*Flu jab 65+*	*Care satisfaction*	*Early readmissions*	*Falls*	*Supported residents ratio*	*Percentage pop over 65*
Conversion to binary scores									
Barking and Dagenham	0	0	1	0	0	1	1	1	1
Barnet	1	1	1	1	0	0	0	0	1
Bexley	1	1	1	0	1	1	0	1	1
Brent	1	1	1	1	1	0	0	1	1
Bromley	1	1	1	1	1	1	0	1	1
Camden	1	1	0	1	1	1	1	0	1
Croydon	0	0	0	0	0	1	1	1	1
Ealing	0	1	1	0	0	1	1	0	1
Enfield	0	1	1	1	1	0	0	0	1
Greenwich	0	0	1	1	1	1	0	1	1
Hackney	0	0	0	1	1	0	0	1	0
Hammersmith and Fulham	0	0	0	0	0	1	1	1	0
Haringey	0	1	1	0	0	0	0	0	0
Harrow	1	1	0	1	0	0	0	0	1
Havering	1	0	0	0	0	0	0	0	1
Hillingdon	1	1	1	0	0	1	0	1	1
Hounslow	0	0	1	0	1	1	1	0	1
Islington	0	0	0	1	1	0	1	1	0
Kensington and Chelsea	1	1	0	0	0	1	1	0	1
Kingston upon Thames	1	1	1	0	1	0	0	0	1
Lambeth	0	0	1	0	0	1	1	1	0
Lewisham	0	0	0	0	0	0	0	1	0
Merton	1	1	0	0	0	0	0	1	1
Newham	0	0	1	1	1	0	0	0	0
Redbridge	1	1	0	1	1	1	1	0	1
Richmond upon Thames	1	1	0	1	1	1	0	0	1
Southwark	0	0	0	0	0	1	1	1	0
Sutton	1	1	0	0	1	0	1	0	1
Tower Hamlets	0	0	0	1	0	0	1	1	0
Waltham Forest	0	0	1	1	1	1	1	0	1
Wandsworth	0	0	1	0	1	1	1	1	1
Westminster	1	1	0	1	0	1	1	1	1

Table 4.8 QCA truth table for meso case study, 2011

London borough	*Female life ex 65*	*Male life ex 65*	*Early winter deaths*	*Flu jab 65+*	*Care satisfaction*	*Early readmissions*	*Falls*	*Supported residents ratio*	*Percentage pop over 65*	*Cluster*
Bexley	1	1	1	0	**1**	**1**	0	1	**1**	1
Redbridge	1	1	0	1	**1**	**1**	1	0	**1**	1
Waltham Forest	0	0	1	1	**1**	**1**	1	0	**1**	1
Greenwich	0	0	1	1	**1**	**1**	0	1	**1**	1
Wandsworth	0	0	1	0	**1**	**1**	1	1	**1**	1
Hounslow	0	0	1	0	**1**	**1**	1	0	**1**	1
Bromley	1	1	1	1	1	1	0	1	1	2
Brent	1	1	1	1	1	0	0	1	1	2
Barnet	1	1	1	1	0	0	0	0	1	2
Kingston upon Thames	1	1	1	0	1	0	0	0	1	2
Hillingdon	1	1	1	0	0	1	0	1	1	2
Sutton	1	1	0	0	1	0	1	0	1	2
Merton	1	1	0	0	0	0	0	1	1	2
Havering	1	0	0	0	0	0	0	0	1	2
Enfield	0	1	1	1	1	0	0	0	1	2
Haringey	0	1	1	0	0	0	0	0	0	2
Camden	**1**	**1**	**0**	1	1	1	1	0	**1**	3
Richmond upon Thames	**1**	**1**	**0**	1	1	1	0	0	**1**	3
Westminster	**1**	**1**	**0**	1	0	1	1	1	**1**	3
Harrow	**1**	**1**	**0**	1	0	0	0	0	**1**	3
Kensington and Chelsea	**1**	**1**	**0**	0	0	1	1	0	**1**	3
Ealing	**0**	**1**	1	0	0	1	1	0	1	4
Barking and Dagenham	**0**	**0**	1	0	0	1	1	1	1	4
Lambeth	**0**	**0**	1	0	0	1	1	1	0	4
Islington	**0**	**0**	0	1	1	0	1	1	0	4
Croydon	**0**	**0**	0	0	0	1	1	1	1	4
Hammersmith and Fulham	**0**	**0**	0	0	0	1	1	1	0	4
Southwark	**0**	**0**	0	0	0	1	1	1	0	4
Lewisham	**0**	**0**	0	0	0	0	0	1	0	4
Newham	**0**	**0**	1	**1**	1	**0**	0	0	**0**	5
Hackney	**0**	**0**	0	**1**	1	**0**	0	1	**0**	5
Tower Hamlets	**0**	**0**	0	**1**	0	**0**	1	1	**0**	5

Table 4.9 QCA truth table for cluster 2, 2011, reordered to examine previous cluster sub sets

London borough	*Female life ex 65*	*Male life ex 65*	*Early winter deaths*	*Flu jab 65+*	*Care satisfaction*	*Early readmissions*	*Falls*	*Supported residents ratio*	*Percentage pop over 65*	*Cluster sub set*
Bromley	1	**1**	**1**	1	**1**	1	**0**	1	**1**	A
Kingston upon Thames	1	**1**	**1**	0	**1**	0	**0**	0	**1**	A
Enfield	0	**1**	**1**	1	**1**	0	**0**	0	**1**	A
Sutton	**1**	1	**0**	**0**	1	**0**	1	**0**	**1**	B
Havering	**1**	0	**0**	**0**	0	**0**	0	**0**	**1**	B
Brent	1	**1**	1	1	1	0	**0**	1	1	C
Barnet	1	**1**	1	1	0	0	**0**	0	1	C
Hillingdon	1	**1**	1	0	0	1	**0**	1	1	C
Merton	1	**1**	0	0	0	0	**0**	1	1	C
Haringey	0	**1**	1	0	0	0	**0**	0	0	C

Cluster 4 is a large cluster with only one prime implicant, but with four near misses that need consideration. The first near miss is male life expectancy at age 65, where only Ealing scores above threshold with a score of 18.7. However, examination of Table 4.7 shows this score to be at the mean threshold point and only 0.1 below the median of 18.8. For this reason, the score is overruled and becomes a below threshold prime implicant for this cluster. The second near miss is for the borough of Islington, the only place to score above threshold (72%) for those aged 65 and over having a flu jab. The Islington score is distributed close to the mean (71.6%), but above the median of 71.2%. The standard deviation is 2.3%, and several other London boroughs have similar scores rated above the threshold and so the score is not overruled. The third near miss is the ratio of falls where only Lewisham is below threshold with a score of 2295.4, where the mean is 2328.9, the median is 2330.3 and the standard deviation is 354.4. Several boroughs are scored higher than Lewisham and have a below threshold rating and so this score is not overruled. The final near miss is Ealing and it is below threshold on the number of supported residents with a score of 359.3 where the sample mean is 547.6 and the median 547.9 Ealing is not located near to the central tendency used to set the threshold and so the score is not overruled.

Cluster 5 is a small homogeneous cluster with only three boroughs who share five prime implicants.

Table 4.10 Boolean simplification, meso case study, 2011

Clusters	*Boolean simplification*
Cluster 1	CARE SATISFACTION * EARLY READMISSIONS * POP OVER 65
Cluster 2a	MALE LIFE EX * EARLY WINTER DEATHS * CARE SATISFACTION * falls * POP OVER 65
Cluster 2b	FEMALE LIFE EX * early winter deaths * flu jab 65+ * early readmissions * supported residents * POP OVER 65
Cluster 2c	MALE LIFE EX * falls
Cluster 3	FEMALE LIFE EX * MALE LIFE EX * early winter deaths * POP OVER 65
Cluster 4	female life ex * male life ex
Cluster 5	female life ex * male life ex * FLU JAB 65+ * early readmissions * pop over 65

Because of the rolling back of cluster 2, Table 4.10 presents the Boolean simplification in seven separate groupings.

Cluster 1 appears to be a misnomer, in that a shared strong positive sense of most older people reporting they are satisfied with the amount of care they receive is not matched with preventing readmissions after hospital discharge (where this cluster scores above threshold). These are London boroughs with relatively high proportions of their populations being aged 65 and over.

Cluster 2 as a whole is able to report different aspects of good life expectance. Cluster 2a has higher male life expectancy and also reports a shared positive sense of older people reporting they are satisfied with care received, but the cluster is above threshold for early winter deaths. While the older population is a relatively high feature of the borough, falls are below threshold.

Cluster 2b reports higher female life expectancy, below threshold problems (like early readmissions, early winter deaths), but also below threshold activities for flu jabs and supported residents.

Cluster 2c has an above threshold male life expectancy and a low level of falls. Cluster 2 as a whole, while diverse, has themes of above threshold scores for life expectancy and a tendency to report better health outcomes, such as lower falls, but this is not always consistent (for example, with a mixed picture on early winter deaths).

Cluster 3 has above threshold life expectancy and this is associated with below threshold winter deaths.

Cluster 4 has below threshold life expectancy. There is not a strong association with other variables, but it has several near misses that could not be overruled. The threshold evidence in Table 4.8 shows a tendency towards lower satisfaction with services and take up of the flu jab and higher likelihood of falls and early readmissions.

Cluster 5 has the same below threshold life expectancy as cluster 4, but above threshold flu jabs and below threshold readmissions following discharge. These are more positive service outcome aspects considering the boroughs share above threshold relative older population sizes.

At this stage of the DPS for 2011, it appears there is some increased fragmentation to the patterns developing in the first time period of 2010, although there is still some evidence of differences in service uptake and health outcomes being associated with life expectancy.

Meso case study, 2012

The same DPS process is repeated with the same cases and variables one year later in 2012, to examine evidence of change.

The agglomeration schedule in Table 4.11 indicates an initial increase in the coefficient between clusters 7 and 8. This gives the first indication of the optimal number of clusters.

The icicle plot in Figure 4.6 indicates the first pairings of boroughs in the cluster agglomerations. The first pair to be selected as the most similar is Westminster and Camden, followed by Waltham Forest and Haringey. Next are Brent and Barnet and then Lewisham and Lambeth.

The dendrogram in Figure 4.7 assists with the selection of the optimal number of clusters for the next stage in the analysis. This meso local government DPS case study has already revealed a difficulty with identifying a meaningful conceptualisation of larger clusters and that smaller clusters of London boroughs are likely to have more homogeneity and meaningful social explanation when related to variable scores. There has so far been some lack of consistency in patterns, especially for the larger clusters. One of the dangers with Cluster Analysis (CA), when it uses larger numbers of cases, is that it can generate larger clusters that are mathematical artefacts rather than useful social categories (Everitt, 1993). Nevertheless, it is important to acknowledge that the dendrogram (Figure 4.7) for the 2012 data demonstrates a hierarchy of both three large clusters and eight smaller clusters. The follow up QCA can be used to explore the characteristics of both these structures.

This cluster structure is summarised below.

Cluster 1a	Camden, Westminster, Harrow and Kensington and Chelsea
Cluster 1b	Hillingdon, Merton, Haringey, Waltham Forest, Barnet and Brent
Cluster 2a	Bexley, Havering, Bromley, Enfield and Richmond upon Thames
Cluster 2b	Croydon, Ealing, Sutton, Kingston upon Thames, and Redbridge
Cluster 3a	Newham, Wandsworth, Hackney,
Cluster 3b	Lambeth, Lewisham, Southwark
Cluster 3c	Hammersmith and Fulham, Islington, and Hounslow
Cluster 3d	Greenwich, Tower Hamlets and Barking and Dagenham

Table 4.11 Agglomeration schedule for meso case study, 2012

Stage	*Cluster Combined*		*Coefficients*	*Stage Cluster First Appears*		*Next Stage*
	Cluster 1	*Cluster 2*		*Cluster 1*	*Cluster 2*	
1	6	32	.771	0	0	16
2	13	30	1.801	0	0	14
3	2	4	3.211	0	0	14
4	21	22	4.763	0	0	8
5	16	23	6.467	0	0	20
6	7	8	8.307	0	0	15
7	24	31	10.480	0	0	9
8	21	27	13.150	4	0	21
9	11	24	15.891	0	7	30
10	3	15	18.758	0	0	13
11	12	18	21.902	0	0	19
12	14	19	25.075	0	0	16
13	3	5	28.318	10	0	22
14	2	13	31.799	3	2	20
15	7	28	35.372	6	0	25
16	6	14	40.175	1	12	26
17	10	29	45.388	0	0	23
18	9	26	50.835	0	0	22
19	12	17	56.772	11	0	21
20	2	16	63.240	14	5	26
21	12	21	69.854	19	8	27
22	3	9	77.193	13	18	28
23	1	10	84.690	0	17	27
24	20	25	93.025	0	0	25
25	7	20	104.608	15	24	28
26	2	6	119.924	20	16	29
27	1	12	139.335	23	21	30
28	3	7	161.358	22	25	29
29	2	3	185.431	26	28	31
30	1	11	210.475	27	9	31
31	1	2	279.000	30	29	0

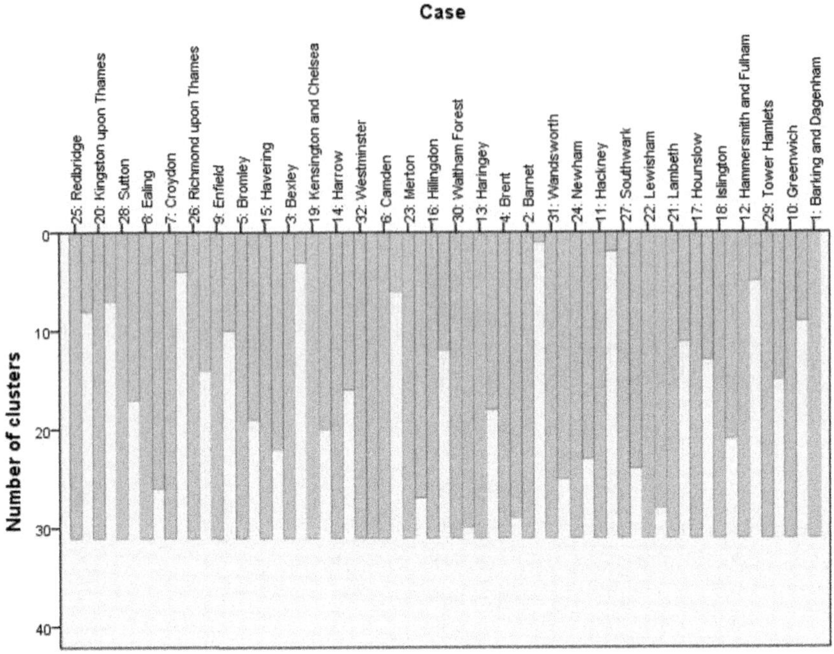

Figure 4.6 Icicle plot of cluster formulation: meso case study, 2012

Table 4.12 shows the process of converting the scale variables for the 2012 data to the binary structure required for the QCA. As in the previous examples, the median and mean results in this table provide the threshold for the researcher's decision about the allocation of binary scores.

Table 4.13 reveals the QCA truth table to test the binary scores against the cluster outcomes, and to examine the relationship between variables and cluster definition. Final prime implicant decisions are also indicated in Table 4.13.

Cluster 1a has three prime implicants.

Cluster 1b is a larger cluster with six boroughs and it has two prime implicants, but there are also three near misses for consideration. The first of these is Hillingdon's score of 21.6 years for female life expectancy at age 65. The sample mean is 21.9 and the median 21.7. The standard deviation is 1.0 with a distribution close to the mean. Given that Hillingdon's score is only 0.1 below the median it is appropriate to overrule the near miss and to make this variable an above threshold prime implicant for the cluster.

The second near miss is Merton's score of 71.1% for the percentage aged 65 and over who have received a flu jab, where it is the only borough in cluster 1b coded as below threshold. The sample mean is 72.3% and the median is 72.6% and the standard deviation is 2.7. Merton is not the closest borough to mean that is ranked below threshold. For this reason, the score is not overruled.

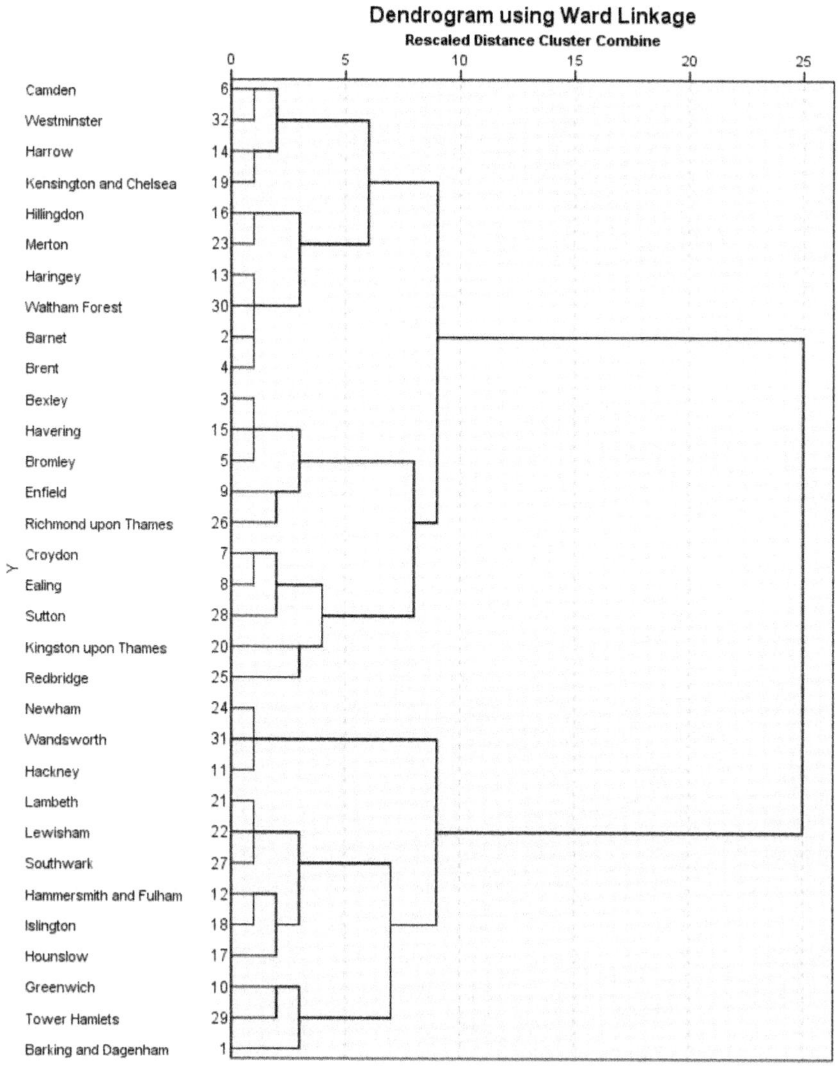

Figure 4.7 Dendrogram of cluster formulation: meso case study, 2012

The third near miss is Haringey's below threshold score of 9% for the percentage of the population aged 65 and over. The mean is 10 and the median is 10 with the distribution close to the mean (standard deviation = 3). Given there are four other boroughs with a score of 9% in the sample recorded as below threshold, it is not appropriate to overrule Haringey's score.

Cluster 2a and 2b both have five boroughs and each has four prime implicants. Cluster 2b has three near misses, but given it is a relatively small cluster, these are not considered.

Table 4.12 QCA meso case study, 2012: conversion of meso data variables to binary scores

London borough	*Female life ex 65*	*Male life ex 65*	*Early winter deaths*	*Flu jab 65+*	*Care satisfaction*	*Early readmissions*	*Falls*	*Supported residents ratio*	*Percentagepop over 65*
Barking and Dagenham	20.4	17.4	34.5	72.3	38.4	13.3	2335.6	871.0	0.10
Barnet	22.5	20.2	19.9	74.1	39.8	11.7	2265.3	493.0	0.14
Bexley	21.8	19.0	14.6	68.8	43.0	11.5	1782.4	547.8	0.16
Brent	22.8	19.3	24.9	72.4	38.7	12.1	2285.5	480.4	0.11
Bromley	22.2	19.7	18.8	73.7	40.6	11.6	1623.0	336.2	0.17
Camden	24.0	20.3	18.1	73.2	39.4	13.3	2318.2	456.3	0.11
Croydon	21.5	19.1	18.6	68.5	40.5	12.6	2318.2	212.0	0.13
Ealing	21.7	19.2	23.4	69.9	40.5	12.3	2923.3	285.7	0.11
Enfield	22.0	19.4	24.0	74.6	40.5	10.3	1441.7	513.5	0.13
Greenwich	20.9	17.6	35.0	75.4	38.2	11.4	1731.1	717.6	0.10
Hackney	21.3	18.5	3.8	75.9	43.1	11.9	2389.1	347.4	0.07
Hammersmith and Fulham	21.6	18.5	25.0	68.9	33.9	13.1	3082.5	665.2	0.09
Haringey	22.6	19.4	15.8	74.1	39.7	12.5	2170.5	458.2	0.09
Harrow	23.5	21.1	6.9	74.1	37.6	12.1	2104.2	339.7	0.14
Havering	21.8	18.8	21.3	72.8	38.5	12.0	1985.5	675.7	0.18
Hillingdon	21.6	19.0	9.9	72.3	35.5	12.3	2375.7	553.8	0.13
Hounslow	21.6	18.7	14.3	64.8	32.7	12.8	2522.1	661.6	0.11
Islington	21.3	17.6	21.7	73.8	31.9	12.2	2883.0	606.9	0.09
Kensington and Chelsea	23.5	20.9	18.4	70.3	38.8	12.8	2272.6	138.3	0.13
Kingston upon Thames	21.7	19.4	38.2	68.4	40.7	11.4	1630.5	348.1	0.13
Lambeth	21.6	18.0	16.3	68.9	39.8	12.1	2625.7	728.8	0.08
Lewisham	21.1	18.1	16.9	70.1	40.0	12.7	2205.0	612.9	0.09
Merton	21.8	19.0	14.1	71.1	32.8	11.3	2431.9	420.8	0.12
Newham	20.8	18.1	12.3	73.5	44.3	10.7	2355.9	480.4	0.07
Redbridge	21.7	19.4	37.5	74.6	50.0	12.9	2193.4	323.0	0.12
Richmond upon Thames	23.1	20.0	15.2	76.9	45.9	11.6	2032.6	503.9	0.14
Southwark	22.0	18.2	15.6	71.9	40.1	13.0	2941.2	770.8	0.08
Sutton	21.6	19.3	12.6	71.1	46.6	12.4	2438.2	153.0	0.15
Tower Hamlets	20.7	17.3	21.0	76.8	40.1	11.3	2574.7	654.7	0.06
Waltham Forest	21.8	19.1	15.7	73.8	39.7	13.1	2410.3	412.3	0.10
Wandsworth	21.1	18.2	3.2	72.0	44.1	11.6	2667.5	554.0	0.09
Westminster	23.8	20.9	20.2	74.8	41.2	12.8	2295.7	472.7	0.11
Mean	*21.9*	*19.0*	*19.0*	*72.3*	*39.9*	*12.1*	*2300.4*	*493.6*	*0.1*
Median	*21.7*	*19.1*	*18.2*	*72.6*	*39.9*	*12.2*	*2318.2*	*486.7*	*0.1*

London borough	*Female life ex 65*	*Male life ex 65*	*Early winter deaths*	*Flu jab 65+*	*Care satisfaction*	*Early readmissions*	*Falls*	*Supported residents ratio*	*Percentagepop over 65*
Conversion to binary scores									
Barking and Dagenham	1	0	1	1	0	1	1	1	1
Barnet	1	1	1	1	0	0	0	1	1
Bexley	1	0	0	0	1	0	0	1	1
Brent	1	1	1	1	0	0	0	0	1
Bromley	1	1	1	1	1	0	0	0	1
Camden	1	1	0	1	0	1	1	0	1
Croydon	0	1	1	0	1	1	1	0	1
Ealing	1	1	1	0	1	1	1	0	1
Enfield	1	1	1	1	1	0	0	1	1
Greenwich	0	0	1	1	0	0	0	1	1
Hackney	0	0	0	1	1	0	1	0	0
Hammersmith and Fulham	0	0	1	0	0	1	1	1	0
Haringey	1	1	0	1	0	1	0	0	0
Harrow	1	1	0	1	0	0	0	0	1
Havering	1	0	1	1	0	0	0	1	1
Hillingdon	0	1	0	1	0	1	1	1	1
Hounslow	0	0	0	0	0	1	1	1	1
Islington	0	0	1	1	0	1	1	1	0
Kensington and Chelsea	1	0	1	0	0	1	0	0	1
Kingston upon Thames	1	1	1	0	1	0	0	0	1
Lambeth	0	0	0	0	0	0	1	1	0
Lewisham	0	0	0	0	1	1	0	1	0
Merton	1	1	0	0	0	0	1	0	1
Newham	0	0	0	1	1	0	1	0	0
Redbridge	1	1	1	1	1	1	0	0	1
Richmond upon Thames	1	1	0	1	1	0	0	1	1
Southwark	1	0	0	0	1	1	1	1	0
Sutton	0	1	0	0	1	1	1	0	1
Tower Hamlets	0	0	1	1	1	0	1	1	0
Waltham Forest	1	1	0	1	0	1	1	0	1
Wandsworth	0	0	0	0	1	0	1	1	0
Westminster	1	1	1	1	1	1	0	0	1

Table 4.13 QCA truth table for meso case study, 2012

London borough	*Female life ex 65*	*Male life ex 65*	*Early winter deaths*	*Flu jab 65+*	*Care satisfaction*	*Early readmissions*	*Falls*	*Supported residents ratio*	*Percentage pop over 65*	*Cluster*
Westminster	**1**	1	1	1	1	1	0	**0**	**1**	1a
Harrow	**1**	1	0	1	0	0	0	**0**	**1**	1a
Camden	**1**	1	0	1	0	1	1	**0**	**1**	1a
Kensington and Chelsea	**1**	0	1	0	0	1	0	**0**	**1**	1a
Barnet	**1**	**1**	1	1	**0**	0	0	1	1	1b
Brent	**1**	**1**	1	1	**0**	0	0	0	1	1b
Waltham Forest	**1**	**1**	0	1	**0**	1	1	0	1	1b
Haringey	**1**	**1**	0	1	**0**	1	0	0	0	1b
Merton	**1**	**1**	0	0	**0**	0	1	0	1	1b
Hillingdon	**0**	**1**	0	1	**0**	1	1	1	1	1b
Enfield	**1**	1	1	1	1	**0**	**0**	1	**1**	2a
Bromley	**1**	1	1	1	1	**0**	**0**	0	**1**	2a
Richmond upon Thames	**1**	1	0	1	1	**0**	**0**	1	**1**	2a
Havering	**1**	0	1	1	0	**0**	**0**	1	**1**	2a
Bexley	**1**	0	0	0	1	**0**	**0**	1	**1**	2a
Redbridge	1	**1**	1	1	**1**	1	0	**0**	**1**	2b
Ealing	1	**1**	1	0	**1**	1	1	**0**	**1**	2b
Croydon	0	**1**	1	0	**1**	1	1	**0**	**1**	2b
Sutton	0	**1**	0	0	**1**	1	1	**0**	**1**	2b
Kingston upon Thames	1	**1**	1	0	**1**	0	0	0	**1**	2b
Newham	**0**	**0**	**0**	1	**1**	**0**	**1**	0	**0**	3a
Hackney	**0**	**0**	**0**	1	**1**	**0**	**1**	0	**0**	3a
Wandsworth	**0**	**0**	**0**	0	**1**	**0**	**1**	1	**0**	3a
Southwark	1	**0**	**0**	**0**	1	1	1	**1**	**0**	3b
Lewisham	0	**0**	**0**	**0**	1	1	0	**1**	**0**	3b
Lambeth	0	**0**	**0**	**0**	0	0	1	**1**	**0**	3b
Islington	**0**	**0**	1	1	**0**	**1**	**1**	**1**	0	3c
Hammersmith and Fulham	**0**	**0**	1	0	**0**	**1**	**1**	**1**	0	3c
Hounslow	**0**	**0**	0	0	**0**	**1**	**1**	**1**	1	3c
Barking and Dagenham	1	**0**	**1**	**1**	0	1	1	**1**	1	3d
Tower Hamlets	0	**0**	**1**	**1**	1	0	1	**1**	0	3d
Greenwich	0	**0**	**1**	**1**	0	0	0	**1**	1	3d

Table 4.14 Boolean simplification, meso case study, 2012

Clusters	*Boolean simplification*
Cluster 1a	FEMALE LIFE EX * supported residents * POP OVER 65
Cluster 1b	FEMALE LIFE EX * MALE LIFE EX * care satisfaction
Cluster 2a	FEMALE LIFE EX * early readmissions * falls * POP OVER 65
Cluster 2b	MALE LIFE EX * care satisfaction * supported residents * POP OVER 65
Cluster 3a	female life ex * male life ex * early winter deaths * CARE SATISFACTION * early readmissions * FALLS * pop over 65
Cluster 3b	male life ex * early winter deaths * flu jab 65+ * SUPPORTED RESIDENTS * pop over 65
Cluster 3c	female life ex * male life ex * care satisfaction * EARLY READMISSIONS * FALLS * SUPPORTED RESIDENTS
Cluster 3d	male life ex * EARLY WINTER DEATHS * FLU JAB 65+ * SUPPORTED RESIDENTS

The Cluster 3 sub clusters a – d all have three members. Given the low membership of each, near misses are not considered for each sub cluster. Cluster 3a has seven prime implicants. Cluster 3b has five prime implicants. Cluster 3c has six prime implicants. Cluster 3d has four implicants.

As regards the higher level, with three summary clusters in the later stage of the agglomeration, Table 4.13 indicates that cluster 1 has no prime implicants but there are several near misses across its 10 member structure. One of these near misses (female life expectancy at aged 65+ for Hillingdon) has already been overruled in the analysis above. This therefore results in one prime implicant for cluster 1. Cluster 2 has one prime implicant. Cluster 3 is the largest agglomeration with 12 members. It has one prime implicant. The smaller clusters add important detail to the emergent patterns.

Meso case study: conclusions

Cases

The meso case study is characterised by a relative lack of stability in cluster membership. A large number of cases move clusters during the short time period studied (2010–2012). In addition, the cluster definitions are relatively unstable, in that the agglomeration gradient is relatively even and not indicating sharp definition points for the optimal number of clusters. The research in this case study faces challenges with summarising larger clusters with few homogenous factors. In the main it has proved better to consider smaller clusters that reflect the diversity of case experience, but sometimes change their memberships and allegiances over time.

Table 4.15 Variable trends: meso case study, 2010–2012

	Female life ex 65	*Male life ex 65*	*Early winter deaths*	*Flu jab 65+*	*Care satisfaction*	*Early readmissions*	*Falls*	*Supported residents ratio*	*Percentage pop over 65*
Mean 2010	21.3	18.4	17.2	70.8	38.4	11.6	2220.8	592.5	0.11
Mean 2011	21.7	18.7	18.7	71.6	39.3	12.0	2328.9	547.6	0.11
Mean 2012	21.9	19.0	19.0	72.3	39.9	12.1	2300.4	493.6	0.11
Change	∧	∧	∧	∧	∧	∧	~	∨	stable

Compared to the macro case studies in Chapter 3, there is less evidence of cases remaining in the same clusters over all time periods. In this case study, less than one third of the cases remain in the same cluster. These boroughs are: Bromley, Havering and Enfield, Hillingdon and Merton, Newham and Hackney, and Hammersmith and Fulham and Islington. Only one of these stable case groupings are immediate geographical neighbours: Newham and Hackney. So, while the cross sectional clusters reveal some geographical relationships within clusters, this is not evidence of these geographical relationships remaining in the longer term. The relationship between cases is relatively unstable.

Variables

Table 4.15 shows the overall direction of change for the trend in average variable scores for the whole sample over the three year period 2010–12. Much of the sample variable data is characterised by incremental change with marginal changes in the overall trend. For example, marginal upward improvements in life expectancy. Despite the increasing life expectancy, early winter deaths and falls increase. The drop in the number of residents who are financially supported in residential care by their London boroughs after the financial crisis and resulting local government cuts is noteworthy. In conclusion, given the relatively short period of time studied (2010–2012) the variable change patterns look to be relatively unstable.

Patterns

Table 4.16 shows where London boroughs share the same above or below threshold score on any one variable consistently over the three year period studied (2010–12). Blank cells indicate a changing result over the three year period that is not stable. Near misses and associated overruling of threshold scores are included.

The resulting Table (4.16) has been ranked by the life expectancy variables so that the boroughs recording above threshold on both female and male life expectancy are at the top of the table, and then followed by those boroughs that displayed consistently above threshold in one of these scores. In the middle of the table are the boroughs that scored contradictory results (ie: Havering). In the bottom half of the table are the boroughs that consistently scored below threshold on the life expectancy variables.

There is least stability over time in the case and variable patterns for the level of care satisfaction and early winter deaths (less likely to be consistently above or below threshold in Table 4.16). There is no apparent pattern with how these two variables compare to other more stable variables. There is a relatively high degree of stability over time in the other social and health care activity and outcome variables. More than half of the case-to-variable patterns over time in these variables are stable over the three year period. The proportion of those aged 65 and over receiving flu jabs looks to be more consistently above threshold in those boroughs with consistently high life expectancy, although there are exceptions, like Kingston upon Thames.

The number of falls amongst older people in the boroughs does show some reverse pattern with the life expectancy, so that boroughs with higher life expectancy that is consistent over time have below threshold numbers of falls over time (Brent, Barnet, Bromley, Kingston upon Thames, Richmond upon Thames and Harrow). Similarly, the ratio of supported residents in care homes shows some of this pattern with areas that have high life expectancy that is consistent over time being less likely to be consistently supporting above threshold numbers of older people in care homes over time (ie: Kingston upon Thames, Harrow). In fact, this relationship looks to be a clearer pattern when examining the influence in the bottom half of the table, so where boroughs with consistently below threshold scores for life expectancy can be seen to consistently support above threshold ratios of their older populations in care homes (examples being Hammersmith and Fulham, Islington, Greenwich and Tower Hamlets).

Future research and the possible plotting of QCA outcome variables could include relative inequality of income, wealth and household and family structure variables. This might further insights to the existing patterns. The current DPS concludes that both case and variable patterns are relatively unstable in the time period studied.

Table 4.16 Longitudinal truth table: meso case study

Overall threshold stability	*Female life ex 65*	*Male life ex 65*	*Early winter deaths*	*Flu jab 65+*	*Care satisfaction*	*Early readmissions*	*Falls*	*Supported residents ratio*	*Percentage pop over 65*
Brent	Above	Above				Below	Below		Above
Barnet	Above	Above		Above			Below		Above
Camden	Above	Above		Above		Above			Above
Westminster	Above	Above		Above		Above			Above
Bromley	Above	Above	Above	Above			Below		Above
Kingston upon Thames	Above	Above	Above	Below			Below	Below	Above
Richmond upon Thames	Above	Above	Below	Above	Above		Below		Above
Harrow	Above	Above	Below	Above	Below		Below	Below	Above
Hillingdon	Above	Above				Above			Above
Kensington and Chelsea	Above					Above		Below	Above
Bexley	Above			Below			Below	Above	Above
Haringey		Above			Below		Below	Below	Below
Enfield		Above	Above	Above		Below	Below		Above

Sutton		Above	Below	Below			Above	Below	
Merton		Above	Below	Below		Below			Above
Waltham Forest				Above		Above	Above	Below	
Redbridge				Above	Above	Above		Below	Above
Ealing				Below		Above	Above	Below	Above
Havering	Above	Below				Below	Below		Above
Southwark		Below		Below		Above	Above	Above	Below
Barking and Dagenham		Below	Above			Above	Above	Above	
Croydon	Below			Below		Above	Above		Above
Hounslow	Below	Below					Above		Above
Hammersmith and Fulham	Below	Below				Above	Above	Above	Below
Islington	Below	Below		Above			Above	Above	Below
Greenwich	Below	Below		Above			Below	Above	
Tower Hamlets	Below	Below		Above		Below		Above	Below
Newham	Below	Below		Above	Above	Below		Below	Below
Lewisham	Below	Below		Below				Above	Below
Wandsworth	Below	Below		Below	Above		Above	Above	Below
Lambeth	Below	Below		Below	Below		Above	Above	Below
Hackney	Below	Below	Below	Above	Above	Below			Below

5 Micro case study example

Older people in Sweden

This chapter examines the use of DPS to explore dynamic change in micro case studies with individual people. Micro approaches are underdeveloped with quantitative case based methods (Rihoux, et al., 2011).

Micro case study: older people in Sweden born in 1918

The first case study in this chapter examines a sub sample of the easySHARE data-set used in Chapter 3 for the first macro case study (Börsch-Supan, et al., 2016; Gruber, et al., 2016). That case study used aggregate nation level data scores to compare countries as cases. In contrast, this case study takes a small sub sample of easySHARE data at the individual respondent level, but from the same data-set. The selection criteria for the sub sample of respondents is all those born in 1918 and resident in Sweden. For the first wave, 2004, there are 30 older people included. At this point the respondent's average age is 86 years. The aim is to then track the same sub sample in the later waves 2, 4 and 5. The later samples get smaller due to some of the respondents being unavailable. This could include them being too ill to take part, or deceased at the later data collection waves.

The selection of variables is designed to maximise the use of available scale data and to minimise the use of variables with missing values. Case numbers are set up to distinguish the respondent's sex, where a case number beginning with 0 is a man and a case number beginning with other integers are female. The resulting list of variables is used in the Cluster Analysis (CA) is shown in Table 5.1

Table 5.1 List of variables used in the micro case study

- Number of children
- Number of grandchildren
- Self-perceived health score (where higher score indicates the person has more concerns about their own health)
- Number of chronic diseases
- How often talked to a medical doctor in the last 12 months
- Mobility index
- Number of days per week when alcohol consumed in the last three months
- Household income based on European percentiles

Micro case study, wave 1, 2004

Table 5.2 demonstrates the gradient of change in the coefficient scores. It marginally increases between stages 4 and 5, suggesting that this is likely to be an optimal point to consider the meaningfulness of the clusters selected.

Figure 5.1 shows the icicle plot for the agglomeration process and the pairs of respondents who are selected in the early stages of the CA as being most similar.

Table 5.2 Agglomeration schedule for individual respondents, micro case study, 2004

Stage	*Cluster Combined*		*Coefficients*	*Stage Cluster First Appears*		*Next Stage*
	Cluster 1	*Cluster 2*		*Cluster 1*	*Cluster 2*	
1	5	29	.276	0	0	7
2	15	25	1.064	0	0	28
3	14	21	2.131	0	0	10
4	6	17	3.364	0	0	16
5	3	20	4.995	0	0	10
6	8	19	6.790	0	0	20
7	5	26	8.671	1	0	15
8	7	23	10.599	0	0	11
9	2	18	12.559	0	0	21
10	3	14	14.712	5	3	13
11	7	27	17.617	8	0	18
12	1	10	20.895	0	0	16
13	3	30	24.281	10	0	19
14	12	28	27.823	0	0	24
15	5	16	31.637	7	0	21
16	1	6	35.542	12	4	23
17	4	24	40.181	0	0	24
18	7	22	45.253	11	0	20
19	3	13	52.246	13	0	23
20	7	8	59.265	18	6	25
21	2	5	68.104	9	15	22
22	2	11	78.461	21	0	28
23	1	3	88.902	16	19	26
24	4	12	100.631	17	14	25
25	4	7	116.622	24	20	27
26	1	9	136.715	23	0	27
27	1	4	160.799	26	25	29
28	2	15	191.894	22	2	29
29	1	2	232.000	27	28	0

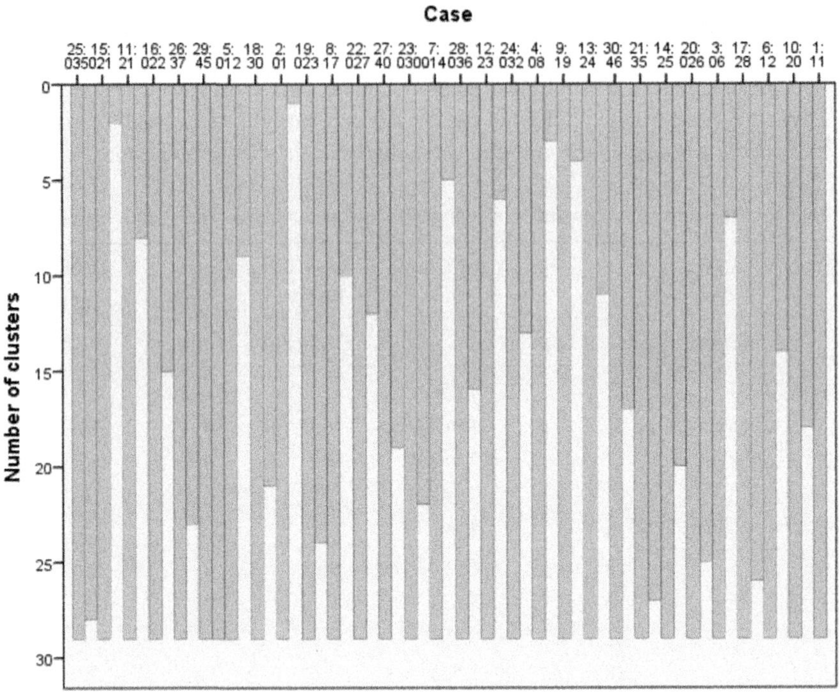

Figure 5.1 Icicle plot of cluster formulation: micro case study, 2004

The first two to be selected as similar are cases 45 and 012. The second pair is 035 and 021, two men. The third agglomeration is between case 35 and 25, two women

The dendrogram in Figure 5.2 suggests that a three or four cluster structure might compromise similarity and cluster integrity by only linking minimal differences given the size of the sample. For example, the top third of the dendrogram looks likely to be two homogenous clusters, where there is a discrete pair of 021 and 035, rather than one single agglomeration.

Therefore, seven differentiations are proposed for consideration with the QCA variable analysis in Table 5.4, this while also seeking to observe evidence of the five cluster agglomeration suggested by the coefficient scores in Table 5.2.

The proposed cluster structure from the dendrogram is:

Cluster 1	012, 45, 37, 022, 01, 30, 21
Cluster 2	021, 035
Cluster 3	17, 023, 014, 030, 40, 027
Cluster 4	23, 036, 08, 032
Cluster 5	12, 28, 11, 20
Cluster 6	25, 35, 06, 026, 46
Outlier	19

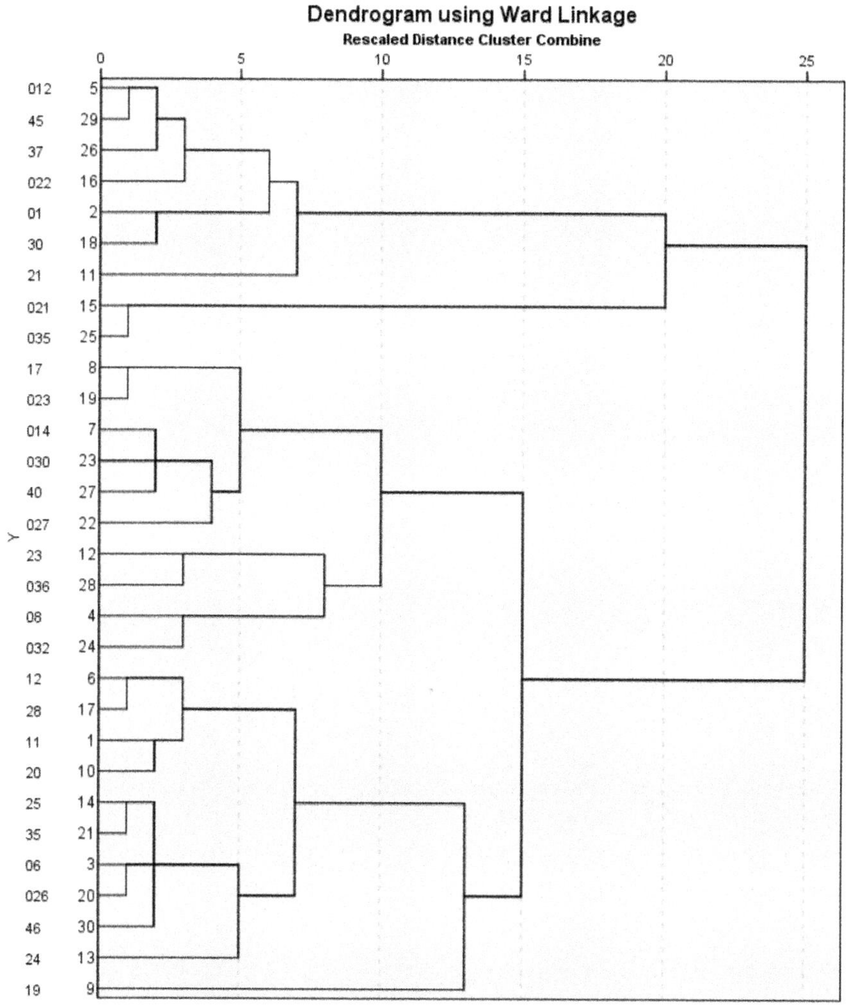

Figure 5.2 Dendrogram of cluster formulation: micro case study, 2004

Two key issues to take forward into the QCA stage of the DPS are whether cluster 1 and cluster 2 are strongly related and whether clusters 5 and 6 are related.

Table 5.4 shows the resulting QCA truth table for the wave 1 cases.

All six clusters have at least one prime implicant before any consideration for near misses. Near misses that are overruled to be prime implicants are indicated in Table 5.4.

Cluster 1 is a large cluster with seven case members, but it has only one prime implicant. There are four near misses for consideration.

Table 5.3 QCA micro case study, 2004: conversion of micro data variables to binary scores

Case ID	*Number of children*	*Number of grandchildren*	*Self-perceived health score*	*Number of chronic diseases*	*Doctor communication*	*Mobility index*	*Alcohol days*	*Household income*
11	1	1	3	1	0	0	5	3
01	4	13	3	1	3	1	7	2
06	2	5	3	0	3	0	1	1
08	2	0	1	3	5	0	6	5
012	3	3	3	1	2	0	4	2
12	1	0	3	1	2	1	2	1
014	2	2	3	2	2	1	1	5
17	1	1	2	3	6	0	1	4
19	1	4	4	4	14	1	2	1
20	1	2	1	2	0	0	4	1
21	5	13	4	2	5	0	1	1
23	4	0	1	1	1	1	3	3
24	2	5	3	0	10	0	2	3
25	1	3	3	1	3	0	3	2
021	2	6	4	0	0	4	1	2
022	5	7	3	2	3	0	4	3
28	1	1	2	2	1	1	1	2
30	3	10	2	2	2	1	6	1
023	1	1	1	2	2	0	1	4
026	2	4	4	1	4	1	2	1
35	2	2	3	2	2	0	2	1
027	1	2	4	5	3	0	1	4
030	2	5	3	2	6	0	1	5
032	2	3	3	1	4	0	7	7
035	2	5	4	0	1	3	2	2
37	3	4	3	2	2	0	7	2
40	3	4	3	4	2	0	1	6
036	3	5	1	0	4	0	1	4
45	3	4	3	1	3	0	4	1
46	3	5	3	3	3	0	1	1
Mean	*2.3*	*4.0*	*2.8*	*1.7*	*3.3*	*0.5*	*2.8*	*2.7*
Median	*2.0*	*4.0*	*3.0*	*2.0*	*3.0*	*0.0*	*2.0*	*2.0*

Case ID	Number of children	Number of grandchildren	Self-perceived health score	Number of chronic diseases	Doctor communication	Mobility index	Alcohol days	Household income
Conversion to binary scores								
11	0	0	1	0	0	0	1	1
01	1	1	1	0	1	1	1	0
06	1	1	1	0	1	0	0	0
08	1	0	0	0	1	0	1	1
012	1	0	1	0	0	0	1	0
12	0	0	1	0	0	1	0	0
014	1	0	1	1	0	1	0	1
17	0	0	0	1	1	0	0	1
19	0	1	1	1	1	1	0	0
20	0	0	0	1	0	0	1	0
21	1	1	1	1	1	0	0	0
23	1	0	0	0	0	1	1	1
24	1	1	1	0	1	0	0	1
25	0	0	1	0	1	0	1	0
021	1	1	1	0	0	1	0	0
022	1	1	1	1	1	0	1	1
28	0	0	0	1	0	1	0	0
30	1	1	0	1	0	1	1	0
023	0	0	0	1	0	0	0	1
026	1	1	1	0	1	1	0	0
35	1	0	1	1	0	0	0	0
027	0	0	1	1	1	0	0	1
030	1	1	1	1	1	0	0	1
032	1	0	1	0	1	0	1	1
035	1	1	1	0	0	1	0	0
37	1	1	1	1	0	0	1	0
40	1	1	1	1	0	0	0	1
036	1	1	0	0	1	0	0	1
45	1	1	1	0	1	0	1	0
46	1	1	1	1	1	0	0	0

Table 5.4 QCA truth table for micro case study, 2004

Case ID	*Number of children*	*Number of grandchildren*	*Self-perceived health score*	*Number of chronic diseases*	*Doctor communication*	*Mobility index*	*Alcohol days*	*Household income*	*Cluster*
022	**1**	**1**	1	1	1	0	1	**1**	1
21	**1**	**1**	1	1	1	0	0	**0**	1
37	**1**	**1**	1	1	0	0	1	**0**	1
01	**1**	**1**	1	0	1	1	1	**0**	1
45	**1**	**1**	1	0	1	0	1	**0**	1
30	**1**	**1**	0	1	0	1	1	**0**	1
012	**1**	**0**	1	0	0	0	1	**0**	1
021	**1**	**1**	**1**	**0**	**0**	**1**	**0**	**0**	2
035	**1**	**1**	**1**	**0**	**0**	**1**	**0**	**0**	2
030	1	1	1	**1**	1	0	**0**	**1**	3
40	1	1	1	**1**	0	0	**0**	**1**	3
014	1	0	1	**1**	0	1	**0**	**1**	3
027	0	0	1	**1**	1	0	**0**	**1**	3
17	0	0	0	**1**	1	0	**0**	**1**	3
023	0	0	0	**1**	0	0	**0**	**1**	3
036	**1**	1	0	**0**	1	0	0	**1**	4
032	**1**	0	1	**0**	1	0	1	**1**	4
08	**1**	0	0	**0**	1	0	1	**1**	4
23	**1**	0	0	**0**	0	1	1	**1**	4
12	**0**	**0**	1	0	**0**	1	0	0	5
11	**0**	**0**	1	0	**0**	0	1	1	5
28	**0**	**0**	0	1	**0**	1	0	0	5
20	**0**	**0**	0	1	**0**	0	1	0	5
46	1	1	**1**	1	**1**	0	**0**	**0**	6
026	1	1	**1**	0	**1**	1	**0**	**0**	6
24	1	1	**1**	0	**1**	0	**0**	**1**	6
06	1	1	**1**	0	**1**	0	**0**	**0**	6
35	1	0	**1**	1	**0**	0	**0**	**0**	6
25	0	0	**1**	0	**1**	0	**1**	**0**	6
19	0	1	1	1	1	1	0	0	7

The first near miss is the number of grandchildren, where only case 012 is below threshold. The mean and median are four grandchildren. The standard deviation is 3.3. Case 012 has three grandchildren. Given the proximity to the threshold the near miss is overruled and number of grandchildren becomes a prime implicant for the cluster.

The second near miss is self-perceived health score, where case 30 is the only case below the threshold. The mean is 2.8 and the median 3. The standard deviation is 1.0. Case 30 scores 2. This is not considered close enough to the central tendency threshold to be concluded as a near miss.

The third near miss is the number of days when alcohol is consumed. Case 21 is the only case in this cluster to be below the threshold. The mean is 2.8 and the median is 2.0. The standard deviation is 2.1. Case 21 scores 1 and is the lower quartile. For this reason, the variable is not upgraded to a prime implicant for this cluster.

The final near miss is household income decile. Only case number 022 scores above the threshold with a score of 3. The mean is 2.7 and the median is 2.0. The standard deviation is 1.7. Given the proximity of case 022 to the threshold, this variable score is considered a near miss and overruled. Household income becomes a prime implicant for the cluster.

Cluster 2 is a pairing of two male cases 021 and 035. They share all variables as prime implicants.

Cluster 3 has six members and three prime implicants and one near miss; that is case 014 being the only case above threshold for the mobility index. There is insufficient difference on the interval scale to justify overruling this score.

Cluster 4 has four cases and shares three prime implicants. Cluster 5 has four cases and shares three prime implicants.

Cluster 6 is a larger cluster with only one prime implicant, but with five near misses for consideration.

The first near miss is for the number of children. Only case 25 is below threshold. The mean is 2.3 and the median 2. Case 25 has only one child. This is not a near miss that can be overruled.

The second near miss is the number of communications with the doctor where only case 35 is below threshold with a score of 2 contacts. The mean is 3.3 and the median is 3.0. The standard deviation is 2.9, indicating a distributed variance. For this reason, the score is overruled and this variable is upgraded to a prime implicant for the cluster.

The third near miss is the mobility index. This is a variable, however, with a limited interval range and a distribution that clusters around lower scores with most respondents scoring zero. As case 026 does have a scoring mobility index when the rest of the cluster score zero, it is not appropriate to rule this as a near miss.

The fourth near miss is the number of days when alcohol is consumed. Case 25 is the only person to score above threshold with a score of 3. Given the mean is 2.8 and median 2 and standard deviation 2.1, it is decided to overrule this score and record alcohol consumption as a below threshold prime implicant for this cluster.

Table 5.5 Boolean simplification, micro case study, 2004

Clusters	*Boolean simplification*
Cluster 1	CHILDREN * GRANDCHILDREN * income
Cluster 2	CHILDREN * GRANDCHILDREN * SELF-PERCEIVED HEALTH * Chronic disease * doctor com * MOBILITY * alcohol * income
Cluster 3	CHRONIC DISEASE * alcohol * INCOME
Cluster 4	CHILDREN * chronic disease * INCOME
Cluster 5	children * grandchildren * doctor com
Cluster 6	SELF-PERCEIVED HEALTH * DOCTOR COM * alcohol * income

The final near miss is the household income. Case number 24 is the only person in the cluster to score above threshold with a score of 3. The mean is 2.7, median is 2.0 and the standard deviation is 1.7. It is decided to overrule this near miss given the proximity to the mean and this variable becomes a below threshold prime implicant for the cluster.

Table 5.5 summarises the prime implicants for the clusters. Clusters 1 and 2 have larger family structures, and lower household incomes, but cluster 2 has evidence of health concerns, despite lower levels of chronic disease and lower levels of communications with doctors.

Cluster 3 has evidence of ill health, despite higher incomes. Cluster 4 is the converse with lower evidence of disease in higher income households. Cluster 5 has small family structures and also lower communications with doctors. Finally cluster 6 has higher levels of self-reported health concerns and higher communications with doctors while also reporting lower levels of household income.

Next the DPS moves to the next available wave of data. This is for 2006. Some cases are no longer available for longitudinal analysis. This may be due to serious illness, death or refusal to continue to take part in the SHARE survey. Two new cases have joined and were not previously available in the 2004 data. These respondents are from the same birth year. They are case numbers 018 and 32. Sixteen cases have progressed from the wave 1, 2004 analysis, to this second wave stage of the analysis.

Micro case study, wave 2, 2006

The agglomeration process for the CA with the wave 2 data is shown in Table 5.6. The coefficient gradient changes more substantially between stages 4 and 5 suggesting that the optimal number of clusters may be 4.

The icicle plot in Figure 5.3 reveals the strongest pairings of cases in the earliest stages of the agglomerations of cases into clusters. First, cases 32 and 036 are joined. Next cases 023 and 17 come together. Then cases 25 and 06 are linked, followed by the pairing of cases 014 and 032.

Table 5.6 Agglomeration schedule for case study, 2006

Stage	*Cluster Combined*		*Coefficients*	*Stage Cluster First Appears*		*Next Stage*
	Cluster 1	*Cluster 2*		*Cluster 1*	*Cluster 2*	
1	10	18	.384	0	0	8
2	5	11	.778	0	0	5
3	2	8	1.699	0	0	7
4	4	15	3.076	0	0	8
5	3	5	5.022	0	2	9
6	12	14	7.271	0	0	9
7	2	6	9.778	3	0	11
8	4	10	13.597	4	1	12
9	3	12	17.592	5	6	11
10	1	7	22.927	0	0	14
11	2	3	28.823	7	9	12
12	2	4	37.549	11	8	15
13	13	17	46.817	0	0	15
14	1	16	56.395	10	0	16
15	2	13	71.760	12	13	16
16	1	2	99.380	14	15	17
17	1	9	136.000	16	0	0

Cluster 1 has two prime implicants. Cluster 2a also has two prime implicants. Cluster 2b is the largest cluster with five members. It already has two prime implicants, but also has three near misses. The first is case 030's score of 6 for the number of grandchildren. This is substantially above the mean of 3.6 (median 2.5) and so the variable is not considered for upgrade. The second near miss is case 35's above threshold score of 4 for communications with doctors where the sample mean is 3.5, median 2.0 and standard deviation 5.4. Given that the scores are distributed and this score is close to the mean the near miss is overruled and this variable becomes a prime implicant for the cluster. The final near miss is case 12's score of above threshold for the mobility index. This variable is not normally distributed with most cases scoring zero. The score for person 12 is not overruled. Cluster 2a and 2b do not share any prime implicants. This is evidence that they are best considered separately.

Cluster 3 is a pairing with four prime implicants. Cluster 4 has three members and shares four prime implicants.

Table 5.9 shows the Boolean simplification for the case study data in 2006.

Cluster 1 members have more children and drink alcohol less often. In addition, Table 5.8 indicates most members in this cluster have more grandchildren and positive self-assessments of their own health. Although they are more likely to

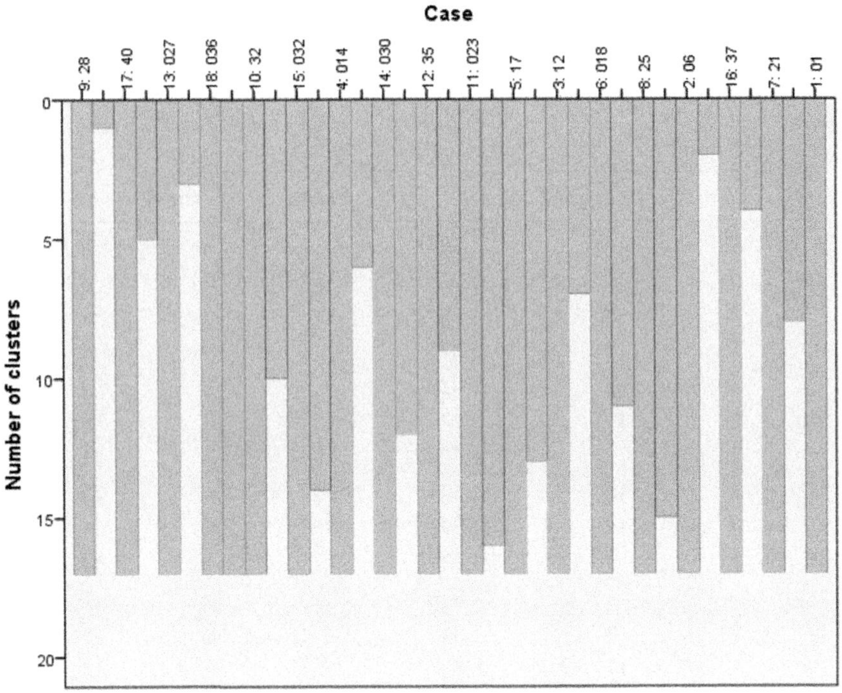

Figure 5.3 Icicle plot of cluster formulation: micro case study, 2006

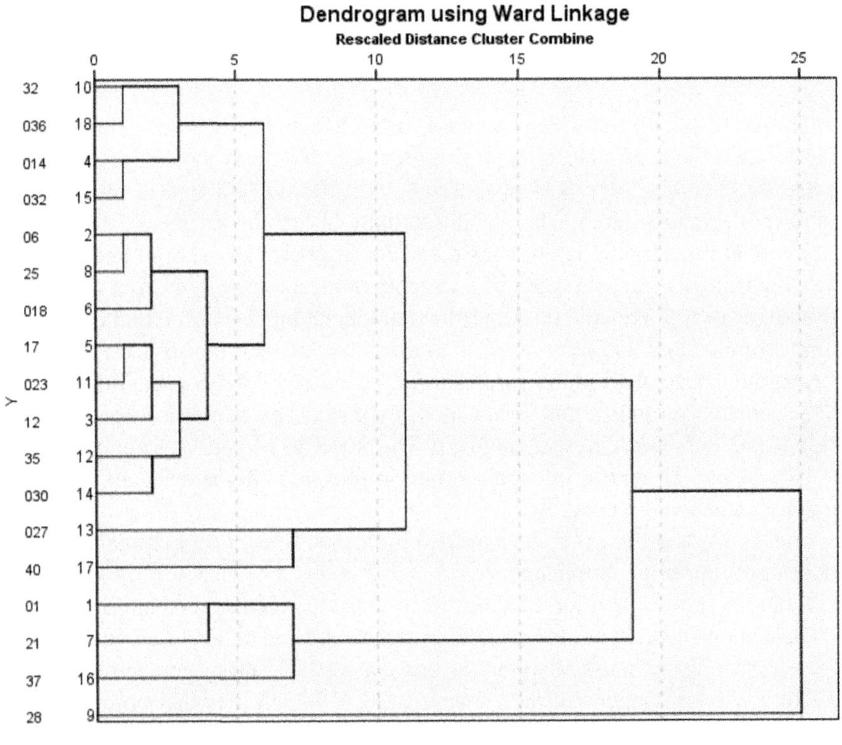

Figure 5.4 Dendrogram of cluster formulation: micro case study, 2006

Table 5.7 QCA micro case study, 2006: conversion of micro data to binary scores

Case ID	*Number of children*	*Number of grandchildren*	*Self-perceived health score*	*Number of chronic diseases*	*Doctor communication*	*Mobility index*	*Alcohol days*	*Household income*
01	4	13	3	1	0	1	7	2
06	2	5	3	0	0	0	2	2
12	1	0	4	3	2	1	1	2
014	2	2	2	2	3	2	1	3
17	1	1	3	2	1	0	1	3
018	1	1	2	0	1	0	1	3
21	5	11	3	1	2	1	1	2
25	1	3	3	0	4	0	3	2
28	1	1	5	5	25	4	1	2
32	3	4	2	1	4	1	1	2
023	1	1	3	2	2	0	1	2
35	2	2	4	1	4	0	1	1
027	1	2	4	5	2	3	1	4
030	2	6	4	1	2	0	1	3
032	2	3	3	3	2	1	1	3
37	3	2	3	2	2	0	7	1
40	3	4	3	2	4	0	1	6
036	3	4	2	1	3	0	1	2
mean	*2.1*	*3.6*	*3.1*	*1.8*	*3.5*	*0.8*	*1.8*	*2.5*
median	*2.0*	*2.5*	*3.0*	*1.5*	*2.0*	*0.0*	*1.0*	*2.0*
Conversion to binary scores								
01	1	1	1	0	0	1	1	0
06	1	1	1	0	0	0	1	0
12	0	0	1	1	0	1	0	0
014	1	0	0	1	1	1	0	1
17	0	0	1	1	0	0	0	1
018	0	0	0	0	0	0	0	1
21	1	1	1	0	0	1	0	0
25	0	1	1	0	1	0	1	0
28	0	0	1	1	1	1	0	0
32	1	1	0	0	1	1	0	0
023	0	0	1	1	0	0	0	0
35	1	0	1	0	1	0	0	0
027	0	0	1	1	0	1	0	1
030	1	1	1	0	0	0	0	1
032	1	1	1	1	0	1	0	1
37	1	0	1	1	0	0	1	0
40	1	1	1	1	1	0	0	1
036	1	1	0	0	1	0	0	0

Table 5.8 QCA truth table for micro case study, 2006

Case ID	*Number of children*	*Number of grandchildren*	*Self-perceived health score*	*Number of chronic diseases*	*Doctor communication*	*Mobility index*	*Alcohol days*	*Household income*	*Cluster ID*
032	**1**	1	1	1	0	1	**0**	1	1
32	**1**	1	0	0	1	1	**0**	0	1
036	**1**	1	0	0	1	0	**0**	0	1
014	**1**	0	0	1	1	1	**0**	1	1
06	1	1	1	**0**	0	**0**	1	0	2a
25	0	1	1	**0**	1	**0**	1	0	2a
018	0	0	0	**0**	0	**0**	0	1	2a
030	1	1	**1**	0	**0**	0	**0**	1	2b
35	1	0	**1**	0	**1**	0	**0**	0	2b
12	0	0	**1**	1	**0**	1	**0**	0	2b
17	0	0	**1**	1	**0**	0	**0**	1	2b
023	0	0	**1**	1	**0**	0	**0**	0	2b
40	1	1	**1**	**1**	1	0	**0**	**1**	3
027	0	0	**1**	**1**	0	1	**0**	**1**	3
01	**1**	1	**1**	0	**0**	1	1	**0**	4
21	**1**	1	**1**	0	**0**	1	0	**0**	4
37	**1**	0	**1**	1	**0**	0	1	**0**	4
28	0	0	1	1	1	1	0	0	5

communicate with the doctor they are also more likely to have mobility problems. Most members of this cluster are men. The cluster is characterised by members who have relatively large extended families with positive outlooks on their heath, despite experiencing some health problems.

Cluster 2a has a low occurrence of chronic diseases and mobility problems with two out of three not communicating with their doctors very often. This small cluster appears to be fairly healthy.

Cluster 2b has low consumption of alcohol and low communications with doctors, but high self-assessment of their concerns about health issues. The majority

Table 5.9 Boolean simplification, micro case study, 2006

Clusters	*Boolean simplification*
Cluster 1	CHILDREN * alcohol
Cluster 2a	chronic disease * mobility index
Cluster 2b	SELF-PERCEIVED HEALTH * doctor com * alcohol
Cluster 3	SELF-PERCEIVED HEALTH * CHRONIC DISEASE * alcohol * INCOME
Cluster 4	CHILDREN * SELF-PERCEIVED HEALTH * doctor com * income

do not report higher size extended families. The mixed scores for chronic disease and mobility issues suggest despite their concerns about their own health, their actual physical health difficulties as a cluster are not low considering their age.

Cluster 3 is a pairing. Their heath seems poor. They self-report health problems and have chronic disease. They share strong household income profiles.

In contrast to the pair in cluster 3, the three people in cluster 4 share poorer household income. They also report health problems in their self-assessment, but have low communications with doctors. Their actual health problems with regard to chronic disease and mobility is mixed.

Given the above classifications, it is hypothesised that the members of cluster 2a will be most likely to survive and remain in the final 2010 cohort.

Micro case study, wave 4, 2010

In wave 4 of the SHARE data only seven cases are available who reside in Sweden and were born in 1918. Six of these respondents were in the previous wave 2, 2006 analysis, but case 08 was not. Nevertheless, case 08 was included in the wave 1, 2004 data.

The coefficients' gradient increases significantly after stage 3 as illustrated in the cluster agglomeration schedule in Table 5.10. The dendrogram in Figure 5.6 also confirms a maximum of three clusters. The first pairing to come together in the stages of analysis in the icicle plot (Figure 5.5) are cases 018 and 12. Next, these are joined by case 014, before the pairing of cases 40 and 32 are agglomerated.

One aspect for consideration in this phase of the DPS is whether clusters 1 and 2 have a linking, and if this can be evidenced by the sharing of shared prime implicants.

Given all the available clusters are small, no mathematical consideration is given to near misses. Table 5.12 shows that cluster 1 shares four prime implicants. Cluster 2 shares six prime implicants and cluster 3 shares three prime implicants. Cluster 1 and 2 do share one prime implicant that is lower alcohol consumption. Cluster 3 also shares one prime implicant with cluster 2, with both clusters having above threshold scores for the number of children.

Table 5.13 summarises the prime implicants for each cluster. Cluster 1 members have smaller extended families. They self-report health problems and mobility

Table 5.10 Agglomeration schedule for micro case study, 2010

Stage	*Cluster Combined*		*Coefficients*	*Stage Cluster First Appears*		*Next Stage*
	Cluster 1	*Cluster 2*		*Cluster 1*	*Cluster 2*	
1	3	5	.958	0	0	2
2	3	4	4.336	1	0	4
3	6	7	8.507	0	0	4
4	3	6	15.317	2	3	6
5	1	2	25.649	0	0	6
6	1	3	48.000	5	4	0

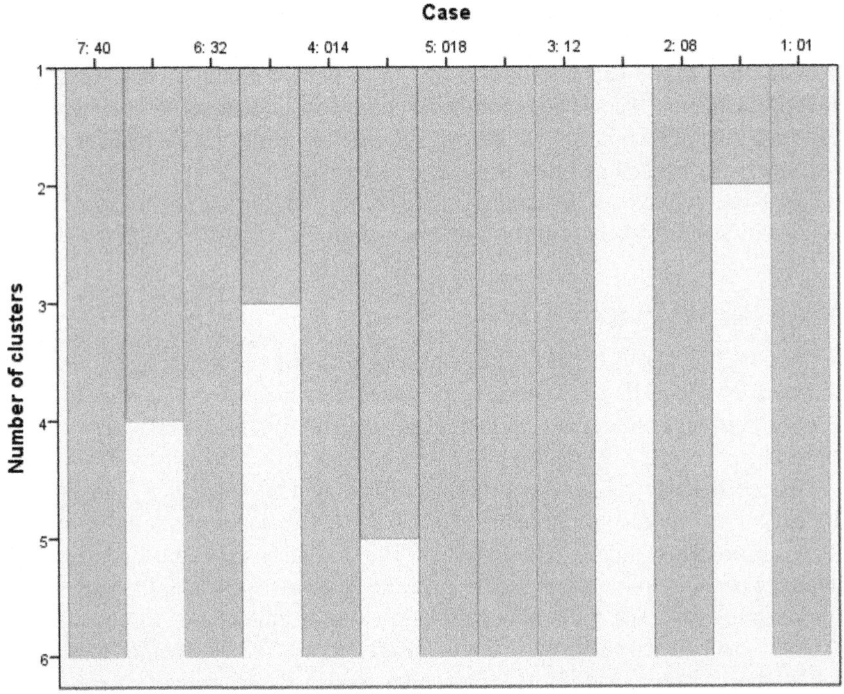

Figure 5.5 Icicle plot of cluster formulation: micro case study, 2010

problems, but in response have low contact with a doctor. They drink alcohol less. Case 018 is in this group, having been in cluster 2b in 2006. This is the only case from that cluster to have been hypothesised to appear in 2010 that remains in the analysis. The health situation of case 018 is now clearly different to the previous situation in 2006.

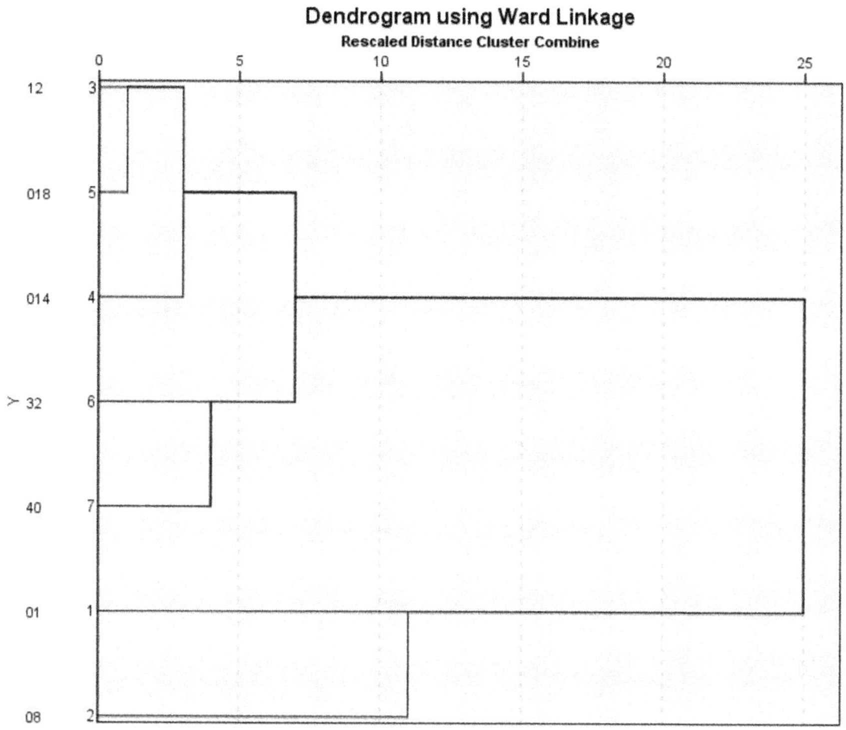

Figure 5.6 Dendrogram of cluster formulation: micro case study, 2010

Cluster 2 members have larger extended families, they self-report health problems and have higher rates of chronic disease. This is associated with above average communications with doctors. They drink alcohol less frequently.

The pair in cluster 3 have larger extended families. They have higher than average household incomes, low levels of chronic disease and mobility problems and are more likely to drink alcohol frequently.

Conclusions for the micro case study

Cases

Most cases move clusters in the time periods studied. In part this lack of similarity over time is determined by the lack of a staple research population over time which is a consequence of the age group selected.

The substantial differences between individuals experience of health and social care, as people grow older, illustrates the diversity of individual experience, even when the sample is reduced to one country and one age group.

Table 5.11 QCA micro case study, 2010: conversion of micro data variables to binary scores

Case ID	*Number of children*	*Number of grandchildren*	*Self-perceived health score*	*Number of chronic diseases*	*Doctor communication*	*Mobility index*	*Alcohol days*	*Household income*
01	4	13	3	1	1	0	7	5
08	2	2	2	0	10	0	6	6
12	1	0	3	1	2	4	1	2
014	2	2	3	2	2	3	1	4
018	1	1	4	1	1	3	1	1
32	3	4	3	1	4	1	1	1
40	3	4	5	2	6	2	1	3
mean	2.3	3.7	3.3	1.1	3.7	1.9	2.6	3.1
median	2.0	2.0	3.0	1.0	2.0	2.0	1.0	3.0
Conversion to binary scores								
01	1	1	1	0	0	0	1	1
08	1	0	0	0	1	0	1	1
12	0	0	1	0	0	1	0	0
014	1	0	1	1	0	1	0	1
018	0	0	1	1	0	1	0	0
32	1	1	1	1	1	0	0	0
40	1	1	1	1	1	1	0	1

Variables

Table 5.14 shows the variable trends influencing the dynamic movement of cases in relation to each other in micro case study 1. It is important to analyse these trends while remembering the structure of the case design, which is that this is a sample of older people who are growing increasingly very old and that the number remaining in the available sample is decreasing each year. This is a key part of the contextual dynamic of the case study. There are constant variables (family structure) that will usually only change because of individual cases exiting the sample at certain time points. These variables are the respondent's number of children and the number of grandchildren. If all the same cases were available to the DPS at each time point, these variables would be close to perfectly stable without change.

Self-perceived health score is incrementally increasing, where an increase in score represents greater health difficulties, but we would expect this given this

Table 5.12 QCA truth table for micro case study, 2010

Case ID	*Number of children*	*Number of grandchildren*	*Self-perceived health score*	*Number of chronic diseases*	*Doctor communication*	*Mobility index*	*Alcohol days*	*Household income*	*Cluster ID*
014	1	**0**	**1**	1	**0**	**1**	**0**	1	1
018	0	**0**	**1**	1	**0**	**1**	**0**	0	1
12	0	**0**	**1**	0	**0**	**1**	**0**	0	1
40	**1**	**1**	**1**	**1**	**1**	1	**0**	1	2
32	**1**	**1**	**1**	**1**	**1**	0	**0**	0	2
01	**1**	1	1	**0**	0	**0**	**1**	**1**	3
08	**1**	0	0	**0**	1	**0**	**1**	**1**	3

Table 5.13 Boolean simplification, micro case study, 2010

Clusters	*Boolean simplification*
Cluster 1	grandchildren * SELF-PERCEIVED HEALTH * doctor com * MOBILITY * alcohol
Cluster 2	CHILDREN * GRANDCHILDREN * SELF-PERCEIVED HEALTH * CHRONIC DISEASE * DOCTOR COM * alcohol
Cluster 3	CHILDREN * chronic disease * mobility * ALCOHOL * INCOME

Table 5.14 Variable trends: micro case study, mean average scores 2004–2010

Year	*Number of children*	*Number of grandchildren*	*Self-perceived health score*	*Number of chronic diseases*	*Doctor communication*	*Mobility index*	*Alcohol days*	*Household income*
2004	2.3	4.0	2.8	1.7	3.3	0.5	2.8	2.7
2006	2.1	3.6	3.1	1.8	3.5	0.8	1.8	2.5
2010	2.3	3.7	3.3	1.1	3.7	1.9	2.6	3.1
Change		∨	∧	∨	∧	∧	∨	∧

is a case study of people born in the same year who are getting older. Somewhat surprisingly, the number of chronic diseases has declined in the last year. This is likely to be because several cases have left the longitudinal study and so those that remain in old age are the fittest survivors. The number of communications with doctors is incrementally increasing through the years and this is again what we would expect, given the increasing old age of the people in the study. Likewise, the mobility index score is increasing to indicate more problems with mobility as the sample age increases. The number of days when alcohol is consumed is relatively stable with some minor fluctuations. Finally, the average household income is increasing and this may represent that those living into very old age are more likely to survive if coming from moderately wealthier households. Given the context of the study, and the long time period studied (for an older population), the changes in variable trends are relatively stable.

Patterns

Tables 5.15 and 5.16 show the interaction of case and variable stability over the years studied with Table 5.15 presenting the conclusions for the five cases that were present in all three years and Table 5.16 comparing 2004 with 2006 only. As would be expected, the family structure variables show most case stability over time, especially with the number of children and this remains constant for all cases. The variable that is most likely to fluctuate for cases over time is the number of communications with a doctor. This shows least stability. Changes in the number of grandchildren is surprising and may reflect changes in older people's reporting as they grew older, and could be partly to do with changing partnerships amongst their adult children. Self-perceived health score is stable over time and reflects a distribution toward above threshold health concerns as is expected with a population of older people. Similarly, alcohol consumption tends to stabilise over time for most respondents and where it does, this reflects below threshold consumption. Respondents with larger families (ie: consistently above threshold for number of children and number of grandchildren) tend to report less occurrence of chronic disease (even if they have reported higher scores for the self-perceived health score). Consistency in above or below threshold for chronic diseases over time does not necessarily associate with consistency of threshold scores reported for mobility problems, as these are often the opposite. For example, in Table 5.16, four cases report stability over time for above threshold number of chronic illnesses but below threshold stability for the mobility problems index. Taken together this demonstrates differing expectations of health with regard to how subjective self-assessments pattern with actual chronic illness and actual mobility problems.

The average number of self-perceived health problems rises as the population grows older, as would be expected. The number of chronic diseases experienced does not necessarily associate with an individual's experience of mobility.

Table 5.15 Longitudinal truth table: micro case study, 2004–2010

Case ID	*Number of children*	*Number of grandchildren*	*Self-perceived health score*	*Number of chronic diseases*	*Doctor communication*	*Mobility index*	*Alcohol days*	*Household income*
12	Below	Below	Above		Below	Above	Below	Below
40	Above	Above	Above	Above			Below	Above
01	Above	Above	Above	Below			Above	
014	Above	Below		Above		Above	Below	Above

Table 5.16 Longitudinal truth table: micro case study, 2004–2006

Case ID	*Number of children*	*Number of grandchildren*	*Self-perceived health score*	*Number of chronic diseases*	*Doctor communication*	*Mobility index*	*Alcohol days*	*Household income*
21	Above	Above	Above				Below	Below
030	Above	Above	Above			Below	Below	Above
40	Above	Above	Above	Above		Below	Below	Above
01	Above	Above	Above	Below		Above	Above	Below
06	Above	Above	Above	Below		Below		Below
036	Above	Above	Below	Below	Above	Below	Below	
032	Above		Above					Above
37	Above		Above	Above	Below	Below	Above	Below
014	Above	Below		Above		Above	Below	Above
35	Above	Below	Above			Below	Below	Below
25	Below		Above	Below	Above	Below	Above	Below
28	Below	Below		Above		Above	Below	Below
17	Below	Below		Above		Below	Below	Above
023	Below	Below		Above	Below	Below	Below	
12	Below	Below	Above		Below	Above	Below	Below
027	Below	Below	Above	Above			Below	Above

Communications with doctors fluctuate much, regardless of the availability of immediate family and the perceived and real experience of one's illness. This last point about service use illustrates the difficulty in targeting primary health services at the point of need, with some who need urgent medical advice and treatment not realising or accepting they need it, while others frequently use such contacts when perhaps a lower level professional advice service might serve them just as well and be less expensive for government to provide.

6 Conclusions

Dynamic Pattern Synthesis (DPS) offers a mixed method for considering small longitudinal datasets over time. It offers a replicable method that can help understand the dynamics of social and economic interactions and identify both stable and unstable patterns. Replication of the same method over time, with the same, or similar, data is at the core of DPS, allowing longitudinal patterns to be observed.

There is scope for the further development of DPS, beyond the definition in this first volume. While the DPS method proposed starts with a multivariate exploration of scale variables that utilises Cluster Analysis (CA), after the binary conversion to the QCA stage it has the potential to be adapted to include other categorical variables with two nominal categories, and can also model another chosen outcome variable. The default approach applied in this monograph is that the QCA stage is used to test the hypothesis of the existence of clusters proposed in the CA (the proposed cluster membership for cases has been used as the QCA outcome variable).

Dynamic Pattern Synthesis and different dynamic typologies

There are three key elements to the concluding stage of DPS and its qualitative interpretation of the synthesis situation for the system it is observing. Firstly, DPS considers variable trends over time, secondly it considers case trajectories over time, and finally it seeks to understand the combined stability patterns of variable and case relationships.

Variable patterns

Variable patterns are considered to be stable, if over time the central tendency of the variable remains similar (this might include some minor fluctuations over time in the values of the central tendency). A variable pattern is unstable if there is a noticeable trajectory of change in the value of the central tendency of the variable. The case studies used in this book show a degree of variable stability with an absence of more extreme changes in variable aggregate scores over the longer term. From the case study evidence, it is relatively unusual for a variable trend to change rapidly in a short space of time. Incremental aggregate variable change is much more likely the norm.

While the central tendency values of variable distributions may look stable they can conceal movement in individual scores within the variable distributions over time. Therefore, aggregate variable trend analysis is a one-dimensional view of variable effects, and in complex systems dynamic interactions may change cases at the micro level, but the sum of micro data changes can 'cancel itself out' in terms of how stability is viewed at the total system level (Dooley & Van de Ven, 1997). Variable change patterns conceal important details about what is happening to cases.

Case patterns

Cases patterns are considered to be stable if cases remain in the same clusters, or very close to the same cluster formations, over time (this in a specific longitudinal analysis). Of interest to the researcher using DPS are cases that move clusters over time. It is possible for cases to remain in the same cluster, even if the variable relationships determining clusters are changing, but this depends to a large extent on a specific cluster of cases experiencing the same variable influences over time.

Some cases do not pair or fit with clusters. These have to be considered as outliers. Some cases remain as outliers and are distinctly different from other cases. One such example was Luxembourg in the second macro case study that examined the implementation of the euro currency. A consideration for future DPS developments is whether persistent outliers like Luxembourg should be excluded. There will be some resulting impact on the remaining shape of cluster formulation when they are excluded. Also, one conclusion of a DPS might be that it is important to follow up with a qualitative study of outliers to understand why they are so different to other cases.

Hierarchical CA is influenced by close pairs that share many similarities. These pairs have a dominant influence on the hierarchical method used and they cannot later be separated once combined. In the case studies where clustering is weak and not persistent over time, such as the meso London borough case study, some strong pairs persist and form an interesting and useful focus for future analysis. One feature of strong pairs is geographical location, and this is not necessarily something that is automatically picked up in the mathematical and logical structure of CA and QCA. In the case studies in this book, geography was not a specified variable. Instead, the researcher took a qualitative contextual approach to space, assuming it was important (as explained in the opening chapter). Strong pairs evidenced in the macro and meso case studies are often geographical neighbours, or near neighbours, but not always.

The stability of case and variable interactions: towards some typologies

At the end of each of the four case studies used in this book, a longitudinal summary truth table was produced to examine case and variable stability across the complete time period studied. These longitudinal truth tables allow for some synthesis about which cases are most consistently similar over time. However, this longitudinal view is not a single reference point overview of stability, as it ignores the detail of the cross sectional perspectives offered at each time point. The summary long view truth table cannot be used alone to summarise the DPS. A qualitative statement about the similarities and differences of cases over time still needs to consider carefully the specific details within the cross sectional analysis. For example, cases that have greater occurrences of variable threshold stability over time are not necessarily those that remain in the same clusters over time. So, even if a case keeps the same threshold relationship with many of the variables it is interacting with, this stability is not necessarily a predictor of the stability of case patterns overall. Therefore, the final qualitative summary of a DPS has to consider several different perspectives and cannot trust one computational chart alone.

To assist the formulation of some ideal typologies of system activity evidenced by DPS, Table 6.1 provides a summary of the resulting types of pattern dynamics. Each possible type is discussed in turn.

Table 6.1 Typologies of dynamic patterns

Type of system dynamics	*Variable pattern*	*Case pattern*	*Nature of dynamic*	*Case study example*
Stable dynamics	Stable	Stable	Cases tend toward staying in the same cluster groupings throughout the DPS and the same variable patterns are associated with the construction of these clusters.	Macro case study 1 (Health and social care in Europe)
Case instability	Stable	Unstable	Most cases experience cluster membership change over time, and there is a lack of consistent change to case cluster patterns. Change is cyclic or random individual variation, with the aggregate variable trends over time being fairly stable at the level of scale (ie: stable sample averages).	Micro case study (Health and social care in Sweden)
Cluster resilience – despite variable instability	Unstable	Stable	Despite considerable change in variable trends, most cases stay in the same clusters over time and case based interactions and similarities are resilient to changes in variables.	Macro case study 2 (European macroeconomics)
System instability	Unstable	Unstable	Many of the cases in the sample experience changes of cluster membership over time and this instability is associated with changes in variable trends and how variables define cluster membership.	Meso case study (London boroughs, local government health and social care for older people)

Stable dynamics

Stable dynamics are demonstrated by relative stability in the aggregate variable change and the relative stability in the relationship between cases over time (in terms of evidence of stable cluster memberships). The best example of stable dynamics in this book is demonstrated by the macro case study 1 in Chapter 3.

It is not straightforward for the researcher to make a binary and qualitative decision about whether a summary of variable changes (as in Table 3.19 for macro case study 1) is either 'stable' or 'unstable'. For example, the researchers' decision about which variables are included in this decision will bias how stable the variable picture is over time, especially if some near constant variables have been included, like the average number of children and grandchildren in each country from a specific population (these variables would not be expected to change very much). Average variable change for a given number of cases does not show the variance and may conceal dynamics within the scores of individual cases (although these will be revealed in case pattern change over time).

The only real basis for a decision about whether a combined pattern of variable change over time is stable or not, is how combined trend data compares to other case studies. There are only four examples presented in this book and DPS is a new method. The qualitative decision of the researcher is based on the number of variables that provide evidence of a considerable scale of change (change that might be described as transformational for its effect on cases), and the scale of transformational change in those variables that are demonstrating change.

What at first sight might appear to be small aggregate changes can be argued to be transformative in the longer term. For example, in the meso London borough, local government case study, in Table 4.15, the population ratio weighting of local government support to older people living in care homes has declined by 17% in three years. Alongside this statistic, early readmissions to hospital have increased 0.5%, the older person's falls ratio has increased 3% and early winter deaths have increased 3%. Taken together and given the relatively short time span of the DPS research (2010–2012) this is concluded to be variable instability. This is a qualitative judgement exercised on the available evidence of quantitative information.

Conversely, in Table 3.19, that summarises average variable trends for macro case study 1 (health and social care in European countries), many of the variables are argued to be stable over time. Some of the variables are relatively constant (average numbers in a family). Nevertheless, average change in variables like self-perceived health, numbers of chronic diseases, quality of life scores and depression indices only change marginally, if at all. In macro case study 1, the variables that change the most are that those that concern the proximity of adult children's living arrangements to their older parents. There is a 7% decline in older adults with children living in the same building and a 4% decline in those children living less than 1 km away from their parents. These are significant and important changes (over time they may well transform the policy agenda and require more funding mechanisms for social care), but taken as a whole, it is concluded for the macro case study 1 that the variable trends are relatively stable. This is because of the marginal movement in the health outcomes over a lengthy time period (2004–2013).

Similarly, in macro case study 1, the cases predominantly remain in the same clusters or hierarchical cluster formations. Only two of the countries (from a sample of 10) change clusters more than once. In the conclusion of the case study, it was argued case movement was marginal (in the context of a stable dataset) rather than being about rapidly changing fundamental differences. For this reason, macro case study 1 is argued to be evidence of system stability.

Case instability

The second typology of system dynamics is case instability. This occurs where there is a distinct lack of evidence of consistent case based patterns of similarity over time. Instead the longer term tendency is for cases to move towards dissimilarity, away from previous similarities.

With the typology of case instability, most individual cases experience cluster membership change over time, and there is a lack of consistent change to case cluster patterns. Case change appears as random variation, perhaps with cyclic patterns, with the variable trends over time being fairly stable at the level of scale (sample averages).

This type of case instability is evident in the micro case study where there are few consistent clusters of older people, but variable aggregate scores over time are stable (Table 5.14). This stability is in the context that the longitudinal DPS in this case study has some changing profile of older adults and not the same profile of cases for each year of study. The case patterns are therefore unstable in comparison to the relative stability in the variable aggregate scores. The variable stability over the full term of the study is characterised by a fluctuation in scores, rather than an increasing or decreasing trend direction. For example, the average days when alcohol is consumed fluctuates, as does the household income (Table 5.14). Also, while the number of chronic diseases reported by the small sample remaining in 2010 decreases, the mobility problem index increases. The degree of variable stability relative to the transient case population is also partly reflected in the longitudinal truth table in Table 5.16. A large proportion of older people born in 1918 in the sample have the same threshold score for variables between the years 2004–2006 (this is before the sample is much reduced in 2010). The lack of case based patterns in the micro case study in part reflects the limited national sample used. There is no regional geography identifier within the national sample. Future DPS research with micro data is likely to find more clustering when local geography can be included and accounted for. Challenges remain for using DPS with micro level data, as has been the case previously with sole use of CA and QCA. A topic for future work is the use of the two step CA as a first exploration with a larger sample of micro data, this is before considering a sub sample focus.

Cluster resilience

The third type of system dynamic is cluster resilience. The defining feature of this dynamic is case based similarity over time regardless of variable trend instability.

Macro case study 2, the 12 countries who initially colaunched the euro monetary union, is an example of cluster resilience despite variable instability. The key feature of the case study over time was the fact that most countries remained in similar pairings and groupings after the financial crisis had hit their economies, though some economic variable trends had changed radically.

System instability

The fourth and final type of instability demonstrated in the case studies is general system instability. This was evidenced in the meso case study of the London borough local authorities and their experience of the health and social care of older people. Most boroughs do not stay in the same clusters and some variables change relatively substantially (while others remain stable). The limits of case pattern stability are demonstrated by a few strong pairs of authorities that remain in the same clusters through the three years of analysis. Not all of these pairs of boroughs are geographic neighbours. Not only are the case patterns unstable, but it has already been argued above that the variable patterns are unstable (Table 4.15).

Reflections on complexity theory and DPS

The final section of the concluding chapter reflects on the relationship between DPS and the key complexity concepts summarised in Chapter 1.

Interactions

Dynamic Pattern Synthesis uses no direct measurements of case interactions. The situation of a case in any one time and place is seen to be resulting from its interaction with other cases and this is a fundamental assumption of DPS based on complexity theoretical explanations, rather than cases assumed to be determined in isolation by variable scores. It assumes that cases are interacting and variable scores reflect these interactions. Nevertheless, the current version of DPS outlined in this book does not provide any direct method for assessing the feedback mechanisms between cases. This is a limitation of the method, and a matter for further consideration. In the case studies in the book, direct measures of interaction are not necessarily relevant to the case studies. For example, at the macro and meso levels the huge complexity of variable interactions between countries makes proxy management and estimation of these interactions exceedingly difficult. In the second macro case study (countries sharing the euro currency) dynamic and interactive relationships between the countries and their actors are taken for granted, given the policy decision for them to share a currency and related institutions like the ECB. In the micro example, people born in Sweden in 1918, the small sample drawn from the country are not assumed to be interactive at a personal level. Nevertheless, in terms of qualitative information influencing the model and its interpretation, it is expected that social expectations about growing older, subjective expectations about health and cultural expectations about what counts as a 'chronic disease' are highly important feedback mechanisms operating as the country context into which the limits of the model are placed. In conclusion, while DPS does not explicitly model or measure interactions, the existence and importance of the presence of interactions is a methodological assumption that needs to be considered in the qualitative reflections. It is a major contextual influence on the mechanisms operating in the DPS model.

Short and long range interactions and feedbacks

Cases are more likely to be influenced by near neighbours than those that are farther away. Therefore, similarities caused by positive, reinforcing feedback often happen in this way. Social scientists often notice and record similarities between family and community members or between groups of countries that are cooperating in proximity to each other. Evidence of near neighbour similarity was demonstrated in the country and local government case studies in this book.

In addition to the importance of short range interactions and feedback, long range interactions are also possible, if less likely. Cases that are not spatial neighbours may still become similar due to other opportunities for cooperative interaction. Examples of such similarity were apparent in some of the case studies.

System openness and dynamics

While the DPS case studies demonstrated elements of system stability and similarity and a tendency for aggregate variable scores to be changing incrementally, rather than exponentially, variable fluctuations and the small-scale movement of cases in relation to each other was a common feature. It was relatively unusual to find variable scores that constantly stayed close to each other. The case studies provide evidence of the fluidity of social system dynamics and the ever-evolving process of change. This challenges the idea of a system equilibrium as cases and what influences their social and economic position and correlation does not settle back to an identical previous state. There is an ebb and flow of incremental change, that requires qualitative and normative judgement about the relative importance of what is being observed. Dynamic Pattern Synthesis is not about identifying mathematical patterns alone, but much more about how social scientists qualitatively interpret these patterns in the context of current historical, social, political and economic change. DPS is both a quantitative and a qualitative method. Social systems are open to processes of constant change, much of which is incremental and evolving, some of this is occasionally transformational. The interaction of cases with each other is dynamic not static.

Case and data patterns

Causality is equifinal. There are many different variable influences on the trajectory of cases and within this matrix of cases and variables diverse patterns and relationships are likely to be evident. In human and social systems, there will often be different patterns that produce the same social or economic outcome.

The paths that cases take are time dependent. Any notion of cause in social science is time asymmetrical and time cannot be reversed (Frisch, 2014). Cases are likely to be subject to elements of path dependency whereby historical events set them on journeys that make them more like other cases in the future. Changes in direction, or exits from these journeys, may be infrequent and episodic. Cases can follow patterns over time, and are not routinely subject to continuous and chaotic forms of uncontrollable instability. Patterns over time are a source of system stability. Such patterns can be interpreted as case based resilience, where the interactive terms between cases include the possibility for keeping them similar and together, regardless of external social and economic change.

Transformational change, demonstrated at scale over time, comes to have a persistent and disruptive effect on the experience of cases. This change may be episodic, rather than continuous, and some cases will not be affected by it and remain resilient to change. For other cases, a period of transformation may represent a major realignment in their relationship with others, so that they have different partners who they regard as similar, and leave behind previous similarities.

Case dynamics and complexity theory

In conclusion, the important developments in the application of complexity theory to the social sciences in the last 25 years have increasingly illustrated the importance of a case based focus and the level of operation of these cases. Cases interact with each other in highly dynamic ways. Finding ways to discover and interpret the nature of these interactive patterns is an important aspect of contemporary social science research. Dynamic Pattern Synthesis seeks to make an original contribution to the vast challenges of this formidable field of research. It has limitations and these limitations are in themselves an expression of the limits to our ability to model complexity, as discussed earlier in this book and acknowledged by seminal complexity researchers like Byrne & Callaghan (2014). Nevertheless, the unique contribution of this monograph is to bring together the benefits of the methods of CA and QCA, two of the most popular contemporary methods used by those with an interest in a case based focus and how cases navigate complexity. The importance of observing patterns over time is vital if we are to make steady progress at understating social and economic change. Synthesis in social science research is as important as analysis. Better health is more likely to be achieved by taking a wide view: understanding genetic history, improving diet, health, relationships and the physical environment and to focus on one factor alone ignores other important contributory factors. Similarly, stable and prosperous economic management depends on understanding the interaction of many elements and creating the best overall environment, rather than focusing on a singular theory and method for managing a variable like price inflation argued to have primacy over others. Cases operate in a complex world and are contingent on many things, not least their relationships with each other. Time and space are the canvases on which case based patterns are painted and appreciated for what they are.

References

Aldenderfer, M. & Blashfield, R., 1984. *Cluster Analysis*. Thousand Oaks, CA: Sage.

Aleskerov, F. et al., 2014. A Method of Static and Dynamic Pattern Analysis of Innovative Development of Russiona Regions in the Long Run. In: M. Batsyn, V. Kalyagin & P. Pardalos, eds. *Models, Algorithms and Technologies for Network Analysis*. s.l.:s.n., pp. 1–8.

Archer, M. S., 1982. Morphogenesis versus Structuration: On Combining Structure and Action. *The British Journal of Sociology*, 33(4), pp. 455–483.

Bar-Yam, Y., 2005. *Making Things Work: Solving Complex Problems in a Complex World*. Cambridge, MA: Knowledge Press.

Benedek, J., Cristea, M. & Szendi, D., 2015. Catching Up or Falling behind? Economic Convergence and Regional Development Trajectories in Romania. *Romanian Review of Regional Studies*, 11(1), pp. 15–34.

Berg-Schlosser, D., De Meur, G., Rihoux, B. & Ragin, C., 2009. Qualitative Comparative Analysis (QCA) as an Approach. In: C. Ragin & B. Rihoux, eds. *Configurational Comparative Methods*. Los Angeles: Sage, pp. 1–18.

Bhaskar, R., 1978. *A Realist Theory of Science*. 2nd ed. Brighton: Harvester Press.

Borenstein, M., Hedges, L., Higgins, J. P. & Rothstein, H. R., 2009. *Introduction to Meta-Analysis*. Chichester: Wiley.

Börsch-Supan, A. et al., 2016. *easySHARE. Release version: 5.0.0. SHARE-ERIC*. s.l.:Data set. DOI: 10.6103/SHARE.easy.500.

Bottle, R., 1996. *The Death of Inflation*. London: Nicholas Brealey.

Boulton, J., Allen, P. & Bowman, C., 2015. *Embracing Complexity: Strategic Perspectives for an Age of Turbulence*. Oxford: Oxford University Press.

Bryman, A., 2004. *Quality and Quantity in Social Research*. London: Routledge.

Bryman, A., 2008. The End of Paradigm Wars? In: P. Alasuutari, L. Bickman & J. Brannen, eds. *The Sage Handbook of Social Research Methods*. London: Sage, pp. 12–26.

Burns, D., 2007. *Systemic Action Research: A Strategy for Whole Systems Change*. Bristol: Policy Press.

Buti, M. & Turrini, A., 2015. *Three Waves of Convergence: Can Eurozone Countries Start Growing Together again?* Brussels: VOX, CEPR.

Byrne, D., 1998. *Complexity Theory and the Social Sciences*. London: Routledge.

Byrne, D., 2002. *Interpreting Quantitative Data*. London: Sage.

Byrne, D., 2004. Complex and Contingent Causation: The Implications of Complex Realism for Quantitative Modelling: The Case of Housing and Health. In: *Making Realism Work*. Abingdon: Routledge, pp. 50–66.

Byrne, D., 2011. *Applying Social Science: The Role of Social Research in Politics, Policy and Practice*. Bristol: Policy Press.

Byrne, D. & Callaghan, G., 2014. *Complexity Theory and the Social Sciences*. Oxford: Routledge.

Carter, B. & New, C., 2004. *Making Realism Work: Realist Social Theory and Empirical Research*. Abingdon: Routledge.

Cartwright, N., 2007. *Hunting Causes and Using Them: Approaches in Philosopy and Economics*. Cambridge: Cambridge University Press.

Castellani, B. & Hafferty, F., 2009. *Sociology and Complexity Science: A New Area of Inquiry*. New York: Springer.

Cilliers, P., 1998. *Complexity and Postmodernism: Understanding Complex Systems*. London: Routledge.

Cilliers, P., 2001. Boundaries, Hiearchies and Networks in Complex Systems. *International Journal of Innovation Management*, 5(2), pp. 135–147.

Cohen, J. & Stewart, I., 1994. *The Collapse of Chaos: Discovering Simplicity in a Complex World*. London: Viking.

Collier, A., 1994. *Critical Realism: An Introduction to Roy Bhaskar's Philosophy*. London: Verso.

Davies, H., 2010. *The Financial Crisis: Who Is to Blame?* London: Polity.

Dooley, K. & Van de Ven, A. H., 1997. Explaining Complex Organizational Dynamics. *Organizational Science*, 10(3), pp. 358–372.

Ebbinghaus, B., 2005. When Less Is More: Selection Problems in Large-N and Small-N Cross-National Comparisions. *International Sociology*, 20, pp. 133–152.

Elliott, E. & Kiel, L., 1997. Nonlinear Dynamics, Complexity, and Piblic Policy Use, Misuse, and Applicability. In: R. A. Eve, S. Horsfall & M. E. Lee, eds. *Chaos, Complexity, and Sociology: Myths, Models and Theories*. London: Sage, pp. 64–78.

Everitt, B. S., 1993. *Cluster Analysis*. London: Arnold.

Ferragina, E., Seeleib-Kaiser, M. & Tomlinson, M., 2013. Unemployment Protection and Family Policy at the Turn of the 21st Century: A Dynamic Approach to Welfare Regieme Theory. *Social Policy and Administration*, 47(7), pp. 783–805.

Frisch, M., 2014. *Causal Reasoning in Physics*. Cambridge: Cambridge University Press.

García-Castro, R. & Ariño, M., 2013. *A General Approach to Panel Data Set-Theoretic Research*, COMPASSS Working Paper 2013–76: www.compasss.org/wpseries/Garcia-CastroArino2013.pdf.

Gelick, J., 1988. *Chaos: Making a New Science*. London: Sphere.

Gerrits, L. M. & Verweij, S., 2013. Understanding and Researching Complexity with QCA. *Evaluation*, 19(1), pp. 40–55.

Gilbert, N., 2008. *Agent-Based Models*. London: Sage.

Gruber, S. et al., 2016. *easySHARE Guide to easySHARE release 5.0.0*, s.l.: mea www.share-project.org/data-access-documentation/easyshare.html.

Haladane, A., 2015. *How Low Can You Go? Speech Given to the Portadown Chamber of Commerce, NI, UK. 18th September*. London: Bank of England. www.bankofengland.co.uk/publications/Pages/speeches/default.aspx.

Harrits, G., 2011. More Than Method?: A Discussion of Paradigm Differences within Mixed Methods Research. *Journal of Mixed Methods Research*, 5(2), pp. 150–166.

Harvey, D. & Reed, M., 1997. Social Science as the Study of Complex Systems. In: L. D. Kiel & E. W. Elliott, eds. *Chaos Theory in the Social Sciences: Foundations and Applications*. Ann Arbor, MI: University fo Michigan Press, pp. 295–324.

Hawe, P., Shiell, A. & Riley, T., 2009. Theorising Interventions as System Events. *American Journal of Community Psychology*, 43, pp. 267–276.

Haynes, P., 1999. *Complex Policy Planning: The Government Strategic Management of the Social Care Market*. Aldershot: Ashgate.

Haynes, P., 2015. *Managing Complexity in the Public Services*. 2nd ed. Oxford: Routledge.

Haynes, P. & Haynes, J., 2016. Convergence and Heterogeniety in Euro Based Economies: Stability and Dynamics. *Economies*, 4(3), pp. 1–17.

Hudson, J. & Kuhner, S., 2013. Qualitative Comparative Analysis and Applied Policy Analysis: New Applications of Innovative Methods. *Policy and Society*, 32, pp. 279–287.

Irac, D. & Lopez, J., 2015. Euro Area Structural Convergence? A Multi-Criterion Cluster Analysis. *International Economics*, 143, pp. 1–22.

Johnson, R. B. & Onwuegbuzie, A. J., 2004. Mixed Methods Research: A Research Paradigm Whose Time Has Come. *Educational Researcher*, 33(7), pp. 14–26.

Kahneman, D., 2012. *Thinking, Fast and Slow*. London: Penguin.

Kauffman, S., 1995. *At Home in the Universe: The Search for Laws of Complexity*. London: Viking.

Kiel, L. D. & Elliott, E., 1997. Exploring Nonlinear Dynamics with a Spreadsheet: A Graphical Vew of Chaos for Beginners. In: L. D. Elliott & E. Kiel, eds. *Chaos Theory in the Social Sciences: Foundations and Applications*. Ann Arbor, MI: University of Michigan Press, pp. 19–29.

Kontopoulos, K., 1993. *The Logics of Social Structure*. Cambridge, MA: Cambridge University Press.

Kvist, J., 1999. Welfare Reform in the Nordic Countries in the 1990s: Using Fuzzy Set Theory to Assess Conformity to Ideal Types. *Journal of European Social Policy*, 9(3), pp. 231–252.

Leong, K., Li, J., Chan, S. & Ng, V., 2009. An Application of the Dynamic Pattern Analysis Framework to the Analysis of Spatial-Temporal Crime Relationships. *Journal of Universal Computer Science*, 15(9), pp. 1852–1870.

Luhmann, N., 1995. *Social Systems*. Translated by John Bednarz, Jr. & Dirk Baecker. Stanford, CA: Stanford University Press.

Major, C. & Savin-Baden, M., 2010. *An Introduction to Qualitative Research Synthesis: Managing the Information Explosion in Social Science Research*. London: Sage.

Maturana, R. & Varela, F. J., 1992. *The Tree of Knowledge: The Biological Roots of Human Understanding*. London: Shambhala Publications.

Montfort, P., 2008. *Convergence of EU Regions: Measures and Evolution*. Brussels: European Commission, Regional Policy.

Morgan, D., 2007. Paradigms Lost and Pragmatism Regained: Methodologial Implications of Combining Qualitative and Quantitative Methods. *Journal of Mixed Methods Reserach*, 1(1), pp. 48–76.

Morgan, D., 2014. Pragmatism as a Paradigm for Social Research. *Qualitative Inquiry*, 20(8), pp. 1045–1053.

Olsen, W., 2014. Comment: The Usefulness of QCA under Realist Assumptions. *Sociological Methodology*, 44, pp. 101–107.

Ormerod, P., 1994. *The Death of Economics*. London: Faber and Faber.

Ormerod, P., 1998. *Butterfly Economics*. London: Faber and Faber.

Ormerod, P., 2012. *Positive Linking: How Networks are Revolutionising Your World*. London: Faber and Faber.

Ormerod, P., Rosewell, B. & Phelps, P., 2009. *Inflation-Unemployment Regimes and the Instablity of the Phillips Curve*. London: Volerra Consulting.

Pastor, D. A., 2010. Cluster Analysis. In: G. R. Hancock & R. Mueller, eds. *The Reviewer's Guide to Quantitative Methods in the Social Sciences*. London: Routledge.

Pawson, R., 2006. *Evidence Based Policy: A Realist Perspective*. London: Sage.

Pawson, R. & Tilley, N., 1997. *Realistic Evaluation*. London: Sage.

Ragin, C., 1987. *The Comparative Method: Moving beyond Qualitative and Quantitative Strategies*. Berkeley, CA: University of California Press.

Ragin, C., 1997. Turning the Tables: How Case-Oriented Research Challenges Variable Oriented Research. *Comparative Social Research*, 16(1), pp. 27–42.

Ragin, C., 1999. Using Qualitative Comparative Analysis to Study Causal Complexity. *Health Services Research*, 34(5), pp. 1225–1239.

Ragin, C., 2009. Qualitative Analysis using Fuzzy Sets (fsQCA). In: B. Rihoux & C. Ragin, eds. *Configurational Comparative Methods: Qualitative Comparative Anaysis (QCA) and Related Techniques*. London: Sage, pp. 87–121.

Ragin, C. & Becker, H., 1992. *What Is a Case? Exploring the Foundations of Social Inquiry*. Cambridge: Cambridge University Press.

Rihoux, B., Rezsohazy, I. & Bol, D., 2011. Qualitative Comparative Analysis (QCA) in Public Policy Analysis: An Extensive Review. *German Policy Studies*, 7(3), pp. 52–82.

Room, G., 2011. *Complexity, Institutions and Public Policy*. Cheltenham: Edward Elgar.

Sandel, M., 2012. *What Money Can't Buy: The Moral Limits of Markets*. London: Penguin.

Sanderson, I., 2000. Evaluation in Complex Policy Systems. *Evaluation*, 6(4), pp. 433–454.

Sayer, A., 1992. *Method in Social Science: A Realist Approach*. 2nd ed. London: Routledge.

Sayer, A., 2000. *Realism and Social Science*. London: Sage.

Schelling, T. C., 1971. Dynamnic Models of Segregation. *Journal of Mathematical Sociology*, 1, pp. 143–186.

Smith, J. & Jenks, C., 2006. *Qualitative Complexity*. London: Routledge.

Thompson, K. E., 2004. *Readings from Emile Durkheim*. Abingdon: Routledge.

Turner, G., 2008. *The Credit Crunch: Housing Bubbles, Globalisation, and the World Economic Crisis*. London: Pluto Press.

Uprichard, E., 2009. Introducing Cluster Analysis: What Can It Teach Us about the Case? In: D. Byrne & C. Ragin, eds. *The Sage Handbook of Case Based Methods*. London: Sage, pp. 132–147.

Urry, J., 2003. *Global Complexity*. Cambridge: Polity Press.

Williams, M. & Dyer, W., 2004. Realism and Probability. In: B. a. N. C., ed. *Making Realism Work*. London: Routledge, pp. 67–86.

Zachariadis, M., Scott, S. & Barrett, M., 2013. Methodolgical Implications of Critical Realism for Mixed-Methods Research. *MIS Quarterly*, 37(3), pp. 855–879.

Index